THE VICTORIANS AT WAR

The Victorians at War

Ian F. W. Beckett

Hambledon and London
London and New York

Hambledon and London
102 Gloucester Avenue
London, NW1 8HX

175 Fifth Avenue
New York, NY 10010
USA

First Published 2003

ISBN 1 85285 275 5

A description of this book is available from the
British Library and from the Library of Congress.

Typeset by Carnegie Publishing, Lancaster,
and printed in Great Britain by Cambridge University Press.

Distributed in the United States and Canada exclusively
by Palgrave Macmillan, a division of St Martin's Press.

Contents

Part Three: Ways of War

Illustrations

Acknowledgements

Quotations from the Royal Archives appear by gracious permission of Her Majesty the Queen. Quotations from Crown copyright material in the Public Record Office appears by permission of Her Majesty's Stationery Office. The author also acknowledges his thanks to the following for allowing him to consult and quote from archives in their possession and/or copyright: the Marquess of Lansdowne, the Marquess of Salisbury, Lord Burnham, the Trustees of the Liddell Hart Centre for Military Archives, the Trustees of the British Library Board, the National Army Museum, News International Newspapers (Times Archive), the Royal Pavilion Libraries and Museums (Hove Reference Library), the National Library of Scotland, the Scottish United Services Museum, the Henry E. Huntington Library, the Sudan Archive of the University of Durham, the Bodleian Library, the Killie Campbell Library of the University of Natal, Devon County Record Office, the Kent Archives Office, and the Warwickshire County Record Office.

Abbreviations

AAG	Assistant Adjutant General
ADC	Aide de Camp
BEF	British Expeditionary Force
BBP	Bechuanaland Border Police
BL	British Library
BSAC	British South Africa Company
BSAP	British South Africa Police
CRE	Commander, Royal Engineers
DAQMG	Deputy Assistant Quartermaster General
FAMP	Frontier Armed and Mounted Police
GCB	Knight Grand Cross of the Order of the Bath
GCMG	Knight Grand Cross of the Order of St Michael and St George
GNP	Gross National Product
GOC	General Officer Commanding
Hatfield	Salisbury MSS, Hatfield House
HBA	Hall Barn Archives Trust
HEHL	Henry E. Huntingdon Library, San Marino, California
Hove	Wolseley Collections, Hove Reference Library
IOL	Oriental and India Office Collections, British Library
IY	Imperial Yeomanry
KAO	Kent Archives Office, Maidstone
KCB	Knight Commander of the Order of the Bath
KCL	Killie Campbell African Library, University of Natal
KCMG	Knight Commander of the Order of St Michael and St George

KCSI	Knight Commander of the Order of the Star of India
KOSB	King's Own Scottish Borderers
LHCMA	Liddell Hart Centre for Military Archives, King's College, London
NAM	National Army Museum
NLS	National Library of Scotland
NNC	Natal Native Contingent
P & O	Peninsular and Oriental Steam Navigation Company
PRO	Public Record Office
psc	Passed Staff College
RA	Royal Archives
RAMC	Royal Army Medical Corps
RE	Royal Engineers
RN	Royal Navy
RVC	Rifle Volunteer Corps
SAD	Sudan Archive, University of Durham
SUSM	Scottish United Services Museum
VC	Victoria Cross

Introduction

Historians walk with ghosts. Military historians perhaps do so even more than others. They are privileged, however, to see what others do not as they tread the deserted banquet-hall of the past, endeavouring to re-populate it with those who have gone before and who might otherwise be forgotten. Military fame, indeed, is a transient affair. Few among one generation's celebrities of any kind will have enduring recognition; and, in the case of soldiers, the paths of glory lead not only to the grave, but also frequently to rapid obscurity. Consider, for example, one of a number of similar Victorian works of hagiography, Arthur Temple's *Our Living Generals*, first published in 1898 and revised in new editions in both October 1899 and January 1900. Despite the publisher's note to the contrary inserted in the third edition, there is no evidence of much updating from the first edition to take account of events in South Africa beyond the summer of 1899. In the third edition, indeed, General Sir Redvers Buller is still to set out for the Cape.

Nonetheless, what is striking is a comment in the last chapter on the then Lieutenant–General Lord Kitchener, proclaiming that no other name had been more frequently mentioned by the 'man in the street' since 1897, 'with the exception perhaps of Sir William Lockhart'. Kitchener, of course, is a figure who still has widespread recognition. One of the seemingly interminable millennium surveys chose Alfred Leete's famous Great War recruiting poster of Kitchener as the most power-ful advertising image of the twentieth century. Who, however, now remembers Lockhart?

Or consider the well-known *Celebrities of the Army*, produced by George Newnes Ltd in 1900, first as a part-work then as a volume in its own right. Some seventy-two soldiers are depicted in full-colour portraits with brief biographies. Few 'men in the street' would recognise any of them now. Perhaps Redvers Buller, Herbert Kitchener, Robert

Baden Powell, Frederick Roberts and conceivably John French, but neither, one suspects, Garnet Wolseley or Evelyn Wood. Indeed, a few years ago, when the inn sign of a London public house named for Wolseley was repainted, the artist mistakenly depicted Cardinal Wolsey! The identity of others, who looked out prominently at their contemporaries from commemorative china, cigarette cards or patriotic buttons at the time of the South African War, such as George White, Lord Methuen, Charles Warren and Andy Wauchope, would simply mystify most people presented with their images today. Equally, many would be hard put to recognise many of those commemorated by statues.

Indeed, in 2000, the Mayor of London, Ken Livingstone, in commenting on statues in Trafalgar Square during the continuing controversy over the 'empty plinth', declared that he had no idea why those of two Victorian generals, Charles Napier and Henry Havelock, were there. Modern historians themselves have also neglected some of the towering personalities of the Victorian army, even where the surviving personal papers are voluminous. Men such as George Cathcart, Colin Campbell, Neville Chamberlain, Charles Gough, Hugh Gough, Frederick Haines, Robert Napier, James Outram, Donald Stewart, George White, Evelyn Wood, even Frederick Roberts, all require modern reassessment. Some particular military dynasties would also repay detailed study. The Goughs, the Napiers, the Chesneys and the Battyes all readily spring to mind.

Some at least of these men will be encountered in this volume which, drawing on largely underused sources, reflects this author's long-term interest in the Victorian army, its leading personalities and their campaigns. It aims to illuminate the internal dynamics of an army, which constituted one of the largest institutions in Victorian Britain for all that neither its officers nor rank and file were representative of Victorian society as a whole. While sharing the characteristics of some other institutions in the sense of being an institution, the army was a closed fraternity whose experience of military service – spent mostly overseas – clearly differentiated soldiers from most of their fellow countrymen. Soldiers, however, naturally shared many of the same aspirations and emotions as their civilian counterparts. Indeed, examples of soldiers' ambition, rivalry and self-promotion are all to be glimpsed alongside examples of their self-effacement, duty and service.

The essays that make up this book are not presented chronologically but grouped in three broad categories. In the first section, Reputations, the emphasis is upon public perceptions of soldiers and of the army. The second section, Generals and Politicians, concentrates upon aspects of military command, including civil-military relations and the interplay of rival 'rings' of soldiers within the army, such as those associated with Garnet Wolseley and Frederick Roberts. The third section, Ways of War, examines aspects of the army's application of military force, but also the impact of two major wars – the Crimean War and the South African War – upon Victorian Britain.

The Empire may or may not have been acquired as a result of absence of mind, but it was the army that had effected much of the Empire's expansion and that had the task of policing that Empire. Many reminders of that military effort remain and one of the many rewards of practising military history – as will become apparent – has been to visit battlefields, fortifications and other sites connected to the Victorian army. I have been fortunate enough over the years to visit a variety of such sites in various parts of the world. Sites such as Isandlwana or Majuba in South Africa, for example, have a special atmosphere arising from the sense of the magnitude of the events that occurred there. Equally, however, a sense of the past can be glimpsed from an encounter with a London statue, an overgrown and forgotten fort in the English countryside, an imaginative museum in Singapore or even a nineteenth-century model of Gibraltar. In part, therefore, this volume also presents reflections prompted by journeys in the present, which have become journeys into the past. In the process, it is hoped that the reader will be able to share some of the author's pleasure of venturing in search of the Victorian army.

Part One

Reputations

1

An English Confederacy

A simple, small square stone in a clearing by a crossroads in a Virginian wood is not the most obvious place from which to consider any aspect of the Victorian army, especially when it more immediately conjures to mind one of those poignant moments for the Southern Confederacy. For this is the site of the 'Lee-Jackson Bivouac', where Robert E. Lee and Thomas 'Stonewall' Jackson conferred by the Orange Plank Road on the night of 1/2 May 1863 following the first day of the battle of Chancellorsville. Jackson and Lee reportedly sat on old cracker boxes as they hatched the plan for Jackson's daring march over narrow back roads to appear unexpectedly on the Union army's right flank the following day. Just as Jackson set out on that following morning, he and Lee exchanged a few last words. A famous and colourful painting by Everett Julio commemorating the scene has pride of place in the magnificent Confederate Museum in Richmond, Lee mounted on his famous grey, 'Traveller', and Jackson restraining his steed as it paws the ground. The battle was to be won, but at the price of Jackson's fatal wounding, ironically by one of his own picquets as he rode back from a reconnaissance.

Why then should this be of any significance for the British army? Quite simply, because of the hold over the consciousness of the Queen's generals of 'those two brilliant champions of a lost cause' as Garnet Wolseley once termed them.[1] Indeed, Wolseley's memoir of Lee, penned for *Macmillan's Magazine* in March 1887, has been described as one of the great classics of Confederate literature, Wolseley listing Lee and Charles Gordon as the only two men whom he had met who realised his ideas of a true hero. More than once, Wolseley was to ascribe to Lee the characteristics of an English gentleman. The great impression Lee and Jackson had made on Wolseley had been evident even earlier in his article for *Blackwood's Edinburgh Magazine* in January 1863, recounting his visit to the Confederacy in the autumn of 1862. George Colley also regarded Lee as a personal hero, while a whole generation of British officers learned, in the somewhat caustic comment of Basil Liddell Hart, 'to be able to enumerate the blades of grass in the Shenandoah Valley'.[2] G. F. R. Henderson's *Stonewall Jackson and the American Civil War*, published in 1898 and which Liddell Hart had specifically in mind, remained a model text for Staff College students well into the 1920s. That other iconoclast of inter-war British military thought, J. F. C. Fuller, was equally critical of the long shadows cast by the Shenandoah.

Significantly, Liddell Hart and Fuller preferred to study Grant and Sherman, whom no one would have likened to English gentlemen. Indeed, when Grant was appointed General-in-Chief of the Union armies in March 1864, he was assuming overall responsibility for the direction of 533,000 men. Seven years later, the Chief of Staff of the German armies, Helmuth von Moltke, was directing 850,000 men in the opening stages of the Franco-Prussian War. By comparison, the largest number of men put into the field by the British army between the end of the Crimean War in 1856 and the opening of the South African War in 1899 was the 35,000 men directed by Wolseley in the occupation of Egypt in 1882, and the actual field force was only 16,000 strong. Even at the height of the South African War, Britain fielded only 450,000 men. Wolseley and his fellow commanders, therefore, operated with far more limited forces than even Lee and Jackson. In that sense, they could afford to admire the leadership qualities of whomever they chose, although this did not necessarily mean that considerable professional demands were not being made upon them.

For one thing, 'small wars' required the conquest of nature as much as the conquest of indigenous opponents. Having needed to cross six hundred miles of Canadian wilderness before the lakes froze during his Red River expedition in 1870, it was understandable that, confronted with the need to complete operations in Ashanti in 1873–74 before the climate took its toll of his European troops, Wolseley wrote: 'I always seem to be condemned to command in expeditions which must be accomplished before a certain season of the year begins.'[3] In advancing over four hundred miles from the Red Sea coast to Magdala in Abyssinia in 1867–68, Sir Robert Napier's expeditionary force of 13,000 men required the logistic support of 14,500 followers and 36,000 draught animals. Even the small Duffla expedition on the heavily forested north-eastern frontier of India in 1874–75 needed 1200 coolies, while, in Zululand in 1879, it was painfully difficult for Lord Chelmsford to assemble the 977 wagons, 10,023 oxen, 803 horses and 398 mules he utilised to support his columns, and all but impossible to make more than ten miles a day. Indeed, Wolseley was to note that, when fully deployed on the march, Chelmsford's baggage train was three or four miles longer than it could actually travel in a day. In the case of Colonel Pearson's column, there were only sufficient oxen to pull 195 of his 384 wagons since each wagon required sixteen oxen, and many of the oxen were then lost when Pearson became besieged at Eshowe. Apart from the toll in lives, Chelmsford's disaster at Isandlwana in January 1879 cost 132 wagons and £60,000 worth of stores, prompting the first major foray back to the scene of carnage in May to recover around forty serviceable wagons.

Railways could help in certain circumstances, as in the expedition to Suakin on the Red Sea coast in 1885 and in the reconquest of the Sudan in 1896–98. Indeed, G. W. Steevens, the military correspondent of the *Daily Mail*, aptly described the Sudan Military Railway as 'the deadliest weapon ... ever used against Mahdism',[4] the 230 miles of single track across the desert from Wadi Halfa to Abu Hamed shortening the journey time from eighteen days by camel and steamer to but twenty-four hours. On the other hand, as in the South African War, dependence upon the relatively few railways could limit strategic options. Thus, in advancing upon the capital of the Orange Free State at Bloemfontein, Lord Roberts was forced to leave the highly vulnerable line of the railway to fall back upon oxen, horses and mules, only for the Boers almost to wreck his efforts by stampeding over three thousand of his oxen at Waterval Drift in February 1900.

Nor did Moltke or Grant have to face the variety of enemies encountered by the British: from European-trained opponents such as the Egyptian army in 1882 to disciplined native armies such as the Zulu, fanatics like the Dervishes of the Sudan, and, almost in a category of their own, mounted Boers armed with modern weapons. Like Grant and Moltke, however, British commanders did have to contend with politicians and Wolseley in particular noted the often disastrous political interference in military operations in the American Civil War. Not without some Caesarist tendencies, Wolseley lamented in his memoir of Lee that the latter had been 'too subservient to those charged with the civil government of his country'. Increasingly, the extension of the submarine telegraph cable through the 1870s and 1880s rendered British commanders subject to the vagaries of political indecision in London, one general officer noting of Wolseley's failure to save Gordon that 'it is ungenerous to forget that nowadays military methods are too often the slaves of political expediency'.[5] In any case, commanders increasingly needed to exercise both military and political judgement, Wolseley himself playing the game astutely, as when he remarked that George Greaves, who had succeeded him in the Cyprus command in 1879, 'had yet to learn that it does not do to insert the whole truth in official correspondence'.[6]

Frederick Roberts learned the hard way, erring in issuing a proclamation in December 1878 during the first phase of the Second Afghan War suggesting the annexation of the Kurram valley. He then reinforced the impression of 'the stupidity he has shown in all non-military matters' in January 1880 by mishandling the summary executions in Kabul of those suspected of complicity in the massacre of the British mission of Louis Cavagnari.[7] By the time of the South African War, however, Roberts was a practised exponent of political skills to the extent that he and his successor, Kitchener, seized effective control of policy. The debt the government owed them in securing its political survival after the exigencies of 'Black Week' also enabled them to dictate the eventual political settlement.

Political considerations intruded largely due to the growing recognition that there was a need to take account of public opinion in an age of popular journalism. Thus, when Lieutenant-General Sir Edward Selby Smyth, who had previously served at the Cape, offered his services in the Zulu War, the Secretary of State for War immediately rejected the appointment of a soldier who was 'hardly well enough known' to take on the job of reversing Isandlwana.[8] Similarly, the feeble Lieutenant-General the Hon. Sir Leicester Smyth, sent to command at the Cape after the Zulu War was safely over and when no new crises were anticipated, was pointedly instructed not to interfere with the command of Sir George Colley in Natal in 1880. He was subsequently ignored when Sir Evelyn Wood was sent out to be Colley's deputy in February 1881; passed over when Colley was killed at Majuba later that month, at which time the public's new hero, Roberts, was sent out to take command; and again overlooked when Sir Charles Warren was appointed to command the expedition to Bechuanaland in October 1884.

Most commanders were hostile to the press, Kitchener famously sweeping out of his tent past the assembled correspondents on one occasion in the Sudan exclaiming: 'Get out of my way, you drunken swabs!'[9] Kitchener's relations with the ubiquitous 'specials' remained poor and it was only the intervention of the government that compelled Kitchener to allow correspondents south of Assouan (Aswan) during the campaign. During the Second Afghan War, Roberts had Maurice Macpherson of the *Standard* removed from the Kurram Field Force for eluding press controls and, in South Africa, he and Kitchener imposed tight regulations in comparison to the somewhat lazy approach of his predecessor, Redvers Buller. At the same time, like Wolseley, Roberts was well aware that the press could be manipulated. Thus he withdrew the Cavalry Division from Kroonstad in May 1900 so he could personally take the town's surrender in view of the assembled press corps.

If commanders faced a range of external pressures, there were also internally-generated difficulties in terms of the mostly casual attitude towards the emergence of a general staff. Pointedly, Wolseley had remarked upon the small size of Lee's personal staff when visiting the Confederate field headquarters, and there was no sense in which the British attempted to emulate the Prussian staff system. Moreover, the personalised approach to command and leadership fuelled the rivalry of the so-called 'rings' around commanders. The struggle ranged widely over issues of imperial strategy and military reform, though neither particular issues nor the positions assumed by individuals with respect to them were necessarily constant as the factions attempted to manoeuvre adherents into particular commands. Wolseley's 'Ashanti Ring', known to some as the 'Mutual Admiration Society', was the best known, but Roberts too had his adherents as, subsequently, did Kitchener. Moreover, the Duke of Cambridge as Commander-in-Chief was equally determined to have his own way with regard to appointments, favouring seniority over 'selection', even after the establishment of a selection board in 1891 to enforce promotion by selection. An amusing apocryphal account of a meeting of the board in a memoir by the future Major-General G. G. A. Egerton, then a captain in the Seaforth Highlanders, has the Duke arriving in a temper:

> 'Well, I suppose we must get on with this new fangled nonsense, go on, read out the names.' At the first name read out, Wolseley said, 'He's deaf'. 'What?' said Evelyn Wood, who was himself as deaf as forty posts, 'Dead?' – 'No,' replied Wolseley, 'D E A F.' 'Humph', answered Wood, 'lot of good officers are deaf.' Later on Wood remarked that a certain officer was a VC, on which Wolseley countered, that he did not in the least consider that fact any claim for advertisement – Wood, of course, being a VC. Then the old Duke chipped in, 'Whose name was that? Oh! Colonel Brown, – oh! Good old fellow! – Yes, certainly, promote him; but that man Jones, No, scratch him out, nasty fellow – I hate him.' [10]

As it happened, Wolseley became associated with some of his leading adherents almost coincidentally in the Red River campaign in 1870, since the choices of Redvers Buller, William Butler, Sir John McNeill and George Huyshe were dictated by those officers available in Canada, only Hugh McCalmont making his own way there to press his services on Wolseley. It would appear, however, that Wolseley was in the habit of keeping a list of able men. Butler, Buller, McNeill, Huyshe and McCalmont, together with Assistant Controller M. B. Irvine, duly appeared in the Ashanti campaign, which marked the real start of the Wolseley ring. Also selected to sail with Wolseley to Cape Coast Castle in September 1873 were Evelyn Wood, Baker Russell, Thomas Baker, Henry Brackenbury, Robert Home, Frederick Maurice and Lord Gifford. When McNeill was wounded, he was replaced by George Greaves, who had shared the same room at the War Office with Wolseley, while George Colley arrived subsequently. Some were clearly chosen for their courage, Wood, McNeill and the expedition surgeon, Dr Anthony Home, all holding the VC. Others such as Brackenbury, Maurice and Colley had earned an intellectual reputation and Wolseley certainly favoured Staff College graduates in all his campaigns. A total of thirty-four psc's served in Egypt in 1882, including fourteen in the headquarters and five out of seven in the intelligence section; twenty on the Gordon Relief Expedition in 1884–85, including six in the headquarters and seven on lines of communication; and no less than eighty psc's were appointed to the staff or despatched on special service to South Africa in 1899, thirty-three being named to the staff of the army corps and the first three divisions.

Wolseley claimed that his staff was selected on merit alone and it was recognised even by his critics that he had a knack of picking able soldiers. On occasions, moreover, he did not have as free a choice as sometimes supposed. When he went to Zululand in 1879, he complained that 'many of the tools I shall have to work with, are not of my own selection, but are men chosen by HRH [Cambridge] & the Horse Guards party'.[11] In Egypt in 1882, the principal field commands were taken by those already intended to command at that year's autumn manoeuvres. Wolseley also felt obliged to take Cambridge's son as private secretary; the Queen's son, the Duke of Connaught, as a brigade commander; the Duke of Teck as a special service officer; and the son of the Secretary of State for War as an ADC. It has also been suggested that the staffing of the Gordon Relief Expedition of 1884–85 showed Wolseley's nepotism and snobbery in taking out relatives including his brother and nephew, and influential courtiers such as Colonel Stanley Clarke and Lord Charles Beresford. Yet this was far from uncommon. Roberts was equally accused of surrounding himself in South Africa with an aristocratic staff. There was in all such criticism a large measure of resentment on the part of those excluded from campaigns and the glory and honour that might derive from them.

Clearly, there was some vindictiveness in the operation of the ring system as in the case of the victimisation by Wolseley and his adherents of non-ringers. Sir Charles Wilson was made the scapegoat for the failure to reach Khartoum in time. He had been thrust into command of the Desert Column after the fatal wounding of a Wolseley favourite, Sir Hebert Stewart, at Metemmeh, and the earlier death of Stewart's deputy, Fred Burnaby at Abu Klea. Yet, equally, there were victims of Roberts such as Dunham Massy, blamed for allowing the Afghan army to escape Kabul in October 1879. Old scores were also settled once Roberts succeeded Buller in the supreme command in South Africa in January 1900, key members of the Roberts's ring such as William Nicholson, Neville Chamberlain and George Pretyman being brought to South Africa. Others already in South Africa, such as Ian Hamilton and Henry Rawlinson, were summoned to join Roberts. Pretyman, indeed, with no apparent sense of irony, announced to a former ADC of Roberts that he anticipated a clean sweep of the rival 'malicious and jobbing clique'.[12]

Of course, the constant employment of a relatively small number of officers did restrict the development of others, Wolseley in particular becoming something of a prisoner of the initial success of his ring, feeling it desirable to employ the same men lest his rejection of them might reflect adversely on his earlier choice. Indeed, Wolseley continued to employ the same men despite his own increasing criticism of their failings. Wood, for example, was never forgiven for signing the peace treaty with the Boers after Colley's death at Majuba in February 1881, while Brackenbury's advocacy of the creation of a general staff was regarded by Wolseley as evidence of Brackenbury's own ambition. Certainly, as the prominent members of Wolseley's ring became more senior, their willingness to work together was subordinated to their own ambitions. Buller was regarded with suspicion by Wolseley for his apparent willingness to accept the office of Commander-in-Chief from the Liberal government ahead of Wolseley in 1895, the subsequent change of government granting Wolseley his long-sought prize. Again, individuals manoeuvring for preferment was hardly unusual. As Buller noted after visiting Roberts in Pretoria in July 1900: 'I found Roberts sitting in one building with his Hindu staff, Kitchener in another with his Egyptian staff, and [Lieutenant-General Sir Thomas] Kelly-Kenny in a third with an English staff, all pulling against each other.'[13]

In the case of the Wolseley ring, however, what made internal dissension so destructive was that Wolseley's command style was built upon the basis of individuals willingly filling specific roles in a kind of orchestrated military collective, with Colley or Greaves as chief of staff, Buller in intelligence, Brackenbury as military secretary, Butler in the field, and so on. Indeed, if a particular individual was not available, Wolseley often lamented that the replacement was not as efficient. Colley's recall to India during the Zulu War, for example, brought Brackenbury's elevation to chief of staff, but Wolseley found him wanting. The year before on Cyprus, Brackenbury's talents as military secretary had been much missed. Yet, while Wolseley's command system was highly personalised, he did plan carefully in advance, in contrast to Roberts who was an indifferent organiser. Moreover, though they were limited in size by continental standards, Wolseley did tend to employ larger staffs than many of his contemporaries. In Zululand, for example, Chelmsford had just fourteen individuals on his headquarters staff for a force of almost 18,000 men, although each of the five columns employed also had about seven staff officers. Nor did Chelmsford employ any intelligence staff, utilising only one civilian in an intelligence capacity. When Wolseley arrived, he gave Major-General the Hon. Hugh Clifford nine assistants on the lines of communication and placed Maurice in charge of intelligence. Similarly, Buller had six assistants for intelligence work in Egypt in 1882 and Sir Charles Wilson five on the Gordon Relief Expedition, including the then young Captain Herbert Kitchener.

Wolseley relied heavily on his chiefs of staff for routine administration, writing on a number of occasions during the Gordon Relief Expedition that he had no intention of attempting to be his own chief of staff: 'it is a very stupid thing in any position in life to keep a dog and bark yourself'.[14] Wolseley's chiefs of staff, however, were not intended to share in decision-making. Buller saw Wolseley for only eight hours in two months once Wolseley went forward to Wadi Halfa in December 1884, leaving Buller 360 miles behind at Korti. Rather similarly, Wolseley allowed little latitude to his subordinates in field command, the problem in the Sudan being that of scale. Wolseley was not allowed as far forward as he would have liked by the government, and the sheer distances involved – it was 1600 miles from Cairo to Khartoum – proved too great for personal control to be exercised. Moreover, the very way Wolseley operated militated against the development of initiative in his subordinates and, without him, they floundered.

Compared to the adoration attracted by his hero Lee, Garnet Wolseley was respected rather than liked and had associates rather than friends. Nonetheless, he was generally successful in coordinating the diverse talents of his chosen subordinates in a way well suited to colonial campaigning. The problem was that improvisation was no substitute for a proper general staff and Wolseley's capacity to manage affairs decreased in proportion to the growth in the scale of operations. In that respect, Grant's operations could have offered many useful lessons but, of course, it was not Grant who caught the imagination of Wolseley but Lee, 'the greatest man I ever conversed with'.[15] That speaks volumes for the understanding of command by arguably the greatest soldier produced by the Victorian army and gives the moment of the Confederacy's high summer at Chancellorsville such unexpected resonance for those who study the British army.

2

Cleansing the East with Steel

Major-General Sir Henry Havelock is not a name well known today, hence the well-publicised recent failure of the Mayor of London, Ken Livingstone, to understand why a statue in Trafalgar Square commemorates him. Perhaps catching the spirit of Livingstone's historical amnesia, leaders of the Sikh community in Southall, also recently called for its Havelock Street to be renamed Gurdwara Road, since 'Havelock was bad, there is no doubt about it. He killed so many innocent people who were protesting against the British Raj'.[1] Apart from the somewhat curious description of the Indian Mutiny of 1857–58 as a 'protest', this also flies in the face of the fact that the Sikhs fought with the British to suppress the Mutiny. Indeed, Sikhs served with the column commanded by Havelock himself in his attempts to relieve first Cawnpore, and then Lucknow. Though now sometimes represented as a nationalist uprising against the British, the Indian Mutiny was confined to the Bengal army and the rebels had no clear concept of their overall objectives or how to translate the sporadic outbreaks of violence into any meaningful wider revolt. Mutiny had arisen from what might be termed bread and butter grievances affecting the sepoys, such as the greater expectation of overseas service and the erosion of former privileges, though there was some sense in which religious practices were also deemed under threat. In the event, however, the newly conquered Punjab did not join the mutiny and it was far from the case that all Bengal sepoys rose in revolt.

It might be added that, as there are some 129 roads, streets, avenues and other thoroughfares named for Havelock in Britain, a wholesale renaming process might cause some difficulties. In 1971, at least, there were still five London public houses named after this strict teetotaler, though Havelock is no longer a common Christian name as it once was.[2] Curiously, seven towns are named after Havelock in the United

States, where he was also once famous and where flags were flown at half-mast in his memory after his death. A number of Union and Confederate units sported 'Havelock caps' – a white canvas headdress with a flap covering the neck – in the American Civil War.[3]

The siege and relief of Lucknow, of course, inspired celebrated poems by Tennyson, who wrote 'Havelock' in 1858 and, much later, 'The Defence of Lucknow' in 1879. John Whittier was another poet who memorialised Lucknow. Indeed, Havelock's fame owed much to the particular circumstances of the time. There was a growing national press with the emergence of popular Sunday weeklies alongside the national dailies such as *The Times* and a burgeoning provincial press. While the national dailies catered primarily for an upper middle-class readership, the weeklies such as *Reynolds's Newspaper* and *Lloyd's Weekly Newspaper* attracted lower middle-class and working-class readers. Moreover, improved communications meant that, despite the disruption in India itself, news now reached Britain far quicker than in the past, the major stations such as Allahabad, from which Havelock's column started out for Cawnpore and Lucknow, being linked to the telegraph. Of course, the prurient nature and morbidity of the Victorians added to the impact of the news of massacre and violation of white women and children, *The Times* apologising to its readers for reporting what was 'painfully interesting' concerning the Cawnpore massacre.[4] The clamour for revenge in Britain was such that it has been argued that the Mutiny represented the 'first national-popular colonial war'.[5] In such circumstances, the efforts of Havelock and his small command to reach Cawnpore and Lucknow was of intense public interest, particularly as it still took some time for each episode in the saga to reach a British public anxious for news. Though the first relief of Lucknow set the seal on Havelock's fame in Victorian Britain, he was just as lauded for his deep Christian faith. Havelock, indeed, was the Christian hero par excellence, another factor which chimed with the times.

Born in Sunderland, the son of a ship builder, Havelock was educated at Charterhouse and intended to enter the law. His difficult relationship with his father, however, cut him off from financial support and he chose to take up the offer of a commission from his elder brother, William, who had been awarded the right of nominating a candidate as a result of his gallantry in the Peninsular War and at Waterloo. Havelock entered the 95th Foot in July 1815. He was always studious – he was known as 'old Phlos' in his schooldays – and chose to learn both Persian and Hindustani before proceeding to India in 1823 with the 13th Foot, into which he exchanged his lieutenancy. Though endowed with some religious convictions by his mother, a fellow officer, James Gardner, apparently aroused Havelock's deeper interest in religion on the voyage out to India. He became acquainted with a number of missionaries while stationed at Calcutta and, after service in the First Burma War, married Hannah, the daughter of a Baptist missionary, Dr Joshua Marshman. It was Marshman who converted Havelock to the Baptist faith in 1829.

In an army hardly known for its religious convictions, Havelock stood out – if that is the best description of someone barely over five feet in height – in reading psalms to troops, issuing Bible tracts and endeavouring to keep his men sober, persisting in what he regarded as his Christian duty despite the scorn of many of his superiors and peers. In fact, Havelock was unpopular with the soldiers not only through his long-winded sermonising, but also because he earned the reputation of something of a martinet. To many, Havelock, who persisted in wearing his medals on all possible occasions, appeared cold and aloof. There is little doubt that his earnestness and proselytising held him back in his career, though he himself attributed his slow progress to the purchase system: he was still only a captain after twenty-three years' service. Certainly, he was of only modest means, and with five children to support – another three had died in infancy – Havelock had almost left the army altogether. In 1847, a serious liver complaint he had picked up in Burma confronted him with the choice of staying in India in order to maintain his military income, but with the possibility of his death leaving Hannah and the children with only a small pension and the purchase value of his commission; or of returning to England to recover at such expense that it would erode all his resources and 'finally sacrificing my prospects in the army by purchase'. In the event, the illness of one of Havelock's daughters compelled Hannah to go back to England with the children in 1849. Havelock followed, returning 'from India as poor, the increased claims on me considered, as I went to it'. Having made a recovery, Havelock again contemplated retirement but, feeling it to be not financially viable, chose to return to India in 1851, leaving Hannah and the children in England.⁶

One newspaper editor described Havelock as 'an old fossil dug up and only fit to be turned into pipe clay'.⁷ To Marshman, however, Havelock was the epitome of the ideal Christian soldier, lionised as such in his weekly newspaper, the *Friend of India*. Havelock's brother-in-law, John Clark Marshman, carried the image still further in his eulogy, *Memoirs of Major-General Sir Henry Havelock*, first published in 1860.

The younger Marshman's vision of Christian Militarism was essentially a middle-class one and, here, Havelock's modest means and background also struck a chord for, following the attack on the supposed aristocratic failures in the Crimea, the national and provincial press was ready for a more lowly hero. Marshman's interpretation of Christian Militarism postulated a direct connection between the private and public spheres, in which Havelock's domestic beliefs and spirituality naturally impacted upon his military duties and reinforced his heroism. In later years, other interpreters of Christian Militarism and other biographers of Havelock would equate heroism more with purely military qualities, whereas Marshman was primarily interested in the intellectual and emotional currents underlining Havelock's beliefs. Havelock thus increasingly became lauded for his secular martial qualities in the same kind of terms that had nearly always applied to other Mutiny heroes such as John Nicholson and William Hodson, whom no one could have considered saintly, and that were applied from the start to later public heroes such as Wolseley, Roberts and Kitchener. In the mid nineteenth century, however, it was Havelock's undoubted Christianity that struck a wider chord throughout Victorian society and beyond. He was equally upheld in these terms as a shining example for emulation in continental Europe.

The idea that the soldier, once universally considered as unfit for polite society, could also be a good Christian had emerged during the Crimean War, but the Mutiny gave it greater impetus in the sense that Christianity itself could be said to be under attack from the perceived bestiality of the mutineers. To the evangelicals, Havelock was ideal material, and, even before Marshman published his biography, all manner of tracts, sermons, odes and lectures on Havelock had already appeared. These included such offerings as *Honouring God, and its Reward: A Lesson from the Life of the Late General Sir Henry Havelock, Havelock the Broad Stone of Honour: A Just Tribute of the Sword and Pen, General Havelock and Christian Soldiership, Ode on the Death of General Sir Henry Havelock,* and *The Soldier and the Saint: or Two Heroes in One. A Christian Lecture in Memory of the Late General Havelock.* Alongside Marshman's biography, there were also three earlier ones – the Rev. W. Owen's *The Good Soldier: A Memoir of Major-General Sir Henry Havelock* (1858), W Brock's *A Biographical Sketch of Sir Henry Havelock* (1858), and James Grant's *The Christian Soldier: Memorials of Sir Henry Havelock* (1858). Brock, a Baptist minister, is estimated to have sold 46,000 copies, while Marshman remained in print for over fifty years, the last edition appearing in 1909. A penny pamphlet, *Who and What is Havelock?* sold over six thousand copies in 1857. Early biographies also appeared in the United States and Germany. Among the plethora of plays, novels and popular songs commemorating the Mutiny, many made reference to Havelock. There was a 'Havelock March' and a 'Havelock Polka Militaire'. His death also coincided with the growth of a degree of enthusiasm among intellectuals for Puritanism, with which Havelock's self-discipline accorded, representing 'an impressive contemporary embodiment of a fashionable literary and aesthetic ideal'.[8]

Alongside Havelock's religious conviction there was his temperance, again hardly typical of the army at the time, especially in India where cheap spirits were plentiful and easily obtained. The Baptists, of course, campaigned against alcohol through such periodicals as the *Soldier's Magazine and Military Chronicle,* first published in 1829. Even before his formal conversion, Havelock and some fellow officers had become known as 'Havelock's Saints' at Rangoon in 1823, the epithet later being transferred to Havelock's men in the 13th Foot, in which he established a Regimental Temperance Society in 1836. Then regimental adjutant, Havelock communicated with other adjutants in British regiments, encouraging them to emulate his example. Some thirty or so such regimental societies existed by 1838, though they do not appear to have spread beyond India and regiments customarily dispensed with them on leaving the subcontinent.[9] After his death, the Havelock Scripture Readers' Fund was launched by the Soldier's Friend and Army Scripture Readers' Society to provide new temperance rooms in barracks in India.

Like Christian Militarism, temperance was a largely middle-class phenomenon in Britain and it was taken up by a number of Rifle Volunteer
units after the revival of the Volunteer movement in 1859. Significantly,
as a temperance corps, George Cruikshank's 24th Surrey RVC was known
as 'Havelock's Own'. The unit failed in 1862 and Cruikshank then raised
the 48th Middlesex (Havelock's Rifles) RVC as a similar temperance
corps later that year. Cruikshank retired as commanding officer in 1868
and the corps dropped the association with Havelock's memory two
years later. In 1862, meanwhile, an old Baptist missionary friend of
Havelock, the Rev. John Gelson Gregson, founded the Soldiers' Total
Abstinence Association at Agra, where Havelock himself had helped
build the chapel. Its work was eventually continued by the Army Temperance Association, which issued medals for each year of successful
temperance. Appropriately, one such medal of the ATA was the Havelock Cross. Less appropriately, perhaps, a Havelock brand of cigarettes
featuring the general's image appeared in the 1880s.

Whatever the eccentricities of his character, no one could doubt that
Havelock possessed just as much courage as a Nicholson or a Hodson,
though his military abilities as displayed in the Mutiny were actually
modest. Havelock took part in the First Afghan War, publishing his
reminiscences of its first phase. After some staff appointments, Havelock
returned to his regiment, serving with it during the defence of Jellalabad
between November 1841 and April 1842. He then accompanied the
so-called Army of Retribution on its march to Kabul to avenge the
disaster that had overtaken the Anglo-Indian army there. For his services,
he received a brevet majority and the CB. There followed service in the
Gwalior campaign of 1843 and the First Sikh War, in which three horses
were shot from under him. More staff appointments followed while
Havelock exchanged into first the 39th Foot and then the 53rd. Having
received a regimental Lieutenant-Colonelcy and a Brevet Colonelcy, he
became Quartermaster-General in India in 1854 and then Adjutant-
General within a few months. Sent to command a division in the Persian
War in 1856, he played a leading role in the operational planning of the
campaign.

Havelock was on his way back to India to resume his duties as
Adjutant-General when the first Mutiny outbreak erupted at Meerut
on 10 May 1857, quickly spreading to Ferozepore and Delhi. Now

sixty-two, Havelock hurried to join the Commander-in-Chief, George Anson, before Delhi, but was shipwrecked off the Singhalese coast on passage to Galle, the overland route from Bombay being closed by the mutineers. Finally reaching Madras, he discovered that Anson had died of cholera and the Commander-in-Chief of the Madras army, Sir Patrick Grant, had been appointed to act in supreme command until Sir Colin Campbell could be summoned from England. Havelock therefore accompanied Grant to Calcutta, where he was introduced to the Governor-General, Lord Canning, on 17 June by Grant, as the man to meet the hour. Lady Canning memorably described the small white-haired man of the leathery countenance: 'No doubt he is fussy and tiresome, but this little, old, stiff figure looks as fit and active for use as if he were made of steel.'[10]

Havelock himself had no doubts that he was God's chosen instrument to suppress the Mutiny, telling his troops on leaving Allahabad that 'We are bound on an expedition whose object is to restore the supremacy of British rule and avenge the fate of British men and women'.[11] Generally, of course, the assumption that British rule had been a liberal and benevolent guardianship suggested an evil conspiracy lay at the root of the Mutiny, and that if imperial control 'grew light or wavering' the 'Hindoo Sepoy' was ever ready to 'slay, to ravage, and spoil'.[12] Small wonder, indeed, that Kipling later wrote of 'remnants of the gallant host', who 'cleansed the East with steel'.

The most immediate problem among many was the relief of Major-General Sir Hugh Wheeler's command at Cawnpore and that of the Chief Commissioner of Oudh, Brigadier-General Sir Henry Lawrence, at Lucknow. Now ranking as Brigadier-General, Havelock hurried up the Grand Trunk Road to Allahabad to command a Moveable Column, forces having already been concentrated there by Colonel James Neill of the 1st Madras Fusiliers, one of the East India Company's European regiments. A vigorous and active soldier, and incidentally another fervent Christian, Neill believed himself more fitted to command the column than Havelock. Relations between Havelock and Neill were difficult from the start. Havelock, who tended to take a gloomier view of the situation than Neill, was referred to by the latter's staff as 'Mr Pomposity'. Both, however, were equally determined to extract retribution among the mutineers and there is no doubt that Havelock approved of the casual brutality already exhibited by Neill's troops on their way to Allahabad. Later in the campaign, indeed, Havelock spoke of the mutineers as 'devils incarnate'.

By the time Havelock had improvised a makeshift relief column of some 1200 men, setting out for Cawnpore on 7 July, Wheeler had already surrendered. Indeed, having accepted safe conduct from the notorious Nana Sahib, Wheeler and his garrison had been massacred on 27 June, and the surviving 125 or so women and children confined to a house known as the Bibighar. Having some inkling that he was already too late, Havelock proceeded slowly at first. The small advance guard commanded by Major Sydenham Renaud, originally dispatched by Neill, was then threatened by the approach of the mutineers from Cawnpore and Havelock quickened his march to affect a junction with Renaud. At Fatehpur on 12 July, Havelock encountered this force and drove it off at small cost, largely through the skilled use of his artillery and the effectiveness of the Enfield rifle musket. It was the first British success since the start of the Mutiny, also satisfying Havelock's long-felt desire to have commanded an army in the field. Another force was driven off on 15 July and Havelock seized the vital bridge across the Pandu (Panda Nudi) river.

At this point, news reached Havelock that, though Wheeler and virtually all of his men were dead, the women and children remained alive. Accordingly, on 16 July, he pressed on despite shortage of supplies and the exhausting heat. The mutineers blocked the main road but Havelock outflanked them near Aherwa, having another horse shot from under him in the action. His force had covered 126 miles in just nine days and fought three major actions. Unknown to him, however, the women and children at Cawnpore had been slaughtered on 15 July, as a result of his forcing of the river, and their bodies thrown down a well.

On reaching Cawnpore on 17 July and discovering the grim scene, the British troops went on the rampage, fuelled by liquor. Havelock undoubtedly lost control of discipline, his removal of all remaining liquor and threat to hang those responsible for plundering having little appreciable effect. Neill, meanwhile, who had remained at Allahabad was now ordered up to take command at Cawnpore with the rank of Brigadier-General under the impression in Calcutta that Havelock's health was failing him. When he got there, he found Havelock strong and healthy, and determined to continue to exercise command. Indeed, Havelock made the situation quite clear, telling the newcomer, 'Now General Neill, let us understand each other, you have no power or authority whilst I am here, and you are not to issue a single order'.[13]

Havelock now proposed to go on to relieve Lucknow, leaving Neill at Cawnpore, where the latter was soon to visit even more brutal retribution on the native inhabitants, though Havelock appears to have been the first to blow mutineers from guns in the advance towards Lucknow. Havelock would dearly have liked to rescue his old friend, Henry Lawrence, but he had already died on 4 July after being mortally wounded by a shell burst in his room at the Residency. The difficult was that Havelock only had some 1200 European troops from the 64th, 78th, and 84th Foot, and Neill's 1st Madras Fusiliers; three hundred Sikhs; and ten guns. Moreover, the troops were already exhausted by their previous exertions in the extreme heat, and cholera had begun to strike. At one point during the subsequent operations, indeed, a medical officer told Havelock his force would be entirely wiped out in six weeks by disease if the current rate of sickness continued. By 20 August, he had only 700 fit men.

Meeting stiff resistance, Havelock had to withdraw back to the Ganges. There was then an extraordinary spat with Neill, who openly criticised his superior, writing to Havelock, 'I deeply regret that you have fallen back one foot'. Havelock resented 'the most astounding words ever addressed by a subordinate officer to his commander', replying that 'I do not want and will not receive any advice from an officer under my command, be his experience what it may'.[14] Havelock also addressed a complaint to Grant, but was sufficiently stung by Neill's criticism to try to advance once more. Neill now changed his mind, fearing the consequences of another advance. In any case, Havelock was compelled to return to Cawnpore twice more, though urged to continue by his son, Harry (later Sir Henry Havelock-Allan), who was acting as his ADC. Havelock's nephew, Charles, was also serving with the Moveable Column.

There are various versions of a speech Havelock delivered at one point during this period and, equally, varying versions as to where precisely it was delivered. According to Havelock's son, it was, 'I am trying you severely, men ... But I know the stuff you are made of. Think of the poor women and children at Lucknow. With God's help we shall save them, or every man of us die in the attempt.' It was apparently met only with a 'low growl', but Havelock said, 'They'll cheer when I show them the enemy and the bugles sound the "charge".'[15] In passing, it should be said that Havelock's son may not have been the most reliable of witnesses. Badly affected by sunstroke while en route to India in 1848, the younger Havelock suffered from what the old *Dictionary of National Biography* delicately referred to as 'periodic fits of mental excitement and eccentricity'. Many indeed, like Wolseley, regarded him as all but insane. Undoubtedly courageous, the younger Havelock took extreme positions on issues such as the value of mounted infantry over cavalry. Indeed, having retired as a Lieutenant-General just before the campaign in Egypt in 1882, Havelock-Allan – he had taken the additional name in 1880 as a condition of a cousin's bequest – tried to persuade Wolseley to give him a military position. Liberal MP for Sunderland from 1874–81 and Liberal and Liberal Unionist MP for South-East Durham from 1885–92 and from 1895 onwards, Havelock-Allan was mortally wounded by a tribesman on a visit to the North West Frontier in 1897.

Meanwhile, Wheeler's old divisional command and the appointment of Chief Commissioner of Oudh had been given to the fifty-four-year-old Major-Gen Sir James Outram, Havelock's former superior in Persia. An energetic and popular commander, Outram was to become known as the 'Bayard of India'. Like Havelock he became associated with temperance, taking up a suggestion by an army chaplain in 1860 to establish Outram Institutes as reading rooms for other ranks, though they were not actually alcohol-free until linked with the Soldiers' Total Abstinence Association in 1887. On arriving at Cawnpore, Outram declared that he would not take away the command from Havelock after all his exertions but would serve merely as a volunteer horseman and in his civil capacity until Lucknow was relieved. In reality, despite his generous gesture, Outram could not wholly restrain himself. According to Havelock's son, this uncertainty undermined his father's confidence for the rest of the campaign and rendered him less decisive.

Another advance was imperative, Lawrence's successor in command at Lucknow, Colonel Inglis, reporting that matters were deteriorating rapidly. Havelock in theory commanded the 2nd Brigade and Neill the 1st Brigade under Outram. Outram certainly gave the direction of the final advance to Havelock but, at one point, appears to have overruled Havelock's wish to make a detour rather than advance directly on the Residency. At another point, Neill, who was killed in the final attack, declined to act on orders conveyed to him by Havelock's son without Outram's direct orders. In turn, Outram lost his temper when Havelock wanted to make the final push on the Residency on 25 September after heavy losses had been sustained forcing the Charbagh bridge, Outram, however, conceded, though he wished to wait until the next day. Havelock's son later claimed that Outram gave up nominal command on this day only so he could win the VC and that Outram told the historian of the Mutiny, Sir John Kaye, this personally in 1863.[16] Havelock's nomination of his own son for the VC came because, according to the latter, he alone obeyed his father's orders that they should ride at the head of their men rather than lead on foot before Cawnpore on 16 July. It was Outram who then recommended the younger Havelock for a second VC following the action before Lucknow on 23 September, the latter reputedly twice saving Outram's life.

On 26 September, the rear guard of the Moveable Column and its sick and wounded were brought into Lucknow. The losses had been heavy – almost a quarter of the force committed. Outram was forced to conclude that, rather than withdrawing with the garrison, they had to stay until a stronger force could reach them. Seen very much as the hero of the first relief of Lucknow, Havelock was given a knighthood and promoted to major-general in September, and made a baronet in November. Significantly, however, these honours were essentially forced upon the government by the pressure brought by the Indian Relief Fund Committee, another middle-class organisation, which had claimed Havelock as its special agent of retribution, and which had been outraged at the grant of just a modest pension to Havelock for his services earlier in the year. It was then the Havelock Memorial Committee that pressed for the statue in Trafalgar Square, a Havelock Memorial Fund being created for the purpose of raising the necessary funds from the public in March 1858 under the presidency of the army's Commander-in-Chief, the Duke of Cambridge.

Havelock was only to learn of the knighthood and the promotion when Grant's successor as Commander-in-Chief in India, Sir Colin Campbell, led the second relief of Lucknow on 14 November 1857.

Havelock never learned that he was a baronet. He had escaped without injury when a shell burst in front of him on the very day of the final relief. He, Outram and others had then risked death in dashing across an open space under heavy fire to greet Campbell, Havelock's son being one of those wounded in the attempt. Havelock, however, contracted dysentery on 20 November. He died on 24 November at the Dilkushah, the former royal hunting seat overlooking the town. Suitably, it was said that his last words to his son were, 'See how a Christian can die'.[17] Havelock was buried under an obelisk in the garden, now a public park. His son received the baronetcy.

3

The Hand on the Throttle

The small cemetery at Mount Prospect in Natal is not much visited, for it lies some way off the main road that runs from Newcastle to Volksrust in the Transvaal through Laing's Nek, and on private land. As from everywhere in this area, however, there is no mistaking the distinctive, seemingly flat-topped, brooding shape of Majuba. Some 2000 feet above the road at Laing's Nek, Amajuba (or the Mount of Doves) as it was known to the Zulu, dominates all. There are fifty-three graves arranged in five rows, together with two monuments to the Gordon Highlanders. Furthest away from the entrance, and also furthest north, in Row B one finds the grave of George Colley, Lord Lytton's erstwhile adviser, killed at Majuba on 27 February 1881. Or, as he had become, Major-General Sir George Pomeroy-Colley, High Commissioner for South-East Africa and Governor of Natal. The knighthood was acquired in 1879 as a result of his services in India, and the additional surname adopted subsequently, Pomeroy being Colley's second Christian name but also the former family name changed as a result of conditions of inheritance. Next to Colley is the grave of Colonel Bonar Deane, Colley's intelligence officer, killed at Laing's Nek on 28 January at the head of the 58th Foot (soon to be the 2nd Battalion, Northamptonshire Regiment) in the last engagement in which a British regiment had taken its colours into action.

This Anglo-Transvaal or First Boer War (1880–81) was a result of increasing Afrikaner resentment at British control of the Transvaal, which had been annexed back in 1877. The British had hoped that the defeat of the Zulu would have reconciled the Boers to the benefits of British rule over an emerging imperial confederation in southern Africa. The attempt, however, to institute a more efficient taxation system – Britain had been able to annexe the Transvaal because of its bankruptcy – had created a new grievance. The situation was then exacerbated by the failure of Gladstone's new administration in Britain to adhere to its electoral promises of leaving the Transvaal. The Boers proclaimed the re-establishment of their republic in December 1880, ambushed a British column en route between Lydenburg and Pretoria, and laid siege to seven small British garrisons in the Transvaal. Colley, therefore, resolved to force his way through to the relief of the garrisons by way of Laing's Nek.

In a strange way, while both victims of the Boers, it might also be argued that Colley and Deane were equally victims of their wives. In the case of Deane, his wife had long tried to keep him 'in a glass case', but, seeing him increasingly unhappy, had then written in support of his employment in South Africa.[1] Though he had recently been on active service in Pondoland, Deane had never been in action and effectively commandeered the 58th when Colley allowed his staff to participate in the engagement. In the way of the Victorian army, when a man died gallantly (however impetuously), the widow was usually treated with enormous respect. That was certainly the case with Mrs Deane. It was so, too, with the widow of the promising Colonel Robert Home, left with six young children, after his death from typhoid in January 1879 while serving with the commission for the delineation of the Bulgarian frontiers. Equally, Major-General Sir Herbert Stewart's wife, widowed for a second time after his lingering death from wounds near Jakdul Wells in the Sudan in February 1885, was also carefully protected. Widows, in turn, had a role to play, several undertaking the task of overseeing their husband's biographies. This was the case with Susan, Countess of Malmesbury, widow of Major-General Sir John Ardagh; Beatrice, Lady Gatacre, widow of Major-General Sir William Gatacre; Lady Stewart, widow of Field-Marshal Sir Donald Stewart; and Charlotte, Lady MacGregor, Major-General Sir Charles MacGregor's second wife, who married him only four years before his premature death from peritonitis in 1887.

To some extent, the appropriate role was also initially played by Lady Colley, who hastened to visit her husband's grave as soon as the hostilities had ended, and over which she had the cross erected that still remains. But Edith Colley raises altogether wider issues with respect to the role of officers' wives in the late Victorian army. Another vignette is called to mind. In October 1880 the very first train had pulled into

Pietermaritzburg in Natal following completion of the line from Durban: no gold had yet been discovered on the Rand to speed the development of railways in southern Africa. It was not so much, however, Colley standing on the footplate that was remarked upon as the fact that the hand at the throttle was that of Lady Colley.

Colley's wedding in 1878 at the age of forty-three to Edith Hamilton, the daughter of Major-General H. Meade 'Tiger' Hamilton, had surprised most at Simla. All recognised her lively intelligence and Colley was to write from Natal that she 'seconds me splendidly, and rows or laughs at the people who come to her with long faces or absurd stories'.[2] So far so good. Yet, as Sir Evelyn Wood also noted in a letter on the very day on which, unknown to him, Colley had been killed, Edith Colley's ambition for her husband 'obliterates apparently every thought of the personal danger which he has undergone'.[3] Indeed, it was widely believed that she had written to Colley after his initial defeats at Laing's Nek and then Ingogo (8 February) to urge him into further action, the letter mysteriously disappearing after his death. Garnet Wolseley, whose chief of staff Colley had been in the latter stages of the Zulu War, subsequently believed that she had married Colley as a matter of convenience rather than love, a conclusion reached in the light of her second marriage and swift and financially productive separation in 1891.

Edith Colley thus stepped, albeit unsuccessfully, beyond the stereotypical perception that wives merely complemented their husbands in the approved manner of Victorian domestic ideology. Clearly, many officers' wives did confine themselves to what is often described as the 'private sphere'. One of Douglas Haig's early biographers, for example, eulogised Lady Haig as having 'fulfilled to perfection the difficult role that falls to the lot of the wife of a great man' and as a 'discreet and sympathetic confidante' who 'devoted every moment of her married life to her husband'.[4] In reality, the Honourable Dorothy Vivian's position as one of Queen Alexandra's ladies-in-waiting, was not without advantage for Haig when he married her in 1905. Moreover, even in a purely domestic role, a wife's domestic competence could be of significance. Lord Cromer specifically requested the appointment of Major-General the Hon. R. A. J. Talbot to the Cairo command in 1898 'as I thought his wife would do the social work well – and that is really all the General here has to do'.[5]

Equally, though as ambitious for her husband as Edith Colley and ever ready to feed Evelyn Wood's already considerable vanity, Lady Wood had the unfortunate drawback of being quite incapable of running an orderly household. Wolseley once complained of Wood's house being as filthy as a railway refreshment room, with Wood oblivious to the noise surrounding him as a result of his deafness, but also seemingly unworried by the appalling food. On another occasion, the Commander-in-Chief, the Duke of Cambridge, complained to Wolseley that he had never experienced such 'an infamous lunch' as that with the Woods – he lamented that a simple chop would have sufficed. Subsequently, he suggested Wolseley advise Wood to put his home in order.[6] Indeed one factor which enabled Wood to secure the Aldershot command in 1888 was that the wife of Wood's principal rival, John Ross, had even greater shortcomings than Mary Wood. Nor did Wood's sister, the minor novelist Anna Steele, assist his cause by some of the speeches she crafted for him. Another of Wood's sisters was to become the notorious Katherine (Kitty) O'Shea, root of the downfall of Charles Stewart Parnell. It does not appear this had any additional influence on Wood's career, though it caused some gossip in 1888–89 when Wood, Anna Steele and Wood's brother jointly contested the will of an aunt, who had left her considerable fortune solely to Kitty. Kitty's divorce from O'Shea assisted Wood's case and Wood may even have encouraged O'Shea to begin the proceedings. There was an out of court settlement on the disputed will in 1892.

Wolseley's wife, Louisa, whom he had married in 1868, was a more than capable partner to her husband. Almost certainly illegitimate, Loo, as she was known to Wolseley, although his endearments also ran to the distinctly curious 'little runterfoozle', was just as determined a character as he was. Interestingly, her social role was performed only in home stations, for she declined to accompany Wolseley on nearly all of his overseas postings. She had little time for Wolseley's occasional philosophical musings on the nature of fame and patriotism, proved especially jealous when other women seemed too friendly towards him, and also spent some lengthy periods away from him after his campaigning days were over. Yet, whatever her apparent shortcomings, she played a significant role in defending Wolseley's interests at home. In 1879, for example, when Wolseley was still in South Africa, she was the intermediary between him and leading Conservatives over the possibility of a peerage. Two years later, she was again negotiating a peerage on her husband's behalf while he was still in Egypt, this time with Liberal Ministers. She passed messages to Wolseley from the Queen during the Gordon Relief Expedition, and in 1893 it was she rather than Wolseley who was sounded out by the Secretary of State for War, Henry Campbell-Bannerman, on the likelihood of Wolseley accepting the Malta command. After Wolseley's serious illness in 1897 she was especially protective of him. Moreover, it was clearly thought that she had an active influence over him for, in 1884 and again in 1899, she was besieged by women trying to get their husbands or sons to the Sudan and South Africa: in 1884 she called them 'camel mammas'.

In reality, there is little to suggest Loo Wolseley was at all influential in the selection of Wolseley's officers or in guiding particular decisions by her husband, though this did not prevent her from exercising independence on occasions, nor being relatively influential in shaping his career. Others were more overt in attempting to wield influence such as Evelyn, Lady Grenfell, whom the then Colonel Sir Francis (later Field-Marshal Lord) Grenfell married in 1887 just after his appointment as Sirdar of the Egyptian army. Grenfell succeeded Evelyn Wood in the appointment and, somewhat confusingly, his new bride was also Evelyn Wood, though actually the daughter of retired Major-General Blücher Wood. Similarly, General Sir William Lockhart's wife was also said to wield considerable influence over her husband. As both Adjutant-General and, later as Commander-in-Chief in succession to Cambridge, Wolseley was frequently subjected to letters from wives seeking employment or preferment for their husbands, not least Princess Helena of Schleswig-Holstein on behalf of her son and the Queen's grandson, Prince Christian Victor. Young Christian Victor was to find an early grave on active service, a victim of enteric (typhoid) in South Africa in October 1900.

Both Lady Randolph Churchill and Lady Jeune (later Lady St Helier) successfully lobbied Evelyn Wood when he was Adjutant-General to get the young Winston Churchill to the Tirah in 1897 and then to the Sudan in 1898. Lady Cunynghame was so incensed by the apparent slight to her husband, General Sir Arthur Cunynghame as Commander-in-Chief at the Cape, by Wolseley's appointment as High Commissioner for Natal in 1875 that she wrote direct to Cambridge demanding the Gibraltar or the Malta commands as proof of the Duke's support. Equally, Adria, Lady Chelmsford also complained bitterly of her husband's treatment after the disasters of the Zulu War, Lieutenant-General Lord Chelmsford having succeeded Cunynghame in the South African command and having then been succeeded by Wolseley in turn. Indeed, the interference of wives was sufficiently common for Colonel the Hon. (later Lieutenant-General Sir) James Dormer, trying to avoid being sent to Malta as DQMG in 1878, to warn his wife, Ella, to stay away from the Military Secretary at the Horse Guards 'for when these things are done at the proper time, & in the right way, nothing does so much harm as wives or female relatives interfering'.[7]

Perhaps the supreme example of female patronage, however, is Nora Roberts, wife of Wolseley's great rival, Frederick (later Field-Marshal Lord) Roberts. Roberts married Nora Bews, the youngest daughter of a retired Scottish soldier, in 1859, at the comparatively young age of twenty-seven. She was just twenty. Bobs was a diminutive figure. She was somewhat taller and, according to Wolseley, who met her for the first time in 1895, 'the commonest and most vulgar looking old thing I have ever seen',[8] a judgement sadly borne out by her photographs. More significantly, when Roberts succeeded him as Commander-in-Chief in 1900, Wolseley wrote to his brother that he was clearing his office 'where she can job & dispense favours to her heart's content, dreadful women'.[9]

Wolseley's impartiality might be questioned, but the sobriquet of 'Bobs and Lady Jobs' was so well known as to suggest Wolseley was far from alone in his view. Even those relatively close to Roberts hint at it. Few letters of Nora Roberts survive, the correspondence between husband and wife having been destroyed – significantly – by one of Roberts's biographers in 1954. It is instructive, however, to compare those that do with Loo Wolseley's voluminous correspondence. While recounting those events at home of immediate professional concern to Wolseley, Loo's letters are often also detailed in their reportage of social and domestic events. By contrast, the one collection of Nora Roberts's correspondence so far located – those letters received by Roberts's former ADC, Viscount Melgund (later Earl of Minto) between 1879 and

1884 – are detailed discussions of military matters. It is almost as if Nora Roberts was acting as her husband's Military Secretary. In South Africa, where Roberts assumed the supreme command in January 1900, there was much talk of petticoat government and it was even suggested by another of Roberts's ADCs, Lord Kerry, that the conversion of Roberts to a much tougher line against Boer women and children owed much to Nora Roberts's arrival in Pretoria.

That arrival was also remarked upon by the Queen. In August 1900 Roberts received a telegram from Lord Lansdowne, the Secretary of State for War, and incidentally Kerry's father, conveying the Queen's concern for the safety of Lady Roberts in the occupied former capital of the Transvaal. Lansdowne, however, was concealing the Queen's real objection, as stated by her private secretary, Arthur Bigge: 'Endless stories, many of which are untrue, reach the Queen respecting Lady Roberts's interference and her influence even exerted on the careers of officers in high command in South Africa.' Thus, if she was not at Pretoria, there could be no possible grounds for accusations 'which are but too common against her'.[10] Indeed, five years earlier, the Queen had described Bobs as 'ruled by his wife who is a terrible jobber' to the extent that she felt he would be unacceptable as Commander-in-Chief at home.[11]

The Queen herself was not beyond promoting the military interests of her own favourites, not least her son, the Duke of Connaught, but she also took her own prerogative immensely seriously, since all promotions to the rank of major-general and above were formally submitted for her approval. No doubt, she was also influenced in her attitude to Nora Roberts by her own social conservatism, resolutely opposing the entry of women to the professions and other means of advancement. Nora Roberts had offended, but she was not unusual or unique, for officers' wives were not necessarily confined by any perception of separate private and public spheres. Nor can it be assumed that marriage automatically implied their subordination or constrained their ambition.

Poor George Colley, himself a modest man, may or may not lie in Mount Prospect a martyr to a wife's ambition. Ironically, the man hurriedly sent out to the Cape to take command after Majuba, but then forced to return straight back to England since peace had already been negotiated by Evelyn Wood, was Roberts, whose wife's ambitions were to have a more successful outcome.

4

The Devil's Pass

It is increasingly difficult to reach the top of the Devil's Pass at Hlobane in Zululand. The mining company that once maintained the unmade roads has ceased business and parts of the main road around the western end of the mountain, which is the easiest approach, have been washed away. The alternatives are a very steep climb up and over the adjacent Ntendeka plateau, or a very long trek across the top of Hlobane itself from the eastern end. Once at the top of the pass, however, it is easy to understand the peril facing Redvers Buller and his irregulars on 28 March 1879 when driven down this precipitous boulder-strewn drop from the top of Hlobane to the lower Ntendeka. It was a cattle raid gone wrong, with mounting opposition from the abaQulusi, whose stronghold Hlobane was, and also from the large Zulu impi which had arrived from the direction of Ulundi (oNdini) during the course of the day. Two Victoria Crosses were won during the descent. Buller himself rescued three men, including Captain Cecil D'Arcy of the Frontier Light Horse, while Major Knox Leet of the 13th Foot, commanding 'Wood's Irregulars', rescued Lieutenant A. Metcalfe Smith, also of the Light Horse. VCs were also won by Lieutenant Henry Lysons and Private Edmund Fowler, both of the 90th Foot, for an engagement in caves on the southern side of Hlobane earlier in the day, though these were not gazetted until 1882. Subsequently, Fowler almost forfeited his VC when, as a sergeant, he was reduced to the ranks for embezzlement in 1887. It is sometimes assumed that Lieutenant Edward Browne of the 24th Foot, attached to the Mounted Infantry, also won the VC at the Devil's Pass. The error seemingly stems from Hlobane being given as the location for the award, but the date being the following day. In fact, Browne won it for saving his commanding officer at Kambula on 29 March, when the impi that had savaged Buller's command was repulsed from Evelyn Wood's entrenched camp.

The awards for Hlobane were not without controversy, for a number of men had risked their lives to save their comrades in that frantic retreat. Indeed, Knox Leet had not been originally recommended by either Wood or Buller, his heroism being highlighted subsequently in a letter to the press from Metcalfe Smith. Indeed, it has been claimed that awards generally for Hlobane – including two Distinguished Conduct Medals – were confined to a 'favoured circle' around Wood and Buller.[1] It is certainly clear that the subsequent awards to Lysons and Fowler owed much to pressure upon Wood from Lysons's father, Sir Daniel Lysons, then Quartermaster-General at the War Office, who had the ear of the Commander-in-Chief at Horse Guards, the Duke of Cambridge, though the award had to await a change in the regulations for the VC.

Under the original warrant of 1856 the VC was available only for 'some signal act of Valour or devotion' or to those whose personal bravery contributed to the success of an operation.[2] It was not awarded, however, for an act of gallantry considered to be merely in the performance of duty until May 1881, the refining of the warrant arising principally from the case of Captain Euston Sartorius of the 59th Foot, who had led an attack on a hilltop position at Shahjui in Afghanistan in October 1879. Sartorius, indeed, was the first beneficiary of the change in interpretation, but Lysons and Fowler soon followed. As it happened, Sartorius's elder brother, Reginald, had won the VC in Ashanti in 1874, making them one of only four pairs of brothers to win the award (the others being Hugh and Charles Gough during the Mutiny, the Bradfords during the Great War and the Turners in the Great War and the Second World War). The Goughs also have the distinction of being one of three families in which fathers and sons won the supreme award, Sir Charles Gough's son, John Gough, gaining his in Somaliland in April 1903. Frederick Roberts won his VC for his gallantry at Khodagunge (Khudaganj) in January 1858 during the closing stages of the Mutiny, while his son, Freddie, won what was technically a posthumous VC at Colenso in December 1899. In the same action of saving the guns at Colenso, Captain (later General Sir) Walter Congreve also won the VC. His son, Brevet Major William 'Billy' Congreve received a posthumous award in July 1916.

Hlobane, however, was not the only action of the Zulu War in which the award of the VC raised issues. Another case in point was the award of three VCs for an engagement on the White Mfolozi on 3 July, in which a patrol led by Buller was attacked by some four thousand Zulus and, again, men had to be rescued. The recipients were Captain Lord William Beresford of the 9th Lancers; Sergeant Edmund O'Toole of the Frontier Light Horse, who assisted Beresford in rescuing Sergeant Fitzmaurice of the 24th Foot attached to the Mounted Infantry; and D'Arcy, whom Buller had rescued at Hlobane and who had apparently been denied the VC himself on that occasion as a colonial officer, but now received it for attempting to rescue Trooper Raubenheim of the Frontier Light Horse. As later recalled by Harcourt Bengough, who had commanded the 2/1st Natal Native Contingent, it was widely believed that Beresford had got himself an appointment in Zululand specifically 'with the resolution of qualifying for the Victoria Cross'.[3] To Beresford's credit, however, he insisted that he would not accept the VC unless it was also awarded to O'Toole. In the case of D'Arcy, Wolseley, who, having succeeded Chelmsford in the South African command, pinned the VC on D'Arcy, believed that the latter should not have received the award since he had not actually succeeded in saving Raubenheim's life.

There was another candidate, however, whose claims for the White Mfolozi were not successful, despite a lengthy campaign pursued on his behalf by his father, who took the matter up with Buller personally. Lieutenant F. M. G. Hutchinson of the 4th Foot had served with the Mounted Infantry and, it was claimed, had participated in the rescue of Fitzmaurice. The campaign had evidently been under way for sometime before the first surviving correspondence between Hutchinson's father and Buller dating from January 1880, Hutchinson senior having written with the apparent support of testimony from Edward Browne. While acknowledging that Hutchinson had acted gallantly, Buller indicated that the line had to be drawn somewhere. Buller also wrote to Browne, however, complaining that, if Browne had points to raise, then he should communicate with him direct rather than at second hand through Hutchinson's father. Buller also professed that, while his recollection of what Hutchinson may or may not have done at the White Mfolozi was 'a matter of doubt', he was absolutely sure that no officer attached to the Mounted Infantry had been present when Fitzmaurice was rescued and there could be no recommendation for the VC.[4] Hutchinson and Browne then maintained that there was no implied criticism of Buller, merely a wish to establish the facts, Hutchinson sending what he claimed was 'a simple statement of fact'.[5] Exasperated by what he saw as Hutchinson's presumption that the VC was his son's personal right, Buller passed the whole correspondence to the Military Secretary at Horse Guards, Sir Alfred Horsford, where the matter clearly ended.

It might be suggested that, as a mere Lieutenant-Colonel, Hutchinson senior did not have the clout of Lysons's father. Nor did Hutchinson's influence equate to that Sir Henry Havelock, whose part in conferring the VC on his own son, Sir Henry Marshman Havelock (later Havelock-Allan), in October 1857 during the Mutiny had raised significant concerns – for all that Havelock had at least theoretically acted on the recommendation of Sir James Outram. What increased the appearance of favouritism was that the recommendation then went to London via the Governor-General and the Court of Directors of the East India Company rather than through the Commander-in-Chief in India. When Havelock was recommended for a bar in 1858, it was rejected on the grounds that it was clear 'that the feeling of the Army in India' was that he 'had not won the Cross when conferred on him by his father' and, therefore, effectively the original award stood for the second act of gallantry.[6]

At the same time that Wolseley presented D'Arcy with his VC, he also presented those won by Lieutenants John Chard and Gonville Bromhead at Rorke's Drift on 22/23 January 1879. Neither man impressed Wolseley and indeed both had been nominated directly by Chelmsford rather than by their immediate superiors, as would have been normally expected. Wolseley, himself fearless in action, clearly doubted that the situation had left the defenders with any other recourse but to fight for their lives, and that this tempered any supposed gallantry. Wolseley also had decided views on the claims being made for Lieutenants Neville Coghill and Teignmouth Melvill, who had been killed at Sothondose's Drift, soon to be renamed 'Fugitives' Drift', carrying the Queen's Colour of the 1/24th Foot from the field of Isandlwana on 22 January. It had become a well-publicised act of heroism, though whether, as reported, Lieutenant-Colonel H. B. Pulleine had given his adjutant, Melvill, any instructions to leave with the Colour, is unknown. Coghill, orderly officer to Brevet Colonel Richard Glyn, the nominal commander of

No. 3 Column, had a badly damaged leg, which rendered him all but immobile. He had clearly left the camp before Melvill and only met up with him at the Buffalo (Mzinyathi) river, riding back into the water to help Melvill when he got into difficulties in the swollen waters. Exhausted, both men were overwhelmed by Zulus, who may well have been natives living on the Natal side of the river rather than those who had pursued the fugitives from Isandlwana.

Wolseley, however, acidly noted that heroes had been made of two men 'who taking advantage of their having horses bolted from the scene of action to save their lives' and, indeed, that 'it is monstrous making heroes of those who saved or attempted to save their lives by bolting ...' Earlier, Wolseley had written of the same incident, 'I don't like the idea of officers escaping on horseback when their men on foot are killed'.[7] Even Chelmsford questioned whether Melvill would have received the VC if he had saved the Colour and himself. Glyn, by contrast, did his utmost to get Melvill and Coghill recognised. Lest it be thought that Wolseley was routinely grudging in the matter of the VC, he was instrumental in pushing the enquiries which resulted in its award to Sergeant Anthony Booth of the 80th, who had directed a fighting retreat by the survivors after the Zulus had ambushed Captain David Moriarty's wagon train escort at the Ntombe drift in March 1879. The difficulty was that, by enhancing Booth's heroism, the conduct of the surviving officer, Lieutenant Henry Harward, who had deserted his men, appeared the more reprehensible. In the event, Booth's citation made no mention of Harward. Wolseley hoped Harward would be convicted at the subsequent court martial and was astonished when he was acquitted, writing that he would have hanged him personally. That there was a court martial at all was largely due to pressure from outside South Africa, Chelmsford having sent Harward back to Pietermaritzburg to appear before a medical board, which conveniently found him unfit for further duty in South Africa. Major-General the Hon. Hugh Clifford, commanding the lines of communication at Pietermaritzburg, was convinced Chelmsford had done so in an to attempt to hush the whole affair up.

As it happened, the original warrant did not allow for the posthumous award of the VC, or rather assuming that it did not became a matter of convention. This not only affected the cases of Coghill and Melville, but also that of Wood's staff officer, Captain the Hon. Ronald Campbell, killed in the same engagement at Hlobane for which Lysons and Fowler were honoured. Consequently, Cambridge wrote to Melvill's father in April 1879 indicating that his son would have won the VC if he had survived. Wood requested a similar letter for Campbell's family but this seems to have been blocked by Wolseley. The convention continued to present difficulties, as in the case of Lieutenant Walter Hamilton of the Corps of Guides, who was recommended for the VC as a result of his gallantry at Fattehabad in Afghanistan in April 1879. Initially, the application for Hamilton was turned down in July 1879 but the VC was then granted on the appeal of the India Office, by which time Hamilton had been killed leading a sortie in defence of Cavagnari's doomed mission in Kabul in September. Consequently, the submission to the Queen was deliberately dated two days before Hamilton's death.

Rather similarly, Freddie Roberts's VC was at least technically posthumous but, as he had died of his wounds two days after Colenso, it could be claimed that he was alive at the time he actually won the Cross. When more cases arose during the South African War, Coghill's father raised the matter once more. The new King, Edward VII, twice refused to relent on the rule but, when Melvill's widow directly petitioned him in December 1906, then relented. The rules were changed, therefore, in January 1907 with Melvill and Coghill honoured, together with two men whose cases dated back to the Mutiny, a case from the Matabele Revolt in Rhodesia in 1897 and another from the North-West Frontier in the same year of 1897.

There were other anomalies, however, in the story of the VC. At Hlobane, Captain F. Duck of the Veterinary Corps performed gallantly and was supposedly recommended by Buller for a VC, only for Chelmsford to refuse to nominate him on the grounds that he had had no right to be there in the first place. Yet Viscount Fincastle won the VC on the North-West Frontier in 1897 when actually present only as a war correspondent, having been released on leave from his regiment specifically on the understanding that he would not be eligible for any campaign medal or reward. Briefly, too, between 1858 and 1881, it was possible to win the VC for acts of gallantry not in the presence of the enemy. The *Sarah Sands* incident, involving a dangerous fire on a troopship in 1857, first raised the issue, but a soldier recommended for his gallantry on that occasion fell foul of the fact that the provision was not retrospective.

One VC was awarded, however, to Timothy O'Hara of the Rifle Brigade for putting out a fire in a railway car full of ammunition in June 1866 during the campaign to contain Fenian incursions into Canada. Five more went to members of the 24th Foot for saving lives in a storm at sea off the Andaman Islands in May 1867. Ironically, one of the five so honoured, Private William Griffiths, was killed at Isandlwana serving with G Company of the 2/24th.

The one VC that was awarded for Isandlwana at the time was to Private Samuel Wassall of the 80th Foot, attached to the Mounted Infantry, who rescued Private Westwood, also detached from the 80th, at Fugitives' Drift. Cases for gallantry awards were also made for three others who escaped the carnage of Isandlwana, namely Captain Alan Gardner of the 14th Hussars, Lieutenant Walter Higginson of the 1/3rd Natal Native Contingent (NNC) and Lieutenant James Adendorff of the same NNC battalion. Higginson had attempted to help Melvill and Coghill but had pressed on to try and find horses when they were too exhausted to continue. Adendorff is a shadowy figure, who managed to reach Rorke's Drift and, despite claims to the contrary over the years, almost certainly did not stay to assist in its defence, despite being specifically mentioned as having done so in Chard's report. Controversy, however, continues to surround the precise moment at which Adendorff left Isandlwana and the route which he took. Indeed, at the time, though the Duke of Cambridge felt initially well disposed towards Adendorff, Chelmsford rejected any award for the only man who fought at both engagements, as his early arrival at Rorke's Drift suggested he had left Isandlwana 'way before he had any right to do so'.[8]

Gardner, attached to the staff of No. 3 Column, was one of only five regular officers to escape the field. The others were the director of transport for No. 3 Column, Captain Edward 'Lucky' Essex of the 75th Foot; Lieutenant William Cochrane of the 32nd Foot, a transport officer of Lieutenant Colonel Durnford's No. 2 Column; Lieutenant Horace Smith-Dorrien of the 95th Foot, another transport officer with No. 3 Column; and Lieutenant Henry Curling of N Battery, 5th Brigade Royal Artillery, the battery attached to No. 3 Column. Having reached the Natal bank of the Buffalo, Gardner conferred with Essex and Cochrane, and wrote a hasty note of warning to the troops at Helpmekaar. Gardner also dispatched two men of the Mounted Infantry, Privates Evans and Whelan, to warn the garrison at the Rorke's Drift mission station. Having reached Helpmekaar, Gardner later claimed that he could find no one to take a second message to Evelyn Wood, commanding No. 4 Column, which had advanced into Zululand from Utrecht. So he went on to Dundee himself. By his own account, Gardner had attempted to rally some mounted Basutos (BaSotho) of the Hlubi Troop of the Natal Native Horse to help hold the right flank of the British line at Isandlwana but they had fled.[9]

It was rumoured, however, that Gardner, who had returned to the camp at Isandlwana early on the fateful morning carrying a message for Pulleine from Lord Chelmsford, had deserted the laager being hastily formed at Helpmekaar. It led to the little ditty recorded by Glyn's principal staff officer, the acerbic Major C. F. Clery, 'I very much fear that the Zulus are near so hang it, I'm off to Dundee'.[10] As in the case of Adendorff, whom Cambridge first thought had been ordered to Rorke's Drift by Gardner, the Duke felt Gardner's conduct in warning Wood merited some reward, but the campaign by some of Gardner's friends to have him awarded the VC proved counterproductive: he received a brevet Majority.

Though he had gained the VC himself, Buller's own view was that the only reward that counted was promotion, writing in February 1879 after Chelmsford had mentioned him in despatches that 'every little helps, for if I am to get anything out of the Zulu War in the way of further promotion I must do a big thing, otherwise I have not a chance, small brevets are easy enough to get, but the plum, of a full Colonelcy is another matter'.[11] Indeed, as Adjutant-General, Buller continued to subscribe to the view that the performance of duty was not sufficient to qualify for a VC and, later still, he declined to recommend the award to another of the eventual Colenso VCs, his own ADC Captain H. N. Schofield, on precisely these grounds. Walter Congreve pointedly remarked that if Schofield was effectively acting under orders to save the guns, the same applied to himself and Freddie Roberts. In any case, Lord Roberts, now Commander-in-Chief at the War Office, and the Secretary of State for War, Brodrick, recommended Schofield in April 1901 over Buller's head and without reference to him. Buller had also resisted what he saw as the blatant favouritism of Sir George White's recommendations of five members of his own regiment, the Gordon Highlanders, for gallantry at Elandslaagte in October 1899.

Interestingly, Knox Leet was put up for a brevet lieutenant-colonelcy by the Duke of Cambridge while the Queen had wanted a brevet for Beresford, which the Duke declined to recommend. On other occasions, both Buller and also Henry Brackenbury told Wolseley that promotion was preferable to the award of the KCB, a position also taken by Sir Gerald Graham when offered a baronetcy.[12] Wolseley himself, who had risen to the rank of colonel without benefit of purchase and as a result of brevets for his own gallantry, similarly turned down a baronetcy after the Ashanti expedition in 1874, as well as refusing a GCB on the grounds that such an advance in the Order of the Bath would offend more senior officers. Already holding a KCMG, Wolseley accepted the KCB and promotion to GCMG, noting that the liberality with which honours had been awarded after Sir Robert Napier's Abyssinian expedition in 1867–68 had unnecessarily inflated military expectations. Lest it be thought Wolseley was entirely altruistic, however, it might also be noted that he felt a baronetcy was only 'a reward reserved for common people',[13] and he entertained some hopes that he might get a peerage. He angled again for a peerage after the Zulu War in order to consolidate his claim to the supreme command in India, and was denied one by the Queen in 1881.

Wolseley finally secured a peerage after his victory over the Egyptian army at Tel el Kebir in 1882, though characteristically angling for a viscountcy rather than a mere barony, which was available to 'every whippersnapper of a diplomatist or party supporter'. Equally, Wolseley, who was never wealthy and lost much money supporting his various relatives, wanted a pension attached to the peerage. He also still wanted promotion 'because I have always thought that the higher I mounted the military ladder the more good I should be able to do the idol that I have always worshipped since I was capable of understanding what love of country meant', his only ambition being to 'see England great'.[14]

Not all took quite the same view as Wolseley. One of his protégés, T. D. Baker, had left the staff at the Horse Guards to take the appointment of Military Secretary to the Viceroy in 1878 in the expectation of advancing his career, only to discover during the first phase of the Second Afghan War that it was George Colley, as Political Secretary, who secured the KCSI for political services, while the Commander-in-Chief,

Haines, only rewarded those directly engaged in military operations. Baker felt he had fallen between two stools, confessing to the Duke of Cambridge that 'being heart & soul in my profession, I cannot but feel somewhat disgusted at the present time, more especially as the opportunities (such as war) rarely offer of allowing one's getting on in the service'. Baker fervently wished he could have reached the Cape to participate in the Zulu War but, in the second phase of the war, he managed to get nominated to a brigade command under Roberts and secured the KCB.[15]

Another of Roberts's brigade commanders, the highly ambitious Charles MacGregor, actively sought, first, the VC and, as this looked increasingly unlikely as he rose in rank, only then pursuing the KCB or the KCSI as an alternative route to prominence. MacGregor was desperate to win the Cross early in his career in the Mutiny and, again, in China in 1860. He wrote to his father on one occasion that he would gladly lose an arm or a leg in order to do so and, on another, that 'I wanted most awfully to see some fighting, and wanted nothing more than to get a chance of getting the Cross'.[16] Constantly thwarted, not least by his quarrels with superiors who might otherwise have recommended him, MacGregor had resolved by 1864 that his best chance for advancement now lay with becoming a sufficient specialist on Central Asian affairs as to make his services indispensable in the event of a major war. Not surprisingly, MacGregor was scornful of what he considered the 'unmanly' and 'unsoldierlike taunt' that Russophobia was driven by 'KCB mania'. Yet, some of the old hopes had not entirely disappeared, his surviving diary for that period of the Second Afghan War between 7 September 1879 and 7 September 1880 containing two references to the possibility of still getting a VC, as well as forty-eight references to his hopes of the KCB or KCSI and seven references to the likelihood of a peerage. Indeed, like an actor approaching Oscar night, MacGregor had a penchant for rehearsing acceptance speeches in reply to imaginary toasts in his honour.

In the event, MacGregor received the KCB in January 1881, becoming Quartermaster-General in India with the local rank of major-general. The rank, however, was not made substantive when MacGregor reached the end of his appointment in 1885 and, passed over for a divisional command, he accepted that of the Punjab Frontier Force. His health was now rapidly failing him with Bright's Disease suspected. He was compelled to leave India in April 1886, dying of peronitis following an operation for an abscess of the liver in Cairo, where he had gone to recuperate, in February 1887. MacGregor died some days before the receipt of the news that he had finally been gazetted a substantive major-general.

MacGregor's recognition that the higher in rank the more unlikely the VC was certainly borne out in practice, Colonel (local Major-General) Ian Hamilton being rejected for the VC for gallantry at Wagon Hill in January 1900 in the continuing belief that the Order of the Bath rather than the VC was the more appropriate reward for someone acting in a superior command position: the principle was not breached until 1917. As Commander-in-Chief, Wolseley, indeed, opposed creating any precedent when the VC had 'never been conferred upon an Officer so high in rank'.[17] Hamilton was doubly unfortunate, having been recommended for the VC after his gallantry at Majuba in February 1881. It was turned down then both on the grounds that he was young and would have plenty of other chances to distinguish himself and also because Evelyn Wood, who made the recommendation, had not actually witnessed the events. Though Hamilton claimed otherwise in his memoirs, referring only to his 'rough luck', it obviously still rankled.

Clearly, the VC was no hindrance to future preferment but it is difficult to judge how far its officer recipients positively benefited in terms of promotion and allocation of commands, particularly when it was increasingly less generously distributed compared with, say, the Crimean War and the Mutiny. There was possibly little absence of coincidence in the appointment of VC holders – John Watson and Herbert Macpherson – to principal commands with respect to the Indian expeditionary force despatched to Malta in 1878. Another VC also accompanied the force, the future General Sir Harry Prendergast commanding the force's contingent of Madras and Bombay Sappers and Miners. Subsequently, Prendergast held the Burma command in the Third Burma War, being replaced in March 1886 by George White, who was junior to him in rank. Macpherson, who was senior to both Prendergast and White, then took over in September. Macpherson's sudden death in October then compelled the Indian government to send out Roberts to assume personal command in Burma.

Indian commands generally were replete with VC winners in this period. In the case of the Second Afghan War, prominent commands were held by Sir Sam Browne, Sir Frederick Maude, John Tytler and Dunham Massy as well as Roberts, the two Goughs, Watson and Macpherson, while two later Commanders-in-Chief in India, White and Sir O'Moore Creagh, won the VC in the war. Apart from Buller, another prominent VC general was Sir Gerald Graham, who commanded the two Suakin expeditions in 1884 and 1885. Only four Field-Marshals have held the VC but three of them – Roberts, Wood and White (the other being Lord Gort) – were Victorian soldiers. Roberts and Wood both won the VC in the Mutiny and attained the baton in 1895 and 1903 respectively. Having won his VC at Kandahar in September 1880, White received his baton on the same day as Wood. It might be concluded, then, that the VC was sufficiently useful in a military career to be desirable. This does not detract in any way from the kind of gallantry required to win it in engagements such as Hlobane. Wood, indeed, considered rescuing comrades in the face of an uncivilised opponent far more worthy than doing so in any European context.

5

The Race for the Peerage

British regimental museums frequently have the capacity to surprise the visitor with the curious or unusual relic of some past encounter. Visitors to the museum of the Royal Gloucestershire, Berkshire and Wiltshire Regiment in the Cathedral Close at Salisbury will find one such exhibit, a proud possession of the Royal Berkshire Regiment and a reminder not only of the one of the heroic last stands of British military history, but also of the circumstances which firmly established Frederick Roberts as a public figure. The relic in question is a stuffed dog, bearing round its neck the Afghan War Medal. Bobby was the pet of a sergeant of the 66th Foot, soon to become the 2nd Battalion, Berkshire Regiment. The sergeant was one of the 'Last Eleven' from the regiment at Maiwand on 27 July 1880, the last stand of the 66th Foot near the village of Khig being one of two heroic incidents which compensated for disaster, the other being the saving of the guns of E/B Battery, Royal Horse Artillery.

While *Saving the Guns* became a celebrated painting by Richard Caton Woodville, another less skilled painting by Frank Feller commemorated the *Last Eleven*. Feller's painting also featured Bobby, who came into Kandahar covered in blood and with a light wound a few days later. Bobby became a celebrity in his own right, being awarded the war medal by Queen Victoria in person when brought back to England. Sadly, Bobby died soon afterwards under the wheels of a hansom cab in Gosport. The men of the 66th who fell at Maiwand were also remembered by a lion monument in Forbury Gardens in Reading, the regimental depot town, the sculptor of which allegedly committed suicide when it was pointed out that the creature's feet were not those of a lion.

To turn from Maiwand itself to its consequences, the defeat there by Ayub Khan of a force from the Bombay army led by Brigadier-General

G. R. S. Burrows on 27 July 1880 created an immediate crisis. With the return of the remnants of Burrows's force, the commander at Kandahar, Lieutenant-General J. M. Primrose, had less than five thousand men to defend a large perimeter against ten thousand or more Afghan regulars and tribesmen, the British defeat having also thoroughly roused the surrounding countryside. Though the degree of real danger to Kandahar and of the decline in morale among Primrose's men have both been exaggerated, a relief would clearly be necessary. In addition, a blow had to be struck against Ayub Khan, younger brother of the former Amir, Yakub Khan, whom the British had ejected from Kabul after Cavagnari's murder, and a bitter rival of the new Amir installed by the British, Abdurrahman. Such a relief attempt and counter-blow could either be mounted from Quetta to the south east or Kabul to the north east. Quetta was the closer to Kandahar and it was logical that the relief should be entrusted to the commander at Quetta, Major-General Robert Phayre. That, however, reckoned without Frederick Roberts.

Roberts had first come to the notice of the wider public commanding the Kurram Field Force in the first phase of the Second Afghan War. Then there was further recognition for Roberts in reoccupying Kabul after Cavagnari and his escort were massacred in September 1880; Roberts going on to repulse a major Afghan attack on his defences at the Sherpur cantonment outside Kabul in December 1880. What was to consolidate his reputation, however, was his celebrated march from Kabul to Kandahar in August 1880. From the start, Roberts was determined to reach Kandahar before Phayre and win what would become known as the 'Race for the Peerage'.

News of Maiwand reached Kabul on 28 July. Roberts had just returned to the city without completing an intended tour of inspection in the Khyber. According to his own account, Roberts returned as a result of a premonition of disaster, 'a presentiment of coming trouble which I can only characterise as instinctive'.[1] Roberts had equally claimed a premonition on his last meeting with Cavagnari. Lieutenant-General Sir Donald Stewart, who had taken the supreme command at Kabul much to the Roberts's chagrin in April 1880, was not inclined to weaken Kabul and send forces to Kandahar, unless it could not be more quickly relieved from Quetta.[2] Indeed, it had already been agreed to begin withdrawing the British garrison from Kabul later that month and

Stewart would have to plan a complicated withdrawal through the Khyber at the height of the hot season. Roberts, however, strongly pressed for a force to be sent from Kabul on the grounds that Phayre had insufficient troops readily available and that the Bombay army could not be trusted with a relief mission. Stewart was persuaded to give Roberts command of a relief since it was evident that Stewart himself would be required to oversee the delicate negotiations with Abdur-rahman for the withdrawal from Kabul – for which Roberts had little aptitude. Roberts himself telegraphed to the Adjutant-General in Simla, George Greaves, to urge the acceptance of the idea. Not only did Stewart yield command to Roberts but he also gave him the pick of the forces available.

The force comprised 10,148 fighting men, consisting of nine infantry battalions, including the 72nd and 92nd Highlanders and the 2/60th Foot; three cavalry regiments, including the 9th Lancers; and three mountain batteries. Nearly all the Indian units were Sikhs, Gurkhas or Punjabis. Baggage was reduced to what was regarded as the absolute minimum, with British soldiers restricted to 30 pounds, native troops to 20 pounds, and followers to 10 pounds. Nonetheless, there were still 8143 followers and 11,224 assorted baggage animals, comprising mules, ponies, donkeys and camels.[3] Roberts was given full military and political powers and, on arrival at Kandahar, would be senior to Primrose, Roberts's local rank of lieutenant-general predating that of Primrose by four months.

The march was not quite the epic portrayed. Leaving Kabul on 8 August, Roberts encountered no opposition, the only real problem being that of supplies and the exhausting heat, the temperature touching 110 degrees Fahrenheit on 29 August. Over the course of twenty-four days – two days were spent entirely at rest – Roberts's force covered 301 miles, the longest day's march being of twenty-one miles and the daily average some 13.7 miles. On most days, the march began at 4.00 or 4.30 a.m., causing some difficulties for those packing and leading the baggage animals since it was still dark at that time of the morning. Some thirty days' supply of tea, rum, sugar, salt and dal were taken, fifteen days' worth of preserved vegetables, five days' worth of bread-stuff and flour, and ten days' worth of mutton on the hoof. The bread-stuff, flour and the sheep were regarded as emergency reserves, with each unit responsible for finding its own additional supplies en route. As it happened, a reasonable amount of corn could be purchased along the route for forage, but there were difficulties of finding firewood in order to cook. Some houses were purchased and pulled down and, on some occasions, recourse was had to roots.

Another difficulty was adjusting the marching lengths between units since, for example, Highlanders had a longer stride pattern than Gurkhas. Ten minutes' rest was allowed every hour, with twenty minutes allowed for breakfast at about 8.00 a.m. At one point, however, the 2nd Brigade was well ahead of its baggage animals. En route, Roberts lost 811 baggage animals while, generally, the daily sick list among the troops averaged around 550 men and 200 followers, though on 23 August Roberts reported that only five men had actually died with four missing believed murdered by tribesmen. On arrival in Kandahar on 31 August, a total of 940 men were admitted to hospital.[4] The acerbic Charles MacGregor, who had been given command of a brigade and himself hoped for a KCB out of the affair, was nonetheless particularly critical of the pace, writing on 26 August: 'The march of this force is that of a disorganised rabble. An Afghan, seeing it, said we were like an Afghan army whereas Stewart's was like a European.'[5]

MacGregor's allusion was to the march of Stewart from Kandahar to Kabul between 27 March and 2 May 1880, in which Stewart had taken a force of 7294 fighting men, 7273 followers and 11,000 baggage animals over the same route in reverse in thirty-seven days but in face of stiff Afghan opposition. Indeed Stewart had fought a sharp action, albeit without great tactical skill, at Ahmed Khel on 19 April. In comparing the two marches subsequently, many contended that Stewart's had been the more difficult, the greater praise accorded to Roberts arising from the circumstances of the relief of Kandahar and the attendant press attention accorded it as a result, as well as the prominence given Afghan affairs in the British general election of April 1880.[6]

It was already clear by the time heliograph communications were opened through the British garrison at Kalat-i-Ghilzai between Kandahar and Roberts's column on 21 August that the city was in no real danger, hence the first full day's halt on 24 August, The second full day's halt on 29 August – the hottest day of the march period – also reflected Roberts's growing awareness that he was going to get to Kandahar before Phayre, which had dictated much of the early relentless pace. Indeed,

writing on 20 August – the day the force marched twenty-one miles –
MacGregor had recorded, 'All this to try, and cut in to Kandahar before
Phayre. This is just like Bobs, he is exposing his force to be defeated in
detail, and Phayre too, whereas, if both got there together the result
must be success ...' On another occasion during the march, MacGregor
concluded that Roberts was simply 'a reckless little brute'.[7] MacGregor
was a malevolent character and, obviously, his views need to be treated
with some caution, but Roberts was to take enormous risks with transport with unfortunate results during the South African War. Compared
to Wolseley, indeed, he was an indifferent organiser.

Just as MacGregor believed Roberts was taking risks to win the race
against Phayre, so the new Viceroy, Lord Ripon, feared that Phayre 'may
be very desirous of winning the race between himself & Sir F. Roberts
for the Kandahar prize'.[8] It was not a view shared by the Commander-
in-Chief in India, Sir Frederick Haines. Though Phayre's force had
initially been seen as the main relief effort, Haines did not believe that
Phayre was particularly motivated by the idea of a race. Haines, though,
was anxious to push Phayre on, as Roberts would be dependent on the
supplies Phayre brought in to Kandahar. Indeed, Phayre was to bring
up ten days' supplies for the Kandahar garrison and a month's supply
for Roberts's force.[9]

Phayre himself, meanwhile, was encountering severe transport problems, higher temperatures and more tribal opposition than Roberts. A
veteran officer of the Bombay army, Phayre had commanded on the
lines of communication between Jacobabad and Quetta during the first
phase of the war, before being nominated as the Bombay representative
on the Eden Commission investigating the organisation of the army in
India as a result of the experience in Afghanistan. Phayre was regarded
as a sound choice to defend the Bombay army against possible reduction,
as he 'is a strong man and has the ability and force of character to make
himself heard'.[10] Promoted to major-general, Phayre was back on the
lines of communication at Quetta for the second phase of the war,
following Cavagnari's murder, and was considered for the command at
Kandahar after Stewart's departure for Kabul. Ripon's predecessor as
Viceroy, Lytton, however, had heard that Phayre had a temper and had
been unable to cultivate cordial relations with the political officers or
the Afghans on the lines of communication. He felt Phayre lacked

sufficient tact and judgement for the command. Equally, Stewart thought Phayre would 'go off the rails' if given his head in Kandahar.[11] Command passed instead to Primrose, a British officer, who had commanded the reserve division of the Kandahar Field Force in the first phase of the war, despite Primrose's obvious poor health.

News of Maiwand reached Phayre on the same day that it reached Roberts, but his available forces – seven infantry battalions and nine squadrons of cavalry regiments – were strung out over the lines of communication and, moreover, consisted only of Indian units, apart from a battery each of the Royal Artillery and Royal Horse Artillery. The 2/11th Foot, however, was on its way to Quetta. Few transport animals were readily available and, in any case, Baluchistan had been suffering drought conditions for almost two years and forage was in particularly short supply. A railway line had been laid towards the Bolan Pass during the earlier part of the war, but it was only single-tracked and was to be greatly strained by the numbers of men now being moved urgently forward. From the railhead at Sibi, most troops had to march the remaining eighteen miles to the Bolan over a desert terrain, in temperatures averaging 120 degrees Fahrenheit and then on to Quetta. Moreover, through the hostility of Marri and Kakar tribes, the main effort beyond Quetta through the Khojak Pass would have to be preceded by pacifying columns. Phayre soon concluded, therefore, that he could not hope to set out for Kabul for at least fifteen days. In the event, he was unable to leave Quetta until 21 August, further complications having arisen from a mutiny of the troops of a British ally, the Khan of Kalat, which necessitated bringing up the 78th Highlanders from Kurrachee (Karachi).

For all practical purposes, the advance only really got underway through the Khojak Pass on 30 August. Realising that Roberts was already almost at Kandahar, Phayre found it appropriate to slow his advance and reduce his own force in order to compensate for the lack of supplies on his own route and in the vicinity of Kandahar. Ripon later praised Phayre's 'admirable self-denial' in doing so.[12] The only purpose now to be served was to advance sufficient troops to secure the supply route into the city. Phayre finally arrived at Kandahar on 6 September, by which time Roberts had dispersed Ayub Khan's army. Given the difficulties he faced, it is remarkable Phayre got there as early as he did. Despite the exhaustion of his own force on reaching Kandahar, Roberts believed that Phayre's men would have been too spent to fight an action had they arrived first. By contrast, the Commander-in-Chief of the Bombay army, Lieutenant-General Warre, felt that, had Roberts waited for Phayre, he would have gained an even more complete victory over Ayub Khan than was achieved on 1 September.[13]

Within two days of Phayre's arrival, Roberts, whose own health was now shaky, had departed, as had MacGregor's brigade, which marched back over Phayre's route to further punish the Marris. Some of Phayre's troops were also detached to continue the work of pacification along the route from Quetta and to give further support to the Khan of Kalat. Roberts had handed command over to the hale and hearty sixty-year-old Phayre. Twelve years younger than Phayre, however, Roberts did not believe that Phayre should exercise the command in the longer term. Indeed, he considered neither Phayre nor Primrose fit for such a position. There were many doubts over Primrose's command at Kandahar and his state of mind in sending a telegram after Maiwand to the effect that Burrows's force had been annihilated. There is little doubt that Roberts found it convenient to exaggerate the degree to which the morale of the Kandahar garrison had declined during its investment by Ayub Khan, but Primrose was clearly ailing and he was removed from command altogether in October 1880. Ripon shared the earlier view of Lytton that Phayre was not at his best dealing with political matters; and, in any case, doubts had now arisen on his organisational abilities as a result of the supply problems faced on his march into Kandahar. Though he had no personal knowledge of Phayre, the Duke of Cambridge also doubted that he was prudent or experienced enough to remain in command, given that he 'had frequently been in hot water when employed politically'.[14] Consequently, Cambridge favoured Major-General John Ross, Roberts's second-in-command, for the billet.

As a result, though formally confirmed in the Kandahar command on 15 October, Phayre was told that it would be only temporary. He was replaced by Major-General Robert Hume, a British officer recently recovered from sunstroke, on 10 November. Phayre returned to his duties on the lines of communication and cooperated well with Hume, who was forced to go on sick leave in September 1880 with an abscess on the shoulder. Having seen Roberts off to Kandahar, Stewart had withdrawn the British garrison from Kabul on 11 August 1880 and overseen the general evacuation of northern Afghanistan, involving the withdrawal of some 24,000 men and all their stores over 170 miles. Again, it was at the peak of the hot season.[15] There was considerable debate as to whether Kandahar should be retained or not, but the government resolved to withdraw in November 1880. Now recovered, Hume oversaw the withdrawal of the last troops on 22 April 1881, taking command at Quetta. Phayre himself, however, had moved to command the Mhow Division in January 1881.

In 1893, when corresponding with the historian W. H. Hanna, General Sir Charles Gough denied that he had ever entertained the idea that he, too, was in a race with Roberts to reach Kabul after Cavagnari's murder. Gough opined, however, that Roberts was no stranger to self-advertisement for, in the opening phase of the war, the Khyber line and not that of the Kurram had been intended as the main thrust, but 'private & personal interests and ambitions carried the day'.[16] Phayre may or may not have believed himself to be involved in another race with Roberts in August 1880 but Roberts most certainly did. Ironically, however, there was to be no peerage. Roberts received the GCB and went on to become Commander-in-Chief in Madras, his fame as 'Our Only Other General' alongside Wolseley now assured. The peerage finally came on his relinquishing his appointment of Commander-in-Chief in India in 1892. Roberts chose the title of Baron Roberts of Kandahar. He was elevated to an earldom during the South African War. His perceived rival, Phayre, who had received the KCB for his part in the relief of Kandahar, had retired with the rank of general three years earlier.

6

Paths of Duty

One of the hidden gems of Paris is the Musée des Plans-Reliefs located in the attic of Les Invalides above the Musée de l'Armée. Entirely renovated and reopened in 1997, and beautifully presented in subdued light, the collection features scale models of strategic fortified towns, mostly to a scale of 1 : 600, ranging in date from the late seventeenth to the mid nineteenth century. A subsidiary collection of relief plans of northern towns is also on view at the Musée des Beaux-Arts in Lille. Yet equal to the impact of the Paris exhibits is the magnificent model of Gibraltar and its defences, also on a scale of 1 : 600, and on show in the Gibraltar Museum in the appropriately named Bomb House Lane. The Gibraltar model shows the defences as they were in 1865. It was executed on the instructions of the then CRE, Major-General Frome, but constructed by Lieutenant Charles Warren, RE, who had undertaken a trigonometrical survey of the Rock as well as supervising the scarping of its eastern face to render it inaccessible. In fact, Warren made two models of Gibraltar, the second being displayed in the Rotunda at Woolwich for many years but now lost.

In themselves, Warren's models provide adequate illustration of the considerable attainments of officers of the Royal Engineers, but his varied career also suggests the ways in which many Victorian army officers were required to fulfil a multiplicity of functions, for Warren was to be engineer, colonial administrator, fighting soldier, archaeologist, politician, and policeman. Indeed, while the military historian may remember Warren primarily for his participation in the Spion Kop disaster in January 1900 during the South African War, archaeologists know Warren best for his excavations in Jerusalem from 1867 to 1870 during what might be termed the heroic age of British archaeology. By contrast, some will recognise him chiefly as the Commissioner of the Metropolitan Police from 1886 to 1888 during the Whitechapel murders of Jack the Ripper, the many conspiracy theories surrounding these events fuelled by the fact that Warren was also a prominent freemason.

Before considering Charles Warren in more detail, however, it should be noted that the achievements of Victorian soldiers in non-military fields were considerable, as the exhibition 'Butterflies and Bayonets', held at the National Army Museum back in 1989 nicely illustrated. Colonel Augustus Henry Lane Fox presented the 14,000 items of his ethnological and weapons collection to the Bethnal Green Museum in 1874. The collection subsequently went to the University of Oxford to be housed in the Pitt-Rivers Museum, the now Lieutenant-General Lane Fox taking the surname of Pitt-Rivers as a proviso of a family bequest in 1880. Pitt-Rivers also campaigned for the preservation of ancient monuments, becoming an Inspector when the Ancient Monuments Act was passed in 1882, and building a second collection of archaeological and other objects, which was displayed in his private museum at Cranborne Chase. Subsequently, much of this second collection passed to the Salisbury and South Wiltshire Museum in the 1970s. Similarly, the collection of Egyptian antiquities at Eton College is that of Major William Joseph Myers, one time Adjutant of the 2nd Bucks (Eton College) Rifle Volunteers, who was killed while serving unofficially with his old regiment, the King's Royal Rifle Corps, at Dundee in Natal in October 1899.

One is accustomed to expect that Victorian officers slaughtered any game that moved, an impression easily reinforced by General Sir Ian Hamilton's memoirs of his days as a subaltern in India and mostly based on letters to his brother, *Listening to the Drums*, with such chapter sub-headings as 'The Boar', 'Quail Shooting', 'Markhor Shooting', 'Encounters with Bears', and 'My First Ovis Ammon'.[1] Yet there were those whose interests went beyond extermination. Thus the collection of Australian fauna in the Royal Cornwall Museum at Truro is that of Hamilton's fellow member of the Roberts ring, Lieutenant-General Sir Reginald Pole-Carew, being collected while 'Polly' was private secretary to the Governor of New South Wales between 1876 and 1879. Earlier, Brevet Lieutenant-Colonel John George Champion, mortally wounded at Balaclava in November 1854, had supplied the Madras, Cambridge and Kew Botanical Gardens with hundreds of new plants he had discovered in Ceylon and Hong Kong. Ironically, Champion died at the notorious Scutari hospital, the medical shambles of the Crimea being presided over at least in theory by the Director-General of the Army Medical Department, Sir Andrew Smith. The latter would doubtless have preferred to be known to history more for the five-volume *Illustrations of the Zoology of South Africa*, published in 1849, and the 1700 specimens he presented to the Natural History Museum in Edinburgh in 1858. So many geological, ethnographical and entomological specimens were presented to the United Service Museum (later the United Service Institution), which had been established in 1831, that its Council resolved in 1858 that it could no longer accept large stuffed animals unless they were specifically connected to a particular military campaign.

Colonel Charles Gordon spent much of his time as CRE on Mauritius in 1881 studying the Coco-de-Mer palm-like tree on the island of Praslin in the Seychelles, presenting specimens to Kew, and concluding from this and other evidence that it had been the site of the Garden of Eden. Following his resignation as Commandant General of the colonial forces at the Cape in 1882, the now Major-General Gordon went travelling in the Holy Land, searching for biblical sites including the true site of Calvary, since he rejected the traditional site beneath the church of the Holy Sepulchre. His pamphlet, *Reflections in Palestine*, edited from his letters to a Prebendary of Exeter, was published while he was besieged in Khartoum. As is well known, a visit from Kitchener after he became a celebrity was about as welcome as one from Queen Mary for collectors of porcelain, both making embarrassingly plain their desire for pieces which caught their attention.

Other soldiers also produced works of note. There were the explorers such as Lieutenant-Colonel Francis Rawdon Chesney, whose two-volume account, *The Expedition for the Survey of the Rivers Euphrates and Tigris*, advocating the opening of a route to India through the Euphrates valley, appeared in 1850. Chesney's earlier report on the feasibility of a Suez Canal inspired Ferdinand de Lesseps, who referred to Chesney as 'the father of the Canal'. William Henry Sleeman, the man who destroyed the power of the Thugee cult in India in the 1830s, produced a great classic of travel writing, *A Journey Through the Kingdom of Oude in 1849–50*, in 1858. Equally, William Butler's *The Great Lone Land* appeared in 1872, recounting his exploration of the North-West Territories on behalf of the Canadian government following the suppression of the Riel rebellion by Wolseley on the Red River in 1870. Butler is wonderfully descriptive of a 'prairie-ocean' wilderness in which he saw 'the world as it had taken shape and form from the Creator'.[2]

Captain (later Colonel) Fred Burnaby's celebrated *A Ride to Khiva*, published in 1876 and recording his trek over snow-covered steppes in defiance of the Tsarist government's prohibition on foreigners entering Central Asia, was followed by *On Horseback Through Asia Minor* in 1877. Francis Younghusband's account of his trip from Peking to Kashmir via Manchuria and the Gobi in 1886, *The Heart of a Continent*, was published ten years later when he was a captain and reprinted four times in its first year. It was but one of many books Younghusband was to write stretching into the 1940s. Younghusband addressed the Royal Geographical Society on his experiences in 1888 and, its youngest ever elected member, was awarded the Founder's Medal two years later. Indeed, the annals of the Royal Geographical Society are replete with contributions by soldiers such as George Hayward, another Founder's Medallist of the Society, who lectured to it on his journey from Leh to Yarkand and Kashgar in the Pamirs in December 1869. A few months later, Hayward was murdered on another expedition in Yasin, his death commemorated in Newbolt's poem, 'He Fell Among Thieves'.

Among other soldiers awarded the Founder's Medal were Chesney, awarded it in 1838 for his work in Syria and Mesopotamia, and the African explorers Captains Richard Burton of the 18th Bombay Native Infantry (1859), John Hanning Speke of the 46th Bengal Native Infantry (1861) and James Grant of the 8th Bengal Native Infantry (1864). RGS Presidents included Major-General Sir Henry Rawlinson (1871–73 and 1874–76), who had received the Founder's Medal in 1840 for explorations in Persia, and General Sir Richard Strachey (1887–89). Younghusband was to be President after the Great War (1919–22), while his predecessor, Colonel Sir Thomas Holditch (1917–19), had also been awarded a Founder's Medal in 1887 for his work in Afghanistan.

In terms of other kinds of investigation, R. E. Crompton of the Rifle Brigade, who had begun by designing a rubber-tired steam engine for use on India's trunk roads in the 1870s, eventually became President of the Institute of Electrical Engineers and a pioneer of the introduction of electric lighting into Britain. The Hon. Edward Noel of the same regiment, besides climbing the Matterhorn and Mont Blanc, wrote

The Science of Metrology or Natural Weights and Measures, challenging the metric system. A noted military theorist, Captain (later Sir) Henry Tyler of the Royal Engineers left the army in 1866, becoming chairman of the Westing House Brake Company and deputy chairman of the Great Eastern Railway Company. Another Royal Engineer, Captain (later Sir) William Abney, who ran the Photography and Chemistry School at Chatham, organised a series of stations throughout the world in 1875 to photograph the transit of Venus for navigational purposes; that established in Egypt also photographically recorded ancient Egyptian sites in a series still extant in the library of the Royal Engineers' Institution. Abney also contributed greatly to the development of the emulsion printing process for photographs, and to colour photography.

More often than not it was the engineers, schooled in a more rigorous scientific education at the Royal Military Academy, Woolwich, than their cavalry and infantry colleagues at the Royal Military College, Sandhurst, who made their mark in other fields, since their professional skills were already likely to draw them into the civil sphere. Earlier in the nineteenth century, Royal Engineers had constructed Canadian canals and tamed Indian rivers in irrigation projects. Such construction continued into the late Victorian period. Colonel Sir Colin Scott-Moncrieff, who had published *Irrigation in Southern Europe* in 1868, and worked on further irrigation projects India, took up the post of Inspector-General of Irrigation in Egypt in 1883. Royal Engineers designed public buildings including Pentonville Prison and the Albert Hall, and it was two former Royal Engineers, Colonel F. Beaumont MP and Captain Thomas English, who were employed to carry out experimental boring of a Channel Tunnel by the South Eastern Railway Company between 1880 and 1882. Engineers were also increasingly employed to delineate frontiers such as that between British Colombia and the United States in 1858 and that between the new Bulgaria and its neighbours after the Russo-Turkish War of 1876–78.

Beyond purely professional concerns or those deriving directly from them, the army's engineers were also prominent in archaeology. With Lieutenant Frederick Maisey of the Bengal Native Infantry, Major Alexander Cunningham of the Royal Engineers excavated the ancient Buddhist site of Sanchi in Madhya Pradesh in 1851. One means by which Warren and others were drawn to the subject was through the auspices of the Palestine Exploration Fund. Initially established in 1865, the fund had resulted directly from the work of another Royal Engineer and controversial soldier, Captain (later Major-General Sir) Charles Wilson, whose reputation was to be destroyed by the blame attributed to him by Wolseley and others for failing to reach Khartoum in time to save Gordon in January 1885, when command of the River Column devolved upon him after the mortal wounding of Herbert Stewart and the death of Fred Burnaby.

Back in 1864, however, having worked on the North American Boundary Commission, Wilson was sent to Jerusalem to survey the city as a basis for improving its water supply, Miss Burdett Coutts having raised funds for the purpose. At the request of the Royal Geographical Society, Wilson had also undertaken to measure the difference of level between the Mediterranean and the Dead Sea. In the course of his survey, Wilson made a number of significant historical discoveries. As a result, A. P. Stanley, the Dean of Westminster, and Sir George Grove, as well known for his writing on the Bible as for his contributions to musicology, conceived of a wider exploration of Palestine as a whole to assist in defending orthodox religion from the challenge from science. Accordingly, Wilson returned to Jerusalem to work for the newly established fund on special leave from the War Office. With Wilson posted elsewhere in 1866, the fund requested the services of another engineer to continue the work, Warren being selected.

Wilson remained a member of the fund's executive committee and was to return to Palestine himself in 1868 to survey the Sinai, identifying Jebel Musa as the biblical Mount Sinai. In 1883 Wilson also helped found the Palestine Pilgrims' Text Society to translate and publish various historical and topographical accounts of Palestine from antiquity to the Crusades, the society being dissolved in 1895 when its planned publication programme was completed. Wilson, who made other visits to Palestine after his retirement in 1898, also continued to lecture on Palestine, contributing articles to *Smith's Dictionary of the Bible* and the *Encyclopaedia Britannica*, with his contributions to issues of the quarterly statement of the fund being published as *Golgotha and the Holy Sepulchre* in 1906, some months after his death.[3]

Warren, meanwhile, began work in Palestine in 1867, somewhat hampered by the Turks, under whose control Palestine fell as part of the

Ottoman Empire, and by the fund's frequent lack of money. Indeed, Warren subsidised his work from his own resources. Warren secured pieces of the so-called Moabite Stone but became best known for his work sinking shafts up to eighty feet below the old city of Jerusalem and tunnelling through vaults, passages and sewers such as the Siloam Tunnel. Warren worked on his stomach by the light of torches or just candles held in the mouth, at constant risk from collapsing walls and roofs, often in near suffocating conditions and, at other times, in freezing water. Credited at the time with restoring the ancient city to the world, Warren's most aptly entitled account, *Underground Jerusalem*, appeared in 1876, Warren also co-authoring *The Recovery of Jerusalem* (1871) and *The Survey of Western Palestine* (1875). Warren was already a keen Freemason, having been initiated whilst at Gibraltar in 1859, and later wrote that he had attended one lodge meeting in 1869 in his excavations below the ruins of the temple of Solomon. Subsequently, Warren helped found the Quatuor Coronati lodge of Masonic research in 1886 with Sir Walter Besant, another luminary of the Palestine Exploration Fund. Warren became the lodge's first Master though he was not a Masonic scholar in any real sense.

'Jerusalem' Warren left Palestine in 1869, serving subsequently on the Griqualand West Boundary Commission in 1877. He was working on the settlement of land claims in the Transvaal when appointed to command a colonial volunteer mounted corps as the outbreak of the Ninth Kaffir (Cape Frontier) War spread native unrest into Griqualand West and Bechuanaland. Invalided home from South Africa with an injured knee in February 1882, Warren was then sent out to Egypt in August 1882 in the wake of Wolseley's occupying army to investigate the disappearance of 'Professor' Edward Palmer, a Fellow of St John's Cambridge, and formerly Lord Almoner's Reader in Arabic rather than a Professor. Together with a Royal Engineer who had travelled extensively, Captain William Gill, and Lieutenant Harold Charrington RN, Palmer had been despatched to the Sinai to collect information on the Arab population and to win their support.

Another Freemason, who had co-authored a book on Jerusalem with Besant, Palmer had earlier worked in Sinai for the Palestine Exploration Fund in 1869–70, being accompanied by another Cambridge man, Charles Tyrwhitt Drake. Drake had gone back to Palestine in 1871 with

Lieutenant Claude Condor of the Royal Engineers to complete the survey of the whole country, but returned home fatally ill with fever three years later, to be replaced by none other than the then Lieutenant Herbert Kitchener. Kitchener was to report in November 1877 that he had personally triangulated 1340 square miles, examined and described 816 ruins, and investigated all known archaeological and geological points of interest. Subsequently, Kitchener lectured on his work to the annual meeting of the British Association for the Advancement of Science in August 1878, the meeting being presided over by Wilson, and passed on to undertake a survey of the newly-acquired island of Cyprus, clashing with its High Commissioner, Wolseley, who wanted only a rough and ready map for tax purposes. The survey of western Palestine by Condor and Kitchener was produced by the Ordnance Survey in 1880 and the three volumes of notes compiled by them were published by the fund between 1881 and 1883 after being edited by Besant and another Royal Engineer, Henry Palmer, who had served in British Colombia and also worked in the Sinai with Wilson.

Edward Palmer, no relation of Henry, had left Suez for Nakhl, half way towards Aqaba on 8 August 1882, carrying £3000 worth of gold but with no escort other than his two companions and two guides. It took Warren until October to verify that Palmer, Gill, Charrington and the two natives had all been murdered at Wadi Sadr only three days after setting out: their remains were recovered from a well and interred in the crypt of St Paul's in April 1883, a memorial plaque still commemorating them there. Warren, meanwhile caught eight of the fifteen Bedouin implicated in the murders, all eight being tried and hanged. Warren returned to head the Surveying School at Chatham but was then chosen to command the expedition to annexe Bechuanaland in 1884–85. He incurred the displeasure of Wolseley in an attempt to be elected as Liberal MP for Sheffield Hallam in November 1885 – he was unsuccessful – but was appointed Governor of the Red Sea Littoral at Suakin, a post later occupied by Kitchener. Warren, however, was only at Suakin for a few weeks before being offered the post of Commissioner of the Metropolitan Police, following the resignation of Sir Edmund Henderson after criticism of the police during various demonstrations. In turn, Warren came under attack when troops were called out to restore order in Trafalgar Square in November 1887, an affair inevitably, if unimaginatively, referred to as 'Bloody Sunday', though no fatalities actually occurred.

Having considered that he had restored police morale, Warren wished to resign but was persuaded to remain by the first of the Whitechapel murders, though he actually had no control over the Criminal Investigation Department tasked with solving the crimes, which reported not to him but direct to the Home Secretary. Much has been made of Warren's Masonic connections with regard to the 'Ripper' speculations, it often being alleged that he indulged in a Masonic conspiracy with the Prime Minister, Salisbury; his Assistant-Commissioner, Sir James Anderson; and the Royal Physician, Sir William Gull, himself sometimes regarded as a suspect by some authors despite his seventy-one years and two strokes, to cover up the involvement of the Duke of Clarence. Inconveniently for the conspiracy theorists, only Warren was actually a Freemason among these alleged conspirators, while the Duke of Clarence, who was a Freemason, was demonstrably in Scotland throughout the period of the murders. Warren certainly ordered the removal of a chalked message incriminating 'Juwes' from a wall near the scene of the fourth of the murders. This is sometimes suggested as a reference to the 'three ruffians' responsible in Masonic ritual for the death of the architect of Solomon's Temple, but this requires some extraordinary leaps of logic and there is little reason to doubt Warren's own explanation that it was to prevent any anti-Semitic disturbances. As it happens, by far the most plausible candidate for 'Jack the Ripper' is a Polish Jew, Kosminski, who was committed to a mental institution.

In the event, Warren left the Metropolitan Police in March 1888, the Home Secretary having objected to an article Warren had contributed to *Murray's Magazine* on policing. There followed a somewhat controversial period as Major-General commanding the Straits Settlements at Singapore, in which he clashed with the civil administration over military expenditure, and then command of Thames District. Warren officially retired in the summer of 1898. For all his accomplishments, Warren had his faults, not least a notoriously foul temper. Warren caused some talk at the annual manoeuvres in the summer of 1895 when deciding to test the weight of a soldier's equipment after several men had fallen out by donning it himself and thus marching past the Duke of Cambridge at the head of his division. The fact that men had fallen out, however, had much to do with Warren's insistence on marching them through the heat of the day. The Under Secretary of State for War, St John Brodrick, reported to the Secretary of State, Lord Lansdowne, that Warren ought to be reprimanded for this and, in any case, was 'impossible', having quarrelled with everyone.[4] Roberts, who had not known Warren previously, soon concluded after reaching South Africa in January 1900 that his 'disagreeable temper unfits him for holding an important position in the field'.[5]

Nonetheless, when war broke out in South Africa, Warren offered his services to Wolseley and was appointed to command the Fifth Division as Lieutenant-General on 7 November 1899, sailing for the Cape later that month. Moreover, he carried a dormant commission to succeed to the overall command should General Sir Redvers Buller be incapacitated in action. It did not assist matters that Warren was on extremely poor personal terms with Buller and was also ordered by Wolseley to assume immediate command of the operations to relieve Kimberley from Lieutenant-General Lord Methuen, only for the orders to be counter-manded by Buller when Warren was already en route from the Cape. Warren did not therefore reach the front in Natal, to which Buller ordered him, until 21 December 1899, Buller already having suffered defeat at Colenso six days earlier.

Warren was certainly to contribute to Buller's defeat at Spion Kop on 23–25 January 1900 but, as Wolseley had remarked when issuing Warren's dormant commission, generals were born not made and he could only send out the best available, into which category Warren fell. Directed to outflank the Boer position on the Tugela (Thukela) by way of Trichard's Drift, Warren proved slow to exploit the lack of opposition on 18 and 19 January. Strengthening Boer resistance led to the decision to attempt to seize the commanding position of Spion Kop (Spioenkop), on which there was only limited information available. A force of some 1700 men under Major-General Sir Edward Woodgate duly seized the summit in the early hours of 24 January but dawn and the clearing of the mist revealed the hastily scraped British trenches to be fatally exposed to Boers on higher positions on Aloe Knoll and partly enfiladed from other Boer positions on Conical Hill and Green Hill. When Woodgate was fatally wounded, Warren ordered up Major-General John Talbot Coke to take command, despite Coke carrying a serious leg injury.

Subsequently, Buller suggested that Lieutenant-Colonel Alec Thorney-croft should command on the summit and Warren agreed without informing Coke. At one stage, Coke, whose injured leg meant that it took him several hours to reach the summit, placed Lieutenant-Colonel Hill in command.

The chaos increased when the signal station established on the summit was destroyed by a Boer shell and messages to and from Warren had to be relayed through Buller's signal station on Mount Alice. Moreover, Warren and Buller were each effectively countermanding the others' orders with respect to attempted reinforcement of the summit. Warren wanted the summit held, but at nightfall Thorneycroft, after a dispute with Hill as to who was in command, directed a retirement at a moment when most of the Boers had also withdrawn. Warren only heard of the retirement after it was too late to stop it, Buller then assuming command in the early hours of 25 January and deciding on retreat back across the Tugela. Warren's force had suffered 322 dead and 563 wounded with another 300 men missing or taken prisoner: the Boers had lost only an estimated 58 dead and 140 wounded.

The arrival of Roberts effectively cancelled Warren's dormant commission and he was first sidelined to a command in Griqualand and then became one of many generals sent home in disgrace. Warren came home to contest Buller's version of events at Spion Kop, since Buller had placed all blame upon him. While Warren was certainly not without blame, Buller had distanced himself from the operation almost from the beginning, having entrusted Warren with the difficult outflanking movement with some 15,000 men while he himself with only 9000 held his positions at Mount Alice and Potgieter's Drift. Whatever the judgement, however, it was the end of Warren's varied military career. Warren turned instead to assisting the Boy Scouts, the Church Lads' Brigade and the Sunday School movement. He died only in 1927.

7

Doing a Billy Hicks

Hollywood rarely gets history right and, indeed, the epic *Khartoum* with Charlton Heston as Gordon and Laurence Olivier reprising his Othello as the Mahdi is no exception. Undeniably, however, there are some well-judged moments in *Khartoum*, not least its opening sequences dealing with the destruction of the Egyptian army commanded by a former British officer, William Hicks, in the wastes of the Sudanese Kordofan in November 1883. Subsequently, Ralph Richardson's Gladstone, nicely capturing the man's combination of sanctimoniousness and cynicism, warns Nigel Greene's Wolseley not to do a 'Billy Hicks on me'. In the House of Lords, Lord Fitzmaurice likened the destruction of Hicks's command to the loss of Pharoah's army in the Red Sea, while Charles Gordon was also to make a comparison between Hicks and Cambyses, whose Persian army had been lost in the sands of the Egyptian desert in the sixth century BC.

According to Gordon, the Mahdists celebrated what they regarded as a victory over British troops, but Hicks was no longer a British officer. He had been commissioned in the Bombay Fusiliers in 1849, subsequently serving in the Mutiny and on Napier's Abyssinian expedition, before retiring from his last appointment as AAG in the Bombay army as a Lieutenant-Colonel and Honorary Colonel in 1880. According to one contemporary account, he was one of three possible candidates for the post of Chief of Staff in the Sudan, his name being picked out of a hat by Valentine Baker.[1] For Hicks, it was a matter both of prestige and pay. He wrote to his wife in January 1883 that he hoped 'to make great things' out of the expedition, qualifying this in a letter to his daughter just after setting out in September 1883 that, 'They say I shall make a good thing of this in a monetary point of view'.[2]

The Khedive had long relied upon a motley band of adventurers to assist in the administration of the Egyptian Sudan. When Charles Gordon was Governor-General of the Sudan between 1874 and 1879, for example, his subordinates included a Swiss, Werner Munzinger; a German, Giegler Pasha; the Italians Romolo Gessi, Emiliani dei Danziger and Messedaglia; and an Austrian, Rudolf Slatin. Hicks had eight Europeans as officers when he met his fate, five of them British, and two European surgeons. In all, eight Englishmen served with him at one time or another. Not all impressed Hicks, who felt most of his European officers were 'washed out'. Colonel the Hon. John Colborne, the son of Lord Seaton, for example, was described as too worn out to be much good and was invalided back to Egypt. Hicks refused to accept him back. Two others – Major Martin and Captain Forrestier-Walker – were also evacuated and, as with Colborne, Hicks had no desire to see Forrestier-Walker return. Colonel Arthur Farquhar, rendered in Hicks's letters as Fargehan, was his Chief of Staff on the last fatal advance. Lieutenant-Colonel de Coetlogon, late 15th Foot, was fortunate enough to be left in command at Khartoum and did not accompany Hicks. Hicks had also taken on a 'wandering Austrian', Captain Herlth, a former Uhlan in the Austro-Hungarian army with over eleven years' military service.[3] Herlth died with Hicks as did a German officer, Baron Seckendorf. The other fatalities were Majors Warner, Massey and Evans; Captain Matyuga; Lieutenant Morris Brody, formerly a Sergeant-Major with the Royal Horse Artillery; and the surgeons, Georges and Rosenberg. Two 'specials' also perished, O'Donovan, war correspondent of the *Daily News*, and Frank Vizitelly, war artist of the *Graphic*, who had accompanied Wolseley on his visit to Confederate headquarters in Virginia in 1862. Frank Power of *The Times* was also meant to accompany Hicks, but, suffering dysentery, returned to Khartoum. Power, however, did not cheat death in the longer term, being murdered with other Europeans when dispatched up the Nile to supposed safety by Gordon in September 1884.

Bennet Burleigh, the war correspondent of the *Daily Telegraph*, who had met Hicks on his way to Egypt, regarded him as gallant and energetic, and not a man to underestimate his foe. Indeed, Burleigh opined that 'it must have been because of some exceptional wrench of circumstances that any command under his leadership was forced to accept destruction at the hands of an uncivilized foe'.[4] Reginald Wingate also considered Hicks able. Hicks himself believed that, despite the many problems he had experienced with his troops, he would be successful in destroying the Mahdist revolt. Like many others, however, Hicks underestimated the challenge represented by the Mahdi. Long-standing resentment against Egyptian rule of the Sudan – first established in the 1820s – had not been modified by Gordon's administration. Indeed, Gordon's attempts to suppress slavery had struck directly at the economy of the Baggara tribes of central Sudan, into which the Mahdi had married. It was apparent, moreover, that the nationalist upheaval in Egypt itself, which was to lead to eventual British intervention and occupation in August 1882, was weakening Egyptian administration.

Mohammed Ahmed, a boat builder turned religious mystic, proclaimed himself the Mahdi or 'Expected One' in the summer of 1881 amid a taxation dispute between himself and the Mudir of Fashoda, Rashid Bey. Expectations of a Mahdi do not in fact not form part of the Koran but are based on a saying attributed to Mohammed, but confined to the Sunni tradition. On 11 August 1881 a small party sent to arrest the Mahdi by the Egyptian Governor-General of the Sudan, Mohammed Rauf Pasha, was overwhelmed. More troops were dispatched from Khartoum, but in December 1881 another government force under Rashid Bey was destroyed, this second defeat triggering increasing insurrection throughout the southern Sudan. There were some subsequent government successes but there were also further significant defeats, as at Jebel Gedir in June 1882 and Bara in September 1882. Both Bara and El Obeid surrendered to the Mahdi in January 1883, delivering to the Mahdists considerable amounts of weapons and ammunition. In February 1883 Abd el Kader Pasha, who had replaced Rauf Pasha as Governor-General, was able to raise the Mahdist siege of a third government garrison at Sennar, a sufficiently successful operation to encourage him to believe that he could follow up the Mahdist retreat. At this point, however, he was superseded through the dual appointment of Ali ed Din Pasha as Civil Governor and the seventy-four or seventy-five year old Suliman Nyasi Pasha as Commander-in-Chief. Suliman's nominal Chief of Staff was Hicks, who arrived in Khartoum by way of Suakin and Berber on 7 March 1883, but, in theory, Suliman had been instructed that Hicks, who held the rank of major-general in the Egyptian army, was to be responsible for all operations. Suliman proved obstructive and was also notably indolent.

Hicks took command of some 5000 men with five guns and two

Nordenfelt machine guns at Kawa in April 1883, Colborne having previously undertaken a reconnaissance there. He advanced to Abu Zed and
repulsed a Mahdist attack at Marabieh in May, largely due to the fact
that the Mahdists were armed largely with spears while Hicks's men had
modern weapons. Hicks, however, believed his theoretical subordination
to Suliman inhibiting, when the latter showed no inclination to follow
his advice. He demanded that he be placed indisputably in command of
the major expedition into Kordofan mooted since at least January to
recapture Bara and El Obeid, the latter almost 350 miles from Khartoum.
While he had favoured a limited advance, Abd el Kader opposed such
a hazardous undertaking. The British, who were in the process of
reorganising the Egyptian army from scratch, also declined to support it
or to offer any military advice. Colonel J. D. H. Stewart of the 11th Hussars,
sent to the Sudan to report on the situation, for example, had specifically
warned against the expedition, as defeat would almost certainly entail
the potential loss of the entire Sudan. Stewart, who was to be killed with
Power, considered it better to remain on the defensive and ensure
holding the Nile. Sir Edward Malet, the British Agent and Consul-
General Egypt until September 1883, also believed Hicks should confine
any operations to the region between the Blue and White Niles.

The British government acting through the Foreign Secretary, Lord
Granville, should have intervened but did not do so for fear of greater
involvement in the Sudan. Indeed, Malet was instructed to inform Hicks
that the British government took no responsibility in the affairs of the
Sudan: while Malet could transmit to the Egyptian authorities any
telegrams sent him by Hicks, he could not offer any opinion with regard
to action on them. No objection was raised, therefore, to Hicks commanding an expedition. Hicks certainly discussed the expedition with
the British GOC in Cairo, Sir Archibald Alison; the Sirdar of the
reconstituted Egyptian army, Sir Evelyn Wood, who also opposed the
expedition; Valentine Baker, who was commanding the Egyptian gendarmerie; and the British Ambassador to the Porte in Constantinople,
Lord Dufferin, who was advising the Khedive on reforms. Alison at least
was sanguine, feeling Hicks seemed accomplished and that his understanding of Asiatic peoples would stand him in good stead.[5] Hicks,
moreover, was apparently prepared to run the risks and, in any case,
believed Khartoum secure.

When his request for sole command was refused, Hicks resigned, an additional factor being a continuing dispute with the Khedival government over his pay and contract, which had still not appeared in August. In late August, however, Suliman was made Governor of the Red Sea Provinces and Hicks agreed to stay, his pay finally settled at 2,000 Egyptian pounds a year and his commission confirmed as Lieutenant-General and Commander-in-Chief.[6] Any expedition, however, required more troops than were currently available to him and Hicks requested 6000 more men and a further E£120,000 to cover the costs, since his troops were well in arrears on pay. Instead, Hicks got only 3000 more men and 40,000 Egyptian pounds. Moreover, as Hicks wrote to Wood, the reinforcements scraped together and sent him by the Egyptian authorities left much to be desired, since they 'can only be collected by dragging from their homes and fields unwilling men, and sending them away in chains'.[7] Indeed, Hicks reported to Wood in June 1883 that fifty-one men intended to serve as artillerymen had managed to desert, even though in chains. In fact, asked to inspect the recruits, Wood had rejected at least six hundred of the first thousand, noting that at least two men pressed into service put lime 'into their eyes to destroy their sight while on parade'.[8]

As it was, many of the Egyptian troops already in the Sudan had been hastily recruited from the remnants of Arabi's army and were hardly committed to the Khedive, even though service took them from unemployment on the streets of Cairo. Hicks would have given much for a British or Indian brigade and tried without success to persuade Wood to send up four battalions of the new army. Bennet Burleigh, indeed, put down Hicks's defeat solely to the fact that the Egyptian soldier was 'worthless'. It was a judgement with which Malet's successor, Sir Evelyn Baring, concurred, as did Frank Power, who thought fifty good men more than capable of routing Hicks's army within ten minutes.

It was not until 9 September that Hicks had collected sufficient transport to contemplate an advance, the force that left Khartoum for Duem (Duaim), about a hundred miles to the south on the White Nile, consisting of about 7000 infantry and 1000 cavalry, with fourteen assorted guns (four of them modern Krupp field guns), six Nordenfelt machine guns, and quantities of the iron spikes known as crow's feet to throw down as a barrier against Mahdist charges. In contrast to the modern weaponry, however, some of the cavalry wore chain mail while many others were irregular Bashi-Bazuks. Besides a baggage train in excess of 5500 camels to carry about sixty days' worth of supplies, Hicks's little army was also encumbered with over 2000 camp followers. Winston Churchill later described it as 'the worst army that has ever marched to war', though, of course, it had achieved a significant small victory at Marabieh, which had lifted morale to some extent. Indeed, Colborne claimed, somewhat improbably, that he had never seen a 'steadier or more patient army'. Things might have been worse if Hicks had not resolved to have the abundant supply of 'poisonous brandy' brought by the frequently drunken O'Donovan broken 'by accident on purpose'.[9]

Having reached Duem on 20 September, Hicks intended to follow a direct route to Bara, about 136 miles distant to the west and over relatively open country inhabited by tribes either friendly or neutral in allegiance. Ali ed Din Pasha, who accompanied the force, however, believed water supplies to be more plentiful on a more circuitous route to the south, a distance to El Obeid of some 250 miles by way of the seasonal watercourse known as the Khor Abu Habli, which could be expected to have water since the rainy season was just ending. This southern route was covered in dense scrub and grass and the tribes were almost entirely hostile. Hicks, who was persuaded to follow the new route, intended to establish posts along his route, quantities of biscuits and ammunition and another thousand camels having been ordered up to Duem in order to organise a continuous supply system. Having advanced only about sixteen miles to some wells at Shatt, however, Hicks was now informed by Ali ed Din Pasha that the troops left at any supply posts would not venture out to guard any supply convoys and that the only recourse was for the force to advance carrying all its own supplies. The various guides taken on by Hicks, moreover, were divided as to which route was the better. Hicks's Egyptian officers were also divided on the best course of action, but Farquhar felt that the planned posts must be abandoned in the circumstances. In his last dispatch, dated from Serakna on 3 October, Hicks explained that he felt there was little alternative, especially as the Nubian tribes south of El Obeid had promised support if Hicks advanced through their territory. In the event, tribal support did not materialise.

Hicks left Shatt on 27 September, venturing into largely unchartered territory, his force advancing in a square formation, with the artillery in the middle, infantry to the sides, and cavalry at front and rear, the whole led by Hicks and his staff. A protective zariba of thorn bushes was formed each night. An earlier undated dispatch from Hicks described his force being dependent upon pools of rainwater, which could be expected only as far as Serakna (Serakhna), some fifty miles beyond Shatt. The heat was intense and no water could be obtained by digging. Villages were deserted, the tribes fleeing with all their food. By 7 October, Hicks had got about forty-five miles south west of Duem, a little beyond Zeraiga and some way short of Serakna. Here the force halted for a few days and O'Donovan sent his final despatch, again emphasising the dependence upon rainwater pools. It represented the last direct communication with Hicks and his men, the last letter from Hicks himself to his wife being dated 4 October. Hicks himself had remarked on leaving Duem that he felt 'like Jesus Christ surrounded by the Jews'.[10] Hicks struggled on as far as Kasghil, another 150 miles to the south west, the diversion ever deeper into Kordofan and away from El Obeid orchestrated by Mahdist agents acting as guides. Hicks knew the guides to be unreliable, some being kept in chains, and lamented the complete absence of information with too few cavalry for proper reconnaissance. All the time, lack of water and heat exhaustion was taking its toll of men, horses and camels. The camels could not be allowed to graze outside of the square and were eventually fed on the straw from the padding of their own saddles. Stragglers were picked off by the Mahdists, informed of the growing weakness of Hicks's men by Gustave (or Adolf) Klootz, Seckendorf's German orderly, who deserted to them. One attack on 3 November as Hicks's force passed through a gorge caused considerable casualties, the Mahdi having now brought his entire army of some 40,000 men from El Obeid. Indeed, the Mahdi sent letters to Hicks offering quarter to those who surrendered.

It is possible that Ali ed Din Pasha declined to go further than the partially filled 'Lake' Rahad and was overwhelmed there, though most reports had him killed with Hicks. Certainly, there had been disagreements between Hicks and his Egyptian subordinates, not least over the reliability of the irregular infantry. Subsequently, Hicks had all civilians accompanying the force disarmed. Hicks seems to have divided his force into three separate squares moving in mutual support, resolving

on the advice of the guides, on or about 3 November, to advance towards
El Obeid via Kashgil. There were various attempted desertions as the
Mahdists closed on Hicks's little army. After some three days without
any water at all and heading in the direction of a reported lake at Fula,
Hicks's remaining force was close to Shakyan when the leading square
was attacked in a wooded valley. Each square was overwhelmed in turn
on 5 November in little more than a quarter of an hour. Barely 300
men survived to be captured. According to the later official history of
the Sudan campaign of 1884–85, Hicks and his staff 'made a brilliant
charge' before being killed. In the approved fashion, Hicks himself was
said to have died with sword in one hand and revolver in the other, he
and his staff having cut their way out of the initial carnage to reach
some cultivated ground. Certainly, it was later said in Kordofan that,
in tribute to his courage at the last, the Baggara were henceforth nick-
named 'Baggar Hicks' or 'the cows driven by Hicks'.[11] The Europeans
were mutilated where they fell, the heads of Hicks and Seckendorf being
sent to the Mahdi as trophies. It is thought that the Mahdi suffered only
500 casualties.

The rumours which began to reach Khartoum and Cairo were not
confirmed until 21 November when a wounded camel driver reached
safety.[12] Subsequently, Reginald Wingate patched together the story from
his agents and a few survivors whom he encountered in later years, such
as Hicks's cook, Mohammed Nur el Barudi. Curiously, a diary of one
of the Egyptian officers killed with Hicks, Abbas Bey, was found on the
battlefield of Omdurman in 1898. Visiting the site, during the winter of
1905–6, Wingate found water within a mile of where Hicks was overwhelmed. Wingate concluded that the authorities had clearly not
appreciated the difficulties of the terrain: 'the dispatch of the expedition,
under the circumstances, can only be characterised as an act of extreme
folly'.[13] The destruction of the Egyptian army's only field force in the
Sudan left just 2000 men holding Khartoum, with other small garrisons
scattered throughout the country. One by one these outlying garrisons
capitulated, Slatin, for example, surrendering at Dara in December to
spend the next eleven years in captivity. The Mahdi had won immense
prestige and, with the defeat of Hicks, brought his arms captures to
almost 21,000 rifles and nineteen guns. The situation worsened still

further in January 1884 when Valentine Baker was defeated at El Teb while trying to relieve Mahdist pressure on Sinkat and Tokar in the eastern Sudan, bringing the total number of troops lost in the Sudan to some 41,000 since Hicks had left Khartoum. As the Mahdist insurrection spread yet further, desperate measures seemed appropriate. Thus did Charles Gordon begin his journey to Khartoum, leaving London on 18 January 1884.

8

The Excitement of Railway Carriages

Taken in isolation, the frequently innocent turn of phrase on the part of contemporaries could easily condemn the late Victorian army as a haven of illegal sexual practices. In March 1879, for example, a thirty-nine year-old unmarried Brevet Lieutenant-Colonel lamented the death of 'a dear good honest loveable creature with whom I have now been living some nine months in closest converse ...'[1] In reality, the writer was Redvers Buller, communicating to his aunt his grief at the death of Robert Barton at Hlobane. Few would claim any sexual improprieties with respect to Buller, though a 'psychohistory' once suggested that Buller's marriage to his cousin's widow at the age of forty-two and the his acquisition, thereby, of a ready-made family of four children implied a mother fixation.

Buller's commanding officer in No. 4 Column in Zululand, Evelyn Wood, has been claimed as a homosexual on the strength of a mis-quotation of one of his letters to Lady Haig in 1909 about a photograph explaining 'part of the attraction' of Douglas Haig as a young officer. It has to be said that Wood's references to another Hlobane casualty, Ronald Campbell, as 'soft, gentle and tender as a girl' and as 'my Ronald' strike somewhat oddly. Wood, however, used these phrases respectively in conversation with the Queen in September 1879, and in a subsequent letter to the Queen in April 1880 after accompanying Campbell's widow to Hlobane whilst escorting the party of the Empress Eugénie to Zulu-land.[2] There is no evidence whatsoever to suggest that Wood was homosexual.

Similarly, despite Kitchener's penchant for flower arranging and for surrounding himself with young unmarried men, the evidence for more than an unfulfilled or sublimated sexual predilection is wholly lacking. It is too often forgotten that Kitchener had been engaged to Hermione, the daughter of Valentine Baker, who died in 1885 aged only eighteen.

Kitchener always wore a locket bearing a miniature of Hermione under his shirt, returning it to her cousin just before his fatal voyage to Russia in HMS *Hampshire* in June 1916. The Queen was certainly satisfied that Kitchener disliked employing married officers simply because 'they are always wanting to go home'.[3] Discouraging marriage, however, was not uncommon. Garnet Wolseley, who had married at thirty-four and, as a result, felt compelled to turn down an offer of appointment as Military Secretary to the Viceroy in 1872 due to his wife's pregnancy, wrote when Buller's marriage was first mooted in May 1875 that he disliked 'his own pet soldiers marrying'. The prospective bride, he insisted, should be told firmly that marriage should be contemplated only 'if she never throws any obstacle in the way of Buller's joining me in any war that I may happen hereafter to be engaged in'.[4] As it happened, Buller did not marry on that occasion.

Some historians, of course, have argued that the export of surplus emotional energy and the rejection of Victorian women were crucial driving forces behind imperial expansion. Inevitably, alleged predilections are produced as evidence, as in the case of Kitchener and Charles Gordon. One of the Gordon's most recent biographers, however, has concluded that Gordon's avowed chastity stemmed from religious conviction rather than sexual inclinations towards the young boys among whom he proselytised. Undeniably, there is the spectre of Hector Macdonald, who committed suicide in a Paris hotel room in March 1903 after being allegedly discovered *en flagrante* with Singhalese boys in a railway carriage in Ceylon.

'Fighting Mac' was a former ranker, commissioned by Frederick Roberts in the field in January 1880 after his heroism during the Second Afghan War, in which, as a Colour Sergeant of the 92nd Highlanders, he had distinguished himself at the Hazardarakht Pass and again at Charasia. A crofter's son from Rootfield near Urquhart, Macdonald had been apprenticed to a draper in Dingwall when he enlisted in June 1870, having previously joined the local Rifle Volunteers. He distinguished himself again at Majuba in February 1881, fighting on with his fists against the Boers before being overwhelmed and captured. Opting for service in Egypt in 1883, Macdonald served first with the Egyptian gendarmerie before transferring to the Egyptian army in 1888. He commanded the 11th Sudanese Battalion, receiving the DSO after the battle of Toski in 1889, and then commanded the 1st Egyptian Brigade in Kitchener's reconquest of the Sudan as a brevet lieutenant-colonel. At Omdurman in September 1898, having repulsed one Dervish attack from the south west, Macdonald famously wheeled his brigade to repulse another from the north. Promoted to brevet colonel for his services at Omdurman, Macdonald was commanding a district in the Punjab when summoned to South Africa to take over the Highland Brigade after Andy Wauchope was killed at Magersfontein in December 1899. Knighted in May 1901, but apparently frustrated at not receiving further promotion, Macdonald applied for and received the command in Ceylon, thus ranking as a local major-general.

By the time Macdonald went to Ceylon, he was already carrying one if not two secrets. In June 1884 he had secretly married Christina Duncan, still only sixteen by what, under Scottish law, was termed a declaration *de praesenti*. Macdonald, however, repeatedly declined to go through with a public marriage ceremony, though Christina bore him a child in March 1888. It was only after she went to court for official recognition of the marriage that it was eventually publicly acknowledged in 1894. Curiously, the War Office still appeared unaware that Macdonald was married at the time of his death. Macdonald was always short of money and that was one reason why he went to Egypt, but he was also escaping Christina, with whom he never lived for any length of time. The other secret, of course, was his homosexuality, rumours of which had first surfaced when he was commanding at Aliwal North in South Africa and was allegedly involved with Afrikaner internees. The rumours arose again in Ceylon in February 1903, a clergyman and a number of schoolmasters complaining officially to the Governor, Sir West Ridgeway, though the true nature and extent of the charges has never come to light. The old edition of the *Dictionary of National Biography* merely refers to 'an opprobrious accusation'. Trying to avoid scandal, Ridgeway packed Macdonald back to England, but Roberts, now Commander-in-Chief at the War Office, ordered him back to Ceylon to face an official enquiry and possible court martial. En route to Marseille, Macdonald paused in Paris at the Hôtel Regina in the Rue de Rivoli. While he was there, the story appeared in English language newspapers, at least one of which Macdonald saw in the hotel lobby on 25 March 1903. He went up to his room and shot himself.

Yet, while acknowledging the undoubted existence of homosexuality within the army, it should be noted that the evidence for serial woman-ising is substantially greater. This is not just a question of venereal rates among the ordinary rank and file, but the general pursuit of native women overseas, which even historians who regard Empire as a subli-mation of or alternative to sex have noted. Wolseley was not alone in having a native mistress while a young subaltern in India in 1859, while Sir Bindon Blood's memoirs come closer than perhaps he imagined to impropriety in his references to Zulu women. One of the greatest contemporary sexual controversies affecting the army was also not a matter of homosexuality in a railway carriage, but of indecent assault in a railway carriage. Indeed, in other ways, it might be regarded as at the opposite end of the spectrum, since there was little comparison in background between the ex-ranker, Macdonald, and Valentine Baker. Curiously, apart from being disgraced in railway carriages, they did have a common connection with Ceylon and the Egyptian gendarmerie.

The former commanding officer of the 10th Hussars and younger brother of the explorer Sir Samuel White Baker, Valentine Baker was AQMG at Aldershot in June 1875, and regarded as one of the most promising officers in the army. The son of a rich West India merchant with extensive estates in Jamaica and Mauritius, Valentine Baker was educated at College School, Gloucester, and by private tutors. He accompanied his elder brother to Ceylon in 1848, Samuel's intention being to establish a new English settlement at Newera Eliya. Valentine Baker, however, soon tired of a planter's life and was commissioned in the Ceylon Rifles, transferring to the 12th Lancers in 1852. He saw service on the Cape Frontier and in the Crimea, obtaining a majority in the 10th Hussars in 1859 and then commanding it from 1860 to 1873. A noted cavalry tactician, Baker observed both the Austro-Prussian War (1866) and the Franco-Prussian War (1870–71). He also travelled in Persia and Central Asia in 1873, but failed to reach his intended destination of Khiva, the prize eventually falling to his friend, Fred Burnaby. Baker had married Fanny Wormald, a squire's daughter, in 1865. All seemed set fair for a glittering career.

On 17 May 1875, however, Baker caught the London train at Liphook and found himself sharing a carriage with young Miss Rebecca Dickin-son, who was travelling without a chaperone. Baker chose to offer no public account of what transpired between Woking and Esher and refused to allow his barrister to cross-examine Miss Dickinson so that her story remained unchallenged. It would appear that he attempted to kiss her, and that in her alarm she climbed half out of the carriage. Baker had then prevented her from falling from the train, in the process of which she had caught hold of his clothes, leaving them in some disarray. Other passengers had become aware of Miss Dickinson's screams and she was rescued from her precarious position when the train stopped at Esher. The rumours that began to fly prevented any question of a cover up and Baker was brought to trial in August 1875. He was cleared of attempted rape but convicted of indecent assault, the judge ruling that a 'kiss that gratifies or incites passion is indecent'.[5] He was fined £500 and sentenced to a year's imprisonment. Incensed, the Queen demanded that he be dismissed the service rather than being allowed to resign.

Baker had influential friends, including the Duke of Cambridge and the Prince of Wales, but they failed consistently to persuade the Queen to reinstate him. Indeed, it may well have been to Baker's disadvantage that the Queen associated him with the Prince of Wales's 'set'. Consequently, after his release from prison, he had to pursue a career in the Turkish and Egyptian services, becoming a major-general in the Turkish gendarmerie and then commanding a Turkish division in the Russo-Turkish War of 1876–78. His fighting rearguard action at Tashkessan brought him promotion to lieutenant-general. Baker returned to England in 1878, penning *War in Bulgaria: A Narrative of Personal Experience*, to follow his earlier account of his travels, *Clouds in the East*, published before his disgrace in 1875. Baker then returned to his Turkish appointment. With the British occupation of Egypt in 1882, Baker was offered command of the newly reconstructed Egyptian army on Wolseley's recommendation. But, by the time he reached Cairo, the government had had second thoughts on the grounds that English officers could not be expected to serve under an officer previously dismissed the service. Evelyn Wood became Sirdar instead.

In the expectation that it would also see active service, Baker accepted command of the Egyptian gendarmerie and thus was to become Macdonald's commanding officer. Seeking to relieve Mahdist pressure on Tokar, however, 3500 of Baker's gendarmerie were dispersed and put to flight at El Teb on 5 February 1884. In the panic-stricken rout, Baker only just escaped with his life as over 2300 of his men were killed. Coupled with the destruction of William Hicks's army, El Teb dealt a shattering blow to Egyptian control of the Sudan. Baker then acted as an intelligence officer on the staff of Sir Gerald Graham's Suakin expedition, being severely wounded in the face at a second engagement at El Teb in February 1884. There was considerable support now for his reinstatement, but the Queen still resisted it. Reverting to command of the gendarmerie, Baker died on a tour of inspection in Egypt of angina pectoralis in November 1887, not knowing that the Queen had finally relented and directed his reinstatement in the British army. His daughter, Hermione, had died two years previously when engaged to Kitchener, her demise followed within a month by the death of his wife.

Baker's case was by far the most prominent, but scandal was never far away. When, as High Commissioner, Wolseley took some of his 'ring' with him to Natal in 1875, he grew alarmed that the sexual indiscretions would jeopardise his mission to persuade the colonial assembly to accept an amended constitution, intended to pave the way for future federation in South Africa. The most ardent suitors were Henry Brackenbury and Lord Gifford VC, though William Butler was also something of a risk for the colony's husbands. Brackenbury had married a thirty-one-year-old widow some fourteen years previously when he himself was only twenty-three, primarily, it would appear, to help clear his debts. According to Brackenbury, he had realised that he had made a mistake within just three months and he had little compunction in playing the field in Natal. Wolseley noted that Brackenbury's love life did not actually interfere with his day to day duties but that even 'his judicial management of the very jealous and suspicious husband in this case may not prevent a serious explosion'. The woman in question appears to have been the wife of 'Offy' Shepstone, son of the colony's Secretary for Native Affairs. By contrast, young Gifford managed to get himself engaged to a Jewish girl with an alcoholic mother and a bankrupt father. Wolseley advised Gifford's family to get him out of the colony as soon as possible – so that he would fall once more into the eminently preferable hands of a woman whom, nevertheless, Wolseley variously described as of 'easy virtue' and 'the *danseuse* who performs at Islington'.

Gifford escaped the apparent trap set him in Natal, but another promising military career that was blighted was that of George Villiers, a cousin to Lady Lytton, who accompanied Lord Lytton to India as the Viceroy's ADC in 1876. Two years later, and now Lytton's Military Secretary and about to be attached to the staff of Frederick Roberts in Afghanistan, Villiers became involved with a doctor's wife. Unfortunately, she also happened to be the sister of the *Daily Telegraph*'s correspondent in Simla. Simla, of course, was a well-known hot-bed of sexual intrigue, later to provide the young Rudyard Kipling with the raw material for many of his stories. The Simla divorce court awarded £2200 damages against Villiers and he was forced to quit India with the expectation of having to settle £400 a year on the woman and even to contemplate marrying her. A similar case was that of Charles à Court (later Repington), whose affair in Cairo in the 1890s with the wife of a prominent civil servant and subsequent forced resignation from the army is well known. By contrast, Sir John Cowans, who was to become Quartermaster-General in 1912 and serve in that appointment throughout the Great War, was highly fortunate to avoid the consequences of his many indiscretions. By way of defence, his biographers noted of his relationships that 'if he did not always turn to the most refined and cultivated he shared that weakness, if it be one, with men even greater than himself'. The first Commander-in-Chief of the BEF, Sir John French had an equal reputation as ladies' man.

William Butler was also cited as one of the five co-respondents in the celebrated Campbell divorce case in 1886, although there is not much evidence that he was actually involved with Lady Colin Campbell. Another of Wolseley's protégés, however, clearly did have a roving eye. George Greaves's first wife died in 1880 while he was Adjutant-General in India. He had already made the acquaintance of Julia Venour, wife of the doctor of the 15th Hussars, and she became his mistress. According to Lady Wolseley, Greaves then took up with a Mrs Rochfort-Boyd in late 1884, living in a *ménage à trois* with wife and husband. Greaves denied that he could possibly be the father of the child she was expecting, however, on the grounds that he had not been back from India long enough. Subsequently, Greaves married Mrs Venour in 1908. Another soldier whose desertion of his wife was brought to the Queen's attention in 1880 was Sir Arthur Hardinge. Even the Commander-in-Chief, the

Duke of Cambridge, had married an actress against his family's wishes in 1847 and fathered three children by her. Moreover, he was also involved in a long-term relationship with Mrs Louisa Beauclerk for over thirty-five years.

What mattered, of course, was how far liaisons or scandals became public knowledge. In the cases of Macdonald and Baker, railway carriages were all too public.

9

War, Truth and History

In early 1901 the British Military Attaché at Brussels and The Hague, Lieutenant Colonel Charles à Court, to be better known later as Charles Repington, corresponded with the former GOC in Natal, Sir George White. Both had been invalided home from South Africa, where à Court had served on the staff of Buller's army corps, and both had been asked to comment on drafts of *The Times History of the War in South Africa*. Understandably, White was preoccupied with what interpretation might be put upon his defence of Natal and Ladysmith. By contrast, à Court astutely recognised the pertinent issues arising from the attempt by the editor of the history, Leo Amery, to write military history contemporaneously with a continuing conflict. It was necessary to try to achieve accuracy, but equally it should neither 'arouse disputes and ill feeling' nor fail to justice 'to a lot of brave fellows'.[1]

Operational history has always raised difficulties of analysis through the fallibility of memory and the 'fog of war', while contemporary history, in turn, is dependent upon sources, which may be neither definitive nor disinterested. The contemporary historian may also consciously or unconsciously mirror certain perceptions of events. Official history, which is often also near contemporaneous, has yet further problems of being, as Basil Liddell Hart characterised it, both patriotic and parochial. As Liddell Hart memorably wrote to the British official historian of the Great War, Brigadier Sir James Edmonds, it was 'official but not history'.[2] In this regard, the early historiography of the South African War provides a useful case study of the evolution of historiographical method. This is particularly so as much of the contemporary literature, not least Conan Doyle's *The Great Boer War*, Amery's volumes for *The Times*, and the official *History of the War in South Africa*, remained standard secondary sources until the 1970s.

The war generated a large literature from the very beginning. In 1902, for example, J. H. M. Abbott, the Australian author of *Tommy Cornstalk*, an account of the Australian Horse, apologised to readers 'in the hope that he may yet perhaps justify himself for feeling to inflict yet another [book] upon a long-suffering public'.[3] Two years earlier, in 1900, the *United Service Magazine* had already reviewed twenty-seven books on the war. It went on to review another seventy-one over the next three years. An early review article by an anonymous British officer in the *American Historical Review* in 1907 concluded that the reading public's interest was in inverse ratio to the accuracy and value of particular accounts. He was especially critical of the immensely popular illustrated histories such as *With the Flag to Pretoria*, *Khaki in South Africa*, and *the Transvaal War Album*. They were composed 'by the scissors and paste process from the columns of newspapers' with representations by artists 'whose acquaintance with battlefields is limited to a study of Napoleonic pictures and melodramas as presented by the suburban stage'.[4]

Certainly, the war resulted in a burgeoning of this kind of popular literature although such illustrated works had also appeared for earlier conflicts such as the Franco-Prussian War, the Russo-Turkish War and the campaigns in Egypt and the Sudan. Public interest, however, was also marked by the healthy sales of large numbers of first-hand accounts, led by those of war correspondents. On the British side alone, 149 correspondents representing forty-seven different newspapers and journals were entitled to the Queen's South Africa Medal. Many soon published their own accounts in book form, including Charles Goodman, H. W. Nevinson, Bennet Burleigh, Edgar Wallace, Winston Churchill and George W. Steevens, whose *From Capetown to Ladysmith* was published posthumously and incomplete after his death from enteric during the siege of Ladysmith. Indeed, one reason why Amery suggested a history to the managing director of *The Times*, Moberly Bell, was to prevent its own correspondents from 'writing huge books of their own'.[5] In the event, at least three of the newspaper's twenty or so correspondents did so anyway.

Many of these early accounts were published before the war had ended and, of course, before all the facts could be fully known. Nevertheless, there was one attempt to produce an accurate contemporary account for the popular market – Arthur Conan Doyle's *The Great Boer War*.

Already well known as the creator of Sherlock Holmes and Brigadier Gerard, the forty-year-old Conan Doyle tried to enlist in the Imperial Yeomanry but was rejected as too old. Consequently, he went out to South Africa in February 1900 as unpaid civil physician to the privately organised Langham Hospital. He served through the severe outbreak of enteric in Bloemfontein and also accompanied Roberts's advance to Pretoria. Along the way he contributed articles to the *Strand* and the *Cornhill* magazines, conceiving of the idea of a full history at an early stage. Intending to stand as a Liberal Unionist candidate in the general election, he returned to England in July 1900, publishing the first edition later that year. A further fourteen impressions had appeared by 1901 and the sixteenth and final version in September 1903.

Conan Doyle used eyewitness accounts and strived for as much accuracy as possible, though also introducing his own ideas on the need to introduce heavier artillery, rifles rather than swords for the cavalry, and a more democratic army backed by a national militia based on initial training in rifle clubs. Later editions were updated by reference to new material, particularly from war correspondents, Conan Doyle concluding in September 1903 that he had seldom had cause to reverse earlier judgements. Indeed, on reading the Official History, which had cost £27,000 to compile, he claimed that 'I cannot find that there was anything in it which I had not already chronicled, save for those minute details of various forces which clog a narrative'. He even claimed that Frederick Maurice, the official historian, had acknowledged that *The Great Boer War* 'had been the spine round which he built'.[6] Even today, Conan Doyle's narrative remains very readable, if impressionistic rather than accurate. He devoted little attention, however, to the guerrilla phase of the war after the fall of the Boer capitals. Moreover, he was also writing from the perspective of a committed supporter of the war, his separate pamphlet, *The Cause and Conduct of the War* selling in excess of 300,000 copies in Britain and over 140,000 abroad and earning him a knighthood.

One source increasingly available to Conan Doyle and others were the memoirs of participants that also began to appear in ever-larger numbers. Indeed, Amery was regularly sent all relevant books published in Britain while compiling *The Times History of the War in South Africa*. The newspaper was in some financial difficulties when the war began and another reason for the history was an attempt to recoup some of the costs of maintaining its correspondents in the field. Though it seems Amery partly suggested the history in jest, Bell sensed a commercial opportunity. Indeed, Bell happily concluded, 'the more the volumes the more the profit, always provided that it is not unnecessarily dragged out'.[7] His commercial partner in the venture, R. B. Marston of Sampson Low, suggested mentioning as many dead officers as possible and including their photographs.

Whereas Bell wanted to turn a quick profit, Amery had a different purpose, eschewing 'the picturesque imaginativeness of style of Dr Conan Doyle' and aiming for 'a really accurate and impartial work'.[8] Reluctantly or otherwise, Bell also came round to the same point of view, though he grew increasingly impatient as the history expanded inexorably. Amery recounts a story in his memoirs that he sent Bell a letter he had received from a wounded officer warmly praising the history, which was being read to him in hospital by his wife. Bell responded by sending a press cutting recording the officer's death 'after long sufferings heroically endured'.[9] The history eventually ran to six volumes and an index – 3498 pages in all – published over nine years. Amery himself worked directly on four volumes and calculated that he devoted the equivalent of five full years to the project, interspersed with his duties as journalist and activities as aspiring politician. Basil Williams and Erskine Childers compiled the fourth and fifth volumes covering the war after the fall of Bloemfontein respectively. It cost an estimated £19,802 for the 29,500 individual volumes printed, and ultimately made a loss.

Part of the reason for the protracted nature of the work was Amery's desire for accuracy. Initial drafts were contributed by *Times* correspondents such as Flora Shaw, Perceval Landon, Alsager Pollock, Bron Herbert (later Lord Lucas), W. F. Moneypenny, and Lionel James, who acted as assistant editor. Occasionally, outsiders were enlisted, including the jurist, A. V. Dicey, and the future Secretary of State for War, Hugh Arnold-Forster. Drafts were then widely circulated to leading participants. In many cases they were willing to help and, if not, circulation often induced the recalcitrant to break silence in their own defence. Sir George White and Charles à Court, for example, were communicating with each other in January 1901 because they were both unhappy with the treatment of the initial campaign in Natal. White indeed complained to Bell, Amery subsequently explaining that the drafts were circulated in proof form in order 'to gain all the additional information possible in the way of notes and corrections, before proceeding to the task of editing them myself'. Amery confessed that he knew initial drafts would contain inaccuracies, which he hoped would be corrected. Comments would help him 'form a better judgement on the forces by studying the view of those who were particularly concerned in the operations'.[10] It might also be said that if, as was often the case, the drafts were critical, it made it more difficult for the participants to ignore them. Later drafts would also be circulated.

Having made contact with White, Amery pressed him closely on the true nature of the telegrams that had passed between him and Buller after Colenso. White, however, would not be drawn on the content of telegrams, which the Secretary of State for War, St John Brodrick, had already refused to reveal to the House of Commons. White was advised not to cooperate too closely with Amery by the Military Secretary, Sir Ian Hamilton, writing on behalf of Roberts, now Commander-in-Chief at home, and Brodrick. Yet ironically Roberts and others from his coterie, such as Hamilton, Brigadier-General Henry Rawlinson and Colonel Henry Wilson, were giving Amery active help. Roberts, for example, declined to show Amery confidential telegrams but made extensive comments on draft chapters, loaned other material, and provided Amery with a letter of introduction when the latter went to South Africa in 1902. Roberts also deputed one of his staff to answer specific questions, and the War Office provided considerable information on the kind of technical issues such as transport covered in the last volume. Indeed, appearing before the Royal Commission on the War in South Africa, chaired by Lord Elgin, Major-General Geoffry Barton revealed that the normal rules with regard to the press were suspended in the case of *The Times* history.[11]

Generally, Amery found it easier to collect information once the Elgin Commission had published its report and evidence in 1903. In any case, Amery's history served the purpose of Roberts and his circle, hence the essential cynicism of the advice proffered to White. Not surprisingly, therefore, the narrative was flawed through its bias against Redvers Buller and in favour of Roberts. Amery, indeed, was to be responsible for orchestrating the press campaign that saw Buller dismissed from the

Aldershot command in October 1901 after Buller tried to defend his conduct of the opening campaigns of the war in public. Similarly, White complained that the narrative ascribed successes to accidents or enemy failings 'rather than to allow any credit to those senior officers to whom blame is meted out with no grudging hand when opportunity offers'.[12] In fact, Amery was quite open about the 'essentially propagandist' spirit in which he compiled the history, in the belief that it served both the public interest and also represented the best instrument for preaching army reform. Thus the celebrated condemnation of the pre-war army, as 'largely a sham' and 'nothing more or less than a gigantic Dotheboys Hall', greatly exaggerated the actual situation.[13] Amery and Childers also misrepresented the role of cavalry, Childers going on to write a reformist tract, *War and the Arme Blanche*, with the assistance of Roberts and the mounted infantry lobby. Interestingly, Amery and Childers differed over the representation of Lord Milner's post-war political reconstruction of South Africa, Childers disassociating himself with the final chapter of his volume when Amery revised it in a fashion more favourable to Milner.

Interpretation of political issues also dogged the official history, delaying the appearance of its first volume until 1906. Initially, a military writer and theorist, G. F. R. Henderson, was charged with producing the official history. Henderson had been appointed Director of Military Intelligence in South Africa by Roberts, but was invalided home just before the battle of Paardeburg. He died in March 1903 while the project was still at a very early stage. Prior to his death, however, Henderson had been given a free hand and, in an attempt to escape the usual conventions, had approached a commercial publisher, Hurst and Blackett, who agreed to take all risks and simply pay a 30 per cent royalty to the Treasury. On Henderson's death, Major-General Sir J. F. Maurice, recently retired, was asked to assume the mantle of official historian.

Official history was well established in Britain. In fact, Maurice had written the official history of the Egyptian campaign of 1882. The first history usually considered to be official was the two-volume *Journal of the Operations Conducted by the Corps of Royal Engineers*, published in 1859 and dealing with the Crimean War. The next, dealing with the Abyssinian expedition of 1867–68, appeared in 1870. Thereafter, most major campaigns resulted in official treatments. Primarily, they were produced by the War Office Intelligence Branch and intended for purely professional purposes. They were not, however, without controversy. The official history of the Zulu War by Major John Sutton Rothwell, for example, helped perpetuate serious distortions in the official version of what had happened at Isandlwana, while Maurice himself glossed over the dispute between Wolseley and Lieutenant-General Sir Edward Hamley during the Egyptian campaign. Colonel H. E. Colvile's official history of the Gordon Relief Expedition took a decidedly partisan view of military criticism of government policy and, in any case, was delayed until 1889 by the revisions demanded by various officers and departments. The six-volume official history of the Second Afghan War, written by Charles MacGregor, was effectively suppressed, conceivably as a result of political sensitivities with regard to Britain's relationship with Afghanistan. A two-volume version was prepared in 1897 but again suppressed; only a bowdlerised single volume was eventually published in 1908. Only one copy of the original is known to exist.[14]

Maurice himself had a particular view of the function of military history, believing that it should not only educate the military reader but also the general public. Apparently, he had discussed the history with George Henderson and they were broadly in agreement with the lines along which Maurice intended to work. Maurice, however, found that he was not to be given the free hand accorded Henderson. Initially, this was largely a financial constraint after the Treasury became alarmed at escalating costs. Henderson had been appointed at an annual fixed salary of £800 to complete the project in three years. The addition of Major G. L. Gretton and Captain M. H. Grant as assistants, however, raised the costs, as did the appointment of two subalterns for six months and another for a year. The Secretary of State for War, Brodrick, estimated that progress was so slow that it would take another twenty-eight years to produce the six or seven volumes anticipated. Consequently, he increased the staffing: at one stage Maurice had twenty-two staff, though this was reduced to fourteen by 1907. Moreover, Maurice wanted £10,000 annually for three years instead of the £1990 offered. The Treasury had also discovered the commercial agreement only by chance and had to pay off Henderson's agent, who had been promised five per cent of the proceeds.

Brodrick himself doubted that much coverage was required of the guerrilla phase of the war and suggested a more general survey. There were also increasing doubts within the Colonial Office as to the proposed treatment of political issues. At the time of his death, Henderson had been working on the first volume on the war's causes. In November 1903, however, this volume was scrapped in its entirety, including a chapter on the British army in 1899, which was subsequently published in the posthumous collection of his writings, *The Science of War*. Four other chapters survive in proof or galley. Brodrick's successor, Arnold-Forster, substituted a new four-volume scheme in November 1903, with just three chapters now devoted to causation. Maurice's conviction, however, that the war was the responsibility of the Boers still compromised the conciliatory attitude now being fostered in South Africa and these three chapters were also deleted in November 1905, though they have survived in proof. Maurice was appalled by the censorship of political issues, which impinged upon military operations. Roberts, however, had been summarily retired as Commander-in-Chief in February 1904 and could do nothing. The former Colonial Secretary, Joseph Chamberlain, was also unable to exert any leverage.

Within the restrictions now placed upon him, Maurice and his researchers went about their work much as Amery and his collaborators had done. Most of the research staff were retired regulars, but a number had served in South Africa. Gretton, actually a militia officer, had been on Henderson's intelligence staff, while Colonel W. D. Jones had been a press censor on Buller's staff. They prepared draft chapters and circulated them in proof for comment, Gretton's central coordinating section providing the primary documents. Obligingly, the covering letter, which accompanied the circulation of proofs, is included in a 'note to the reader' in the second volume, published in 1907. One reason for its appearance was the difficulty that had obviously been encountered in circulating proofs for the first volume, the letter pointing out that indignant corrections arose from want of facts: 'We cannot make bricks without straw; and though the mass of material to be dealt with is very great, it often fails us at important points.' [15] In at least one case, the proofs never reached a key participant since Ian Hamilton was now acting as an official observer of the Russo-Japanese War. He subsequently pointed out a number of errors in the account of Elandslaagte in the first volume. Others were frankly distressed at how their actions were depicted, notably Buller, who roundly condemned a draft on Colenso prepared by Major A. Griffiths as 'the poorest piece of work I had ever read – not only were there in it several statements which were pure invention, and much that was ... only a parody with truth; but I thought it really a bad piece of work as a literary production ... I told him that it was bad history and really indifferent journalism'.[16]

Other difficulties included the varying interpretations as to whether or not it was desirable to tell the whole truth. Major-General Sir William Gatacre, for example, with much to hide following the disaster at Stormberg in 'Black Week', believed that it was better not to publish facts likely to shame units or individuals. By contrast, Roberts declared that the truth was essential but, as with Amery's work, intended that it be his version of the truth. Thus General Sir Reginald Pole-Carew, once a trusted member of the inner circle, pointed out in October 1906 that he had a very different recollection of one particular episode since he usually saw things 'through glasses of a different colour' and could not expect a favourable interpretation of his conduct from Roberts.[17]

It was not perhaps surprising that the toll told on Maurice and he was compelled to retire after completing the third volume, this appearing in 1908 without any author actually credited. The cost was still escalating and the fourth and last volume was published in 1910 after preparation by Grant and two assistants under the auspices of the new Historical Section of the Committee of Imperial Defence. Grant, incidentally, while still a serving regular, had published a memoir of the war, *Words by an Eyewitness: The Struggle in Natal* under the pseudonym 'Linesman' in 1901. He was better known, however, as a writer on landscape painting and a collector of marbles and granites; his son was the distinguished writer on the ancient world, Michael Grant. Four map volumes were also produced. In all, 1050 sets of the whole were officially distributed – no one had actually thought to calculate the cost of such a distribution – and just 4500 sets were sold to the public. Indeed, so calamitous was the paucity of receipts, and those of the subsequent history of the Russo-Japanese War, that the Treasury tried to close the Historical Section down altogether in 1913.

Clearly, the official history was not the valuable history, comprehensible to and educative of the public, for which Maurice and Henderson had hoped. Grant's preface to the last volume, indeed, remarked that an official history 'would be valueless to military students if it could not be referred to for information concerning the minutiae of the campaign; the lesser as well as the greater tactics, the work of units, and even of individual officers and men'.[18] As a result, it was a fairly colourless statement of facts, which was unlikely to modify views formed as a result of reading Amery's far more lucid and livelier prose.

In some ways, while the war had a decided impact in terms of the organisational and other military reforms effected in its immediate aftermath, it was soon overshadowed in terms of professional interest by the Russo-Japanese War. An internal history of the Royal Engineers during the war was prepared in 1904, an official medical survey in 1911, and a veterinary history in 1919, but interest then largely died. There was a brief flurry of memoirs in the late 1920s and 1930s, but no real revival in publishing interest until popular histories appeared in the late 1950s. More often than not, these were utterly dependent upon Amery, the official history and the evidence presented to the Elgin Commission, with all the virtues and vices of these sources. Back in March 1901 à Court had written that 'anyone who ventures to write a complete history of the war will be certainly doomed in this world or the next, and probably in both'.[19] It would not be until the late 1970s and early 1980s that serious attempts were made to do so and, in the process, to escape the shadows cast by Amery, Maurice and their collaborators.

Part Two

Generals and Politicians

10

Command in South Africa

The original significance of the Cape for Britain lay in its control of the route to India as a 'Gibraltar of the Southern Oceans'. The opening of the Suez Canal in 1869 did not diminish this. Retention of the Cape increasingly drew Britain into the affairs of the interior, but the primary role of British forces in South Africa remained the defence of its ports against maritime attack. Indeed, while a permanent military presence was established in Natal in May 1842, the garrison theoretically remained only a temporary expedient throughout the entire period of Natal's existence as a separate colony from 1856 to 1910. In February 1853 Lieutenant-General Sir George Cathcart regarded the Natal garrison as existing only to assist evacuation of the colonists by sea in the event of any native insurrection. Similarly, it was intended to withdraw the garrison five years after the colony's assumption of responsible government in 1893, a factor that increased the reluctance of the Secretary of State for War, Lord Lansdowne, to reinforce Natal when the Boer threat increased in 1896. The War Office Intelligence Division concluded that Durban and Pietermaritzburg were worth holding only for reasons of prestige, while Lansdowne later questioned whether Natal was worth defending at all. In 1899, however, Major-General Sir Penn Symons was persuaded to move forward to Glencoe by Natal's Lieutenant-Governor, Sir Walter Hely-Hutchinson, who feared native unrest and the loss of the Dundee coalfields.

The pressure to keep the imperial garrison small remained a constant. Only the existing native threats to the eastern frontier and the limited resources of Cape Colony in the 1860s had prevented the extension of the policy of withdrawing imperial garrisons applied to Australia, Canada and New Zealand. Since there was relatively little conflict between the end of the Eighth Kaffir (Cape Frontier) War in 1853 and the beginning of the Ninth War in 1877, there was no imperative to increase the garrison. Subsequently, after the flurry of military activity occasioned by the Ninth Kaffir War (1877–78), the Zulu War (1879) and the First Anglo-Boer War (1880–81), there was again little concern for security until relations between Britain and the Boer republics deteriorated in the mid 1890s.

Consequently, with the exception of 1877–81 and 1899–1902, the Cape did not represent a significant command after the departure of Cathcart as Governor, Commander-in-Chief and High Commissioner in 1854. Indeed, no serving soldier was appointed to these offices again and Lieutenant-Generals Commanding appointed to the Cape were frequently undistinguished. Not unexpectedly, when crises arose, the incumbent was often judged unsuitable to conduct operations, although this also reflected political perceptions of the acceptability of particular generals to public opinion. Lieutenant-General Sir Arthur Cunynghame found himself sidelined by the appointment of Major-General Sir Garnet Wolseley as Special Commissioner in Natal in 1875. However, Cunynghame reluctantly accepted that only a better known officer would satisfy public opinion and Wolseley was 'by far the most rising'.[1] What condemned Cunynghame's eventual successor, Lord Chelmsford, as much as his military failure in 1879, was his inability to comprehend the requirements of public opinion, despite attempts by the Commander-in-Chief at Horse Guards, the Duke of Cambridge, to get him to provide a coherent account of his conduct sufficient to refute press criticism. It was, of course, Wolseley who was sent out to supersede Chelmsford in May 1879 with local rank of full general and concurrent appointments as Governor of Natal and the Transvaal and High Commissioner for South-Eastern Africa.

No one could accuse Lieutenant-General Sir William Butler of being undistinguished when he was appointed to the Cape in November 1898 following the sudden death of William Goodenough. Butler's sympathies for the Boers, however, rapidly rendered his position untenable and he was subjected to such public opprobrium on his return to England that, in November 1899, it was thought better that he should not accompany the Queen on a visit to Bristol. No one had much faith in the military abilities of Butler's successor, Lieutenant-General Sir Frederick Forestier-Walker, and he only arrived in South Africa in September 1899. His responsibilities had already been reduced by the appointment of

Lieutenant-General Sir George White to command in Natal since Penn Symons was largely untried. With the arrival of General Sir Redvers Buller to command the army corps at the Cape in October 1899, Forestier-Walker was quickly confined to duties on lines of communication. Buller's supersession by Roberts after his defeat at Colenso on 15 December 1899 was again linked to public opinion, not least the response to Buller's unfortunate post-action telegram advising White to surrender Ladysmith. Wolseley, now Commander-in-Chief and of course a bitter rival of Roberts, accused the Cabinet of simple pandering to the public gallery. After the war, the significance of the South African command faded once more, Lieutenant-General the Hon. Neville Lyttelton, for example, being considered far from brilliant but 'as sound & safe as possible'.[2]

The politics of command selection in major crises was itself immensely complex and the internal manoeuvring between various military factions was intense after Isandlwana in 1879, Majuba in 1881 and Colenso in 1899. In 1879 Cambridge's choice to succeed Chelmsford was General Lord Napier rather than Wolseley. Having failed to prevent this, the Duke was determined to stop Wolseley obtaining the services of George Colley, the Viceroy's Private Secretary in India, as his Chief of Staff. Wolseley secured Colley's services only temporarily before the renewal of the Second Afghan War compelled Colley's return to India, although he was able to ensure Colley succeeded him in 1880. Wolseley was also forced to accept the four major-generals Cambridge had sent out to the Cape in February 1879. Wolseley was similarly frustrated by the appointment of Frederick Roberts to succeed Colley after Majuba. In the event, peace terms were agreed before Roberts arrived, which both Roberts and Wolseley construed as an attempt by Evelyn Wood, who had succeeded to the immediate command, to prevent anyone else gaining kudos from the campaign. In fact, the Cabinet largely tied Wood's hands, but Wolseley never forgave him for what he regarded as a betrayal of Colley's memory. In December 1899 the triumph of Roberts, who had been pressing for the command in South Africa for three years, was complete, albeit tempered by the death of his son at Colenso.

The need to take account of public opinion and the effect of government policy upon operations both emphasise the point that wartime commanders in South Africa had to demonstrate a capability of exercising both political and military judgement. This was especially so prior to the Zulu War, since there was no direct communication between Britain and South Africa until the war speeded the extension of the submarine telegraph cable to Durban from London via Aden in December 1879: there was no direct link between Cape Town and London until 1887. Thus, the news of Isandlwana reached London only on 11 February. In 1852 mail between London and the Cape averaged thirty-three days and, in 1879, when Chelmsford was deep in Zululand, his communications with Cambridge were sometimes taking over fifty days. On the one hand, this compelled the government to trust entirely to Wolseley's judgement in Natal in 1875. It also enabled the High Commissioner, Sir Bartle Frere, to precipitate a war in 1879 that the government wished to avoid. On the other hand, Wolseley found it irksome to be without government instructions when negotiating with the Transvaal Boers in 1879–80, particularly when the new cable to London kept breaking down and dissident Boers compounded the problem by cutting the telegraph wires. By 1899, the problems of communication had been solved, but, ironically, the government vested so much in the success of Roberts and his chief of staff and successor, Major-General Lord Kitchener, that all political control was surrendered to the soldiers.

The fact that England was some six thousand miles from the Cape also presented the problem of the reinforcement. In 1879 it took sixty days for the first reinforcements to be landed at the Cape from the receipt of the news of Isandlwana in London. In June 1899 it was calculated that the voyage to Cape Town would take seventeen days but that, taking into account the requirements of the mobilisation process, two and a half months would elapse before the first troops reached the Cape, although a contingent could reach Natal from India in five weeks. Wolseley and Buller had both repeatedly urged mobilisation preparations to be undertaken, yet it clearly surprised the Cabinet when Lansdowne informed them in August 1899 that it would take four months to assemble a full army corps in South Africa and that it would cost £1 million to reduce the timescale by a month. In the event, the average passage to the Cape in the autumn of 1899 was just over twenty-one days for infantry transports and just over twenty-three days for horse transports, and the army corps was assembled within forty-five days from the date of first embarkation. At least Cape Town had adequate port facilities, but this was not true elsewhere, the sand bars at both East London and Durban preventing ships from entering and necessitating transfer of men and supplies to lighters. Durban was also 730 miles from Cape Town. Natal, therefore, was particularly isolated, as Major-General Sir Percy Douglas noted in July 1865 when advising the colonists that, if they wanted a larger garrison, they should reduce the 'cost of landing reinforcements upon their shores' through granting free use of the steam tug and harbour facilities at Durban.[3] In 1879 supplies were also landed at Port Durnford – merely an open beach where the surf was relatively low – but Wolseley had to abandon his attempt to land there in July and return to Durban after three days when trying to reach the front quickly.

Such difficulties in reinforcing South Africa increased the significance of the limited numbers of imperial troops normally available. Returning from a two month inspection tour of his new command in July 1874, for example, Cunynghame contemplated ensuring the security of 450,000 square miles with only two battalions and an artillery battery supplemented by between 700 and 800 ill-trained men of the Frontier Armed and Mounted Police (FAMP) and a variety of poorly organised volunteer corps. Confronted with an apparent insurrection on the diamond fields of Griqualand West some 700 miles from Cape Town in 1875, Cunynghame's 'Army of the Vaal' consisted of 250 infantry, forty mounted infantry and two guns. Agreeing with Cunynghame that the War Office took little interest in Natal, Wolseley successfully urged that its garrison be increased to a full battalion in face of the potential Zulu threat.

With the outbreak of the Ninth Kaffir War, the imperial forces in South Africa increased to five and a half battalions, the other half battalion being split between Mauritius and St Helena. However, just nine hundred men based at King William's Town in British Kaffraria were actually available for operations against the Gcaleka and Ngqika. In the build up to the Zulu War, Chelmsford received two more battalions, while a third arrived in January 1879. Excluding native units and transport personnel, Chelmsford had 6669 officers and men available in January 1879. The disaster at Isandlwana resulted in substantial reinforcements being despatched, amounting to a further 10,414 officers and men. Not unexpectedly, the garrison was rapidly reduced after the war. Indeed, Wolseley's post-war settlement of Zululand was intended to obviate the necessity of military occupation by dividing it into thirteen rival chiefdoms. When the Transvaal Boers rose in revolt in December 1880, Colley had only 1772 men available in Natal. Some 2839 men from three different battalions and a cavalry regiment had been divided between nine different garrison posts in the Transvaal in August 1880 before Colley initiated a consolidation, abandoning three posts and withdrawing five companies to Natal prior to the outbreak. The six remaining garrisons were all besieged by the Boers, together with a small detachment at Potchefstroom. Colley's field force drew on twelve companies from four different battalions and no more than six companies were engaged in any of the subsequent actions at Laing's Nek, Ingogo and Majuba. Some 16,000 men were in – or on their way to – South Africa when peace terms were agreed.

Thereafter, the garrison fell once more. Wood urged that three and a half battalions be retained in Natal, with a further battalion at the Cape. Three battalions and a cavalry regiment were stationed in Natal after 1882. Usually there were also two and a half battalions at the Cape, but these tended to be even more dispersed through being utilised for expeditions, such as those to Bechuanaland and to support the British South Africa Company (BSAC) forces in Matabeleland and Mashonaland in 1896–97. In June 1895 there were 3932 imperial troops in South Africa, a total that was slowly increased to 5409 by December 1896, although this included the half battalion on Mauritius. As relations with the Boer republics deteriorated, Lansdowne and the Cabinet continued to resist any increase in the garrison. By June 1899 there were still only 10,289 regulars in South Africa. On 9 October 1899 – two days before the Boers invaded Natal – troop strength had been increased to 16,203. Ultimately, a total of 448,725 men was deployed in South Africa between 1899 and 1902.

Consequently, British commanders had little option but to supplement their forces with locally raised units. Initially, some thought had been given to policing the eastern frontier with veterans' settlements. A pioneering settlement had, however, been destroyed by the Xhosa in December 1850. The British German Legion brought to the Cape for the same purpose in December 1856 was subsequently depleted by contingents sent to India and ceased to exist in March 1860. Unfortunately, too, the employment of colonial irregulars could result in friction with colonial administrations. Cunynghame, for example, had hoped to see a Canadian-style militia develop but enjoyed poor relations with the Cape government. Indeed, the Cape's Prime Minister, John Molteno, who successfully restricted imperial forces to guarding the frontiers of the Transkei at the start of the Ninth Kaffir War, had no intention of allowing Cunynghame to become more than 'an ornamental puppet'.[4] Molteno could not, however, prevent Cunynghame assuming control of operations once initial FAMP operations had failed and the Ngqika had risen in the Ciskei. Frustrated by this turn of events, Molteno's 'Minister of War', John Merriman, launched a raid into Thembuland. This precipitated Frere's dismissal of the ministry in February 1878, a few days after Cunynghame had also been removed due to 'the want of cordiality' existing between him and the Cape authorities.[5]

In Natal there were fifteen existing volunteer units in 1879, eight of which agreed to serve in Zululand and thus compensate for Chelmsford's lack of mounted troops. Despite an equal lack of mounted troops, Colley declined to employ any volunteers against the Boers in 1881 in the belief that to do so would lead to an unacceptable escalation of the conflict. At the same time, however, irregulars were being used in the so-called 'Gun War' against the baSotho in Basutoland. One British officer, Frederick Carrington, became particularly associated with irregulars, commanding them in the campaign against the baPedi chief Sekukuni (Sekhukhune) in the Transvaal in 1879 as well as in the Gun War and on Warren's expedition to Bechuanaland. Carrington commanded the new Bechuanaland Border Police (BPP) from 1885–88 and from 1889–93, also training the British South Africa Police (BSAP) in 1889. As a major-general, Carrington was recalled to command the Rhodesian forces during the rebellions in Mashonaland and Matabeleland in 1896–97, the BSAC resisting the use of imperial troops due both to the cost and the probability of the British government insisting on a role in the post-war settlement. Similarly, the Zulu revolt in 1906 was entirely suppressed by colonial forces.

Africans were another possible source of additional manpower. Originally, the Cape Mounted Rifles had been raised from Hottentots to help police the eastern frontier in 1827, but, following a series of mutinies, they had been Europeanised in 1851 and replaced with the FAMP in 1855. The British had found the Mfengu useful allies against the Xhosa and they were again used extensively during the Ninth Kaffir War. Similarly, Wolseley employed about ten thousand Swazis in the campaign against Sekukuni, and Ngwato, Zulus and 'Cape Boys' assisted in the suppression of Matabeleland and Mashonaland in 1896–97. African levies were also enlisted to defend the frontiers of Bechuanaland and Transkei during the Second Anglo-Boer War. In addition to the eight thousand or so blacks raised for service in Zululand with the Natal Native Contingent (NNC) in 1879, it was also intended to raise some 6000 levies for a Border Guard. However, whereas Natal's Lieutenant-Governor, Sir Henry Bulwer, wanted a largely passive defence, Chelmsford envisaged raids into Zululand, which Bulwer feared would only result in damaging counter-raids. The dispute contributed to Chelmsford's replacement.

Even assuming sufficient manpower was available, commanders in South Africa then confronted the problem famously noted by Charles Callwell, namely that campaigns were waged as much against nature as against indigenous opponents. While the discovery of diamonds in Griqualand West in 1867 and then gold on the Rand in the Transvaal in 1886 finally stimulated railway development, there were still only 5024 miles of line in southern Africa by 1899, much of it only narrow gauge and single track. The line between the Cape and Bloemfontein was only completed in 1892, and those from the Cape to Mafeking and from Natal to the Rand only in 1895. The steep climb from the Cape into the interior also meant, for example, that it took thirty-three hours by rail to reach De Aar. The fact that the railway had not yet been extended from Mafeking hamstrung the movement of reinforcements to Rhodesia in 1896–97. The rail network was also of account in operational planning between 1896 and 1899. The route from Natal to Pretoria was only half the distance of that from the Cape to Pretoria but far more difficult because of the rugged terrain of the Biggarsberg athwart the Natal/Transvaal frontier. Advancing along the railway line from the Cape, however, meant advancing into the Orange Free State, whose attitude towards a conflict was uncertain. It might also be added that Ladysmith was originally chosen as a supply depot simply because it was a rail junction.

Initially, some 900 miles of line fell into Boer hands in 1899 and Roberts also resolved to leave the line of the railway in his advance to Bloemfontein. As a result, more traditional means of transport had to be utilised, namely oxen, horses and mules. Animals, however, were subject to vagaries of climate. The summer months from October to March were generally wet, resulting in good pasture but also flooded and impassable rivers, and tracks that quickly became morasses. The dry winter months of April to September guaranteed hard tracks but shortage of water and non-existent pasture. Oxen, therefore, could be used best in summer and horses and mules best in winter, but horses and mules would have to carry their own fodder with them. An additional factor was that horse sickness was a feature of lower altitudes and of the wet months, with only June to September really free of it. While oxen could be used in Natal through the general absence of tsetse fly, they could not be used to the same extent in the Boer republics through the prevalence of rinderpest. Technically, therefore, campaigning was possible throughout the year but each season presented problems.

Seen in this light, although Wolseley believed a campaign should only be mounted in Zululand between May and September, the timing of Chelmsford's initial offensive in January 1879 had some merit. Natal's frontiers would be additionally protected from Zulu counter-raids by flooded rivers. There would also be plenty of pasture for Chelmsford's transport oxen, while late spring rains had delayed the mealie harvest in Zululand and the Zulus themselves would be short of food, four years of drought having generally reduced their resources. Unfortunately, the need to carry everything the army required turned it 'into an escort for its food'.[6] At most, oxen could make only eleven miles a day, since they had to be rested every three to four hours and grazed for five or six hours. Marching from King William's Town to Utrecht in June 1878, for example, a column of five companies, four guns and some mounted infantry led by Wood had taken five hours to get its wagons across the Kei, which was only 80–90 yards wide and four feet six inches deep. Similarly, Chelmsford took nine hours to cross the Amatukulu on 31 March 1879 during the relief of Eshowe. Inevitably, too, sudden demand pushed up the price of oxen, wagons and drivers. As the campaign became prolonged and oxen began to die from lack of pasture, a two thousand strong native carrier corps was raised in July 1879 to supply the First Division from Port Durnford.

Transport problems equally affected the conduct of the Second Anglo-Boer War. Due to rinderpest, it was the horse and mule that bore the brunt of transport in this conflict. In 1878 Buller had reckoned to lose ninety to ninety-four out of every hundred horses not fully acclimatised to South African conditions. The initial campaign against Sekukuni commanded by Colonel Hugh Rowlands had been totally crippled by horse sickness. Losses in horses and mules were appallingly high between 1899 and 1902, amounting to perhaps 350,000 horses (67 per cent) and 50,000 mules.

South Africa was also largely unmapped. Wolseley had taken detailed notes on Zululand in 1875, and read correspondence sent to the Intelligence Department from officers in Zululand before leaving London in 1879, but there were no reliable maps available. In 1881 Colley received maps of the Transvaal from Germany only a month after hostilities had begun, while in 1899 Treasury restrictions had prevented the Intelligence Division from mapping Natal north of Ladysmith. A new one inch to the mile map was hastily prepared based on railway and farm surveys and information flown out of Ladysmith by pigeon: Major-General Fitzroy Hart's belief that a native guide was more reliable than the map contributed to the defeat at Colenso.

For all that campaigns in South Africa were indeed as much against nature as the enemy, commanders also had to take account of the wide variety of opponents encountered. These could be underestimated only with grave results. While aware of the Zulu military system, Chelmsford, for example, clearly expected the Zulus to fight much like the Xhosa and that they would have to be forced into open battle. On the summit of Majuba, Colley is said to have remarked, 'We could stay here for ever'.[7] Yet, even after the events of 1880–81, no one in 1899 expected the Boers to pose a serious threat. Isandlwana, Majuba and the tribulations of the South African War provide adequate testimony to the manifold difficulties of high command in South Africa.

11

Islands in the Sun

Sailing into Malta's spectacular Grand Harbour remains a special experience. So it must have been for some particularly unusual arrivals
in May 1878, these being Indian sepoys. As the 'English barrack in an
oriental sea', India was certainly of great strategic importance to the
Empire in terms of the potential military manpower it provided. Sepoys
had been used outside India since the Mutiny, in China, Abyssinia and
Perak. They had never been used previously in a European theatre,
however, and, if one excludes the Indian contingent sent to Egypt in
1882 and the Sudan in 1884–85, no more Indian troops served west of
Suez until 1914. Indeed, their arrival on Malta and subsequent transfer
to Cyprus was not without its political controversies. Yet the Indian
Expeditionary Force is little known, the officially produced multi-
volume history, *Frontier and Overseas Expeditions from India*, devoting
only two pages to the expedition. In claiming the force returned to
India after a month, it also appears strangely unaware that the majority
of the sepoys went on to Cyprus and some only returned to India in
October 1878.

The arrival of the Indian Expeditionary Force arose from one of the
rounds of the seemingly interminable Eastern Question, which con-
sumed so much political attention throughout the nineteenth century.
Standing by the provisions of the Treaty of Paris, which had concluded
the Crimean War, successive British governments had given general
support to the integrity of the Ottoman Empire. Indeed, notwithstanding
Turkish atrocities against Bulgarian rebels in 1876, of which Gladstone
was to make so much, the Conservative Prime Minister, Benjamin
Disraeli, stood emphatically with the Turks when a Russo-Turkish War
erupted in April 1877. With the fall of Adrianople to the Russians in
January 1878, Disraeli called for a £6 million vote of credit and sent
British ships to Besika Bay when the Turks accepted an armistice, fearing

that Russia would control the Straits and pose a direct threat to the newly acquired British share of the Suez Canal and the route to India. In February, Lord Napier of Magdala and Garnet Wolseley were appointed respectively as Commander-in-Chief and Chief of Staff of any British expeditionary force. In the following month, reserves were called up as the Russian-imposed Treaty of San Stefano promised considerable gains for the Tsar.

That same month, Disraeli also suggested seizing either Cyprus or Alexandretta on the Syrian coast as a *place d'armes* to counter Russian influence and as a base for operations in either Egypt or Asia Minor. The Colonial Secretary, Lord Carnarvon, had resigned on the issue of a vote of credit and Disraeli now lost his Foreign Secretary, Lord Derby, over the suggestion of seizing a base, though Derby himself had actually raised the possibility of bringing Indian troops to Egypt. Indeed, there had been consideration of other alternative bases for some time, including Crete and Lemnos. Later still, the occupation of Mitylene on Lesbos, Acre in Syria or some point in the Persian Gulf was also contemplated as an additional safeguard of the route from Malta to Aden via Suez.

It was intended from the beginning that any *place d'armes* should be secured by Indian troops, the Viceroy, Lord Lytton, having offered troops before any particular destination was chosen. Within the wider context of establishing a base somewhere, the Commander-in-Chief in India, General Sir Frederick Haines, had notified the Duke of Cambridge, Commander-in-Chief at the War Office, on 11 April 1878 that 8000 men could be made available, comprising six battalions, four batteries, a cavalry regiment and four companies of sappers and miners. By the time the orders were issued on 17 April, however, the destination had become Malta and the force structure amended, with two batteries deleted but a second cavalry regiment added. Its purpose was largely political, Carnarvon's successor, Sir Michael Hicks Beach, writing that it would demonstrate 'quickly and decisively to the world that we were able, if need be, to wield the Force of a united Empire'.[1] With no active military role now envisaged, the original commander, the one-armed Lieutenant-General Sir Sam Browne VC, was replaced by Major-General John Ross. Ross had originally been intended to command only the infantry component and this was now placed under Brigadier-General Herbert Macpherson VC, with the cavalry under Brigadier-General John

Watson VC. The sappers and miners from both Bombay and Madras were also placed under the command of Colonel (later General Sir) Harry Prendergast VC of the Madras army. It is unclear whether the accumulation of holders of the VC was in itself significant as an additional political statement or how far it merely indicates the usefulness of the decoration in easing the way to preferment.

The troops were not specially selected other than being those not too widely dispersed and sufficiently close to railways to be embarked quickly. Haines had originally intended to send some British infantry but changed his mind when the expedition became a gesture, though also in the mistaken belief that Cambridge had ruled out weakening the British presence in India at a critical time. Haines felt justified in sending only native infantry due to the presence of British infantry on Malta, but took the precaution of selecting native units of mixed social composition. An additional consideration was to avoid taking troops from the frontier with Afghanistan or from those designated as reserves for possible operations inside Afghanistan. After such matters had been taken into account, the expeditionary force was settled as comprising the 9th Bengal (1st Hodson's Horse) Cavalry, 2nd (Prince of Wales's Own) Gurkhas, 13th Bengal Infantry and 31st Punjab Infantry from Bengal; the 1st Bombay Lancers, 9th and 26th Bombay Infantry and two companies of sappers and miners from Bombay; and the 25th Madras Infantry and two companies of sappers and miners from Madras. The artillery batteries chosen were M battery, 1st Brigade, and F battery, 2nd Brigade, Royal Artillery.

Continuing echoes of distrust twenty years after the Mutiny were also manifest in Haines's insistence that the Martini Henry rifle, now being issued to British troops in India, should not be given to the expeditionary force. Haines justified his decision in terms of the Martini Henry's predecessor, the Snider, having been only recently issued to native units. He was more worried, however, that equality of weapons might affect the perceived balance of power between British and Indian troops, stressing this when, to his disgust, the Martini was issued to the Indians on Malta in June. In other ways, the Military Member of the Viceroy's Council, Major-General Sir Edwin Johnson, and the Commander-in-Chief of the Madras army, Lieutenant-General Sir Neville Chamberlain, also reflected doubts in their concern that the Indian troops should not be retained in the Mediterranean for longer than absolutely necessary.

Chamberlain feared prolonged absence might bring claims for reward or promotion 'far in excess of deserts',[2] while also raising the point that without familiar bazaars, with expensive prices and in restricted surroundings, Malta would be too European for the native taste.

Concerns of a rather different kind greeted the announcement of the expedition in Britain. The Liberals were exercised both by the fact that the decision had been taken but not announced before Parliament's Easter recess, but also, and more substantially, by the claim that bringing Indian troops into Europe violated the Government of India Act and the Bill of Rights. Replying for the government in statements on 6 and 7 May, the Chancellor of the Exchequer, Northcote, maintained that only bringing the Indians to England would violate the Bill of Rights, while the Government of India Act did not apply when the expedition was to be sustained from imperial and not Indian revenues. The Opposition provoked a debate on 27 May but lost both its motion condemning the expedition and also that for establishing a parliamentary committee on the expenditure involved. Nevertheless the government had some concerns over the charge brought by Sir George Campbell, the MP for Kirkcaldy, that Indian troops on Malta could not be disciplined under either the (British) Mutiny Act or Indian legislation. Northcote claimed that the Articles of War applied but, when consulted, the celebrated authority on military law, J. M. Clode, felt these could not be applied to camp followers. India was therefore urged to remedy the legislative deficiency with some urgency.

Parliament had voted £398,000 to convey the expedition to Malta and a further £350,000 to sustain it there. Much of this was expended upon shipping, since the 447 Europeans, 5683 Indians of all ranks, 2340 public and private followers, 1375 horses, 526 ponies and forty-three bullocks required twelve steamers and fifteen towed sailing vessels between them. No less than sixteen companies provided these twenty-seven ships, though the majority were supplied by Nicol & Co. and Finlay Muir & Co. Fifteen of the ships were then retained for the despatch of the force (less Hodson's Horse) to Cyprus. Some of the firms claimed subsequently that payment was withheld unnecessarily pending final calculations and, in fact, payments were not settled until November 1881 when the India Office admitted to the Bombay government that neither Admiralty nor War Office could account for all stores originally despatched.

Another difficulty was an attempt to pass off the conveyance of eighty-seven men, women and children from Bombay to Aden on HMS *Tamar* in September 1878, which had no connection to the expedition.

The expedition was another impressive example of the ability of the army to organise such matters on an ad hoc basis. With the first orders issued on 17 April, it was only eleven days before the first two ships – the steamer *Goa* towing the sailing ship *Duke of Athol* – left Cannanore with the 25th Madras Infantry. All units had had to complete to war establishment while those supplying drafts were also authorised to recruit to fill vacancies. There was no shortage of volunteers, a squadron of the 10th Bengal (2nd Hodson's Horse) completing the 1st and men of the 3rd Gurkhas being taken up to compete the 2nd Gurkhas. The Government of India issued free additional embarkation clothing to native troops and followers, as well as additional pay and forage, camp equipment and stores for three months. The scale of the enterprise might be judged from each native soldier receiving a blanket, two canvas frocks, two pairs of flannel drawers, two banyans or jerseys, two pairs of arm socks and a pair of English boots, while each follower received a blanket, a pair of cloth pyjamas, a greatcoat, a lascar coat, a pair of English or Indian boots, a tin canteen, a haversack, two pairs of woollen socks and two banyans. It would appear that the force did not know of its destination until it embarked.

Speed was essential before seasonal storms affected the Red Sea and made towing all but impossible and, in fact, strong winds were encountered, slowing the passage and necessitating rationing of water. Some ships were less than satisfactory, notably the steamer *St Osyth*, carrying the 2nd Gurkhas, which was inadequate for towing. Ventilation for horses was poor and it had been overlooked that certain castes were not permitted to cook while afloat. Astonishingly, the same problem recurred on passage from Malta to Cyprus and on the return to India. Four cases of cholera then occurred on the *Maraval* while it was passing through the Suez Cabal at the time when Egyptian officials were already alarmed by a typhus outbreak in Turkey. The acting president of the Egyptian Board of Health was persuaded to allow the ship to proceed, but the Italian authorities objected to the Sanitary Council, on which they had representatives, being bypassed. Only a hastily convened meeting allowed quarantine in transit. More bizarre was the accidental poisoning of forty-eight men, three of whom died, of Hodson's Horse on Malta when disinfecting fluid was mistakenly substituted for the daily issue of lime juice. As a result, the regiment was unable to proceed to Cyprus.

Despite the difficulties, however, the Indian contingent was safely established on Malta by the end of May, attracting much interest from the periodicals such as the *Illustrated London News*, which provided sketches of the infantry encampment at Fort Manoel, the cavalry encampment outside Valetta, and various sporting activities. Indeed, the Indian contingent offered to play the garrison at anything they chose, including cricket, football, pigeon shooting, tennis, racquets, polo and running. The *Contemporary Review* also produced a somewhat speculative piece by a retired general, clearly hazy about the class composition of the units selected, which was intended to make the sepoys 'familiar to the English mind'.[3] The Duke of Cambridge journeyed to Malta to inspect the force on 17 June, his praise for the Madras contingent being especially welcomed by Haines and Johnson. Old Bengal hands had criticised the participation of Madras troops while Wolseley had recently presented a paper to the Council of India advocating their abolition. It was somewhat ironic, then, that when Disraeli and his new Foreign Secretary, Lord Salisbury, secured Turkish agreement to British occupation of Cyprus, it was announced on 8 July that Wolseley would command the British and Indian force to be sent from Malta.

Salisbury and Colonel Robert Home of the War Office Intelligence Department had urged the occupation of either Lemnos or Cyprus back in March. There had been some difference of opinion among the government's military advisers, but the choice had narrowed to these options. Nonetheless, Cyprus was regarded as a poor substitute for Egypt, though this would have risked complications with the French. Formal possession was taken of the island by the Royal Navy on 14 July and the first troops sailed from Malta four days later, the sappers and miners going first on the *Canara* to construct landing stages and piers for the disembarkation of the remainder of the force, and to select and prepare camp sites. Timber for piers proved in short supply and some old houses were pulled down as a result. Subsequently, the sappers and miners were employed on road construction.

Initially, the 31st Punjab Infantry was stationed at Limassol, the

13th Bengal Infantry at Paphos, the 9th Bombay Infantry at Larnaca, the 26th Bombay at Famagusta, and the 25th Madras at Kyrenia. The Gurkhas and the Bombay Lancers, who arrived only on 7 August, were stationed close to Nicosia. Wolseley found this convenient since it enabled him to concentrate his three British battalions – the 42nd, 71st and 101st Foot. It had been anticipated that the Indians must be withdrawn before the October rains, but, on 26 July, Wolseley was informed they must be pulled out at once on both political and sanitary grounds. The political reasons were not spelled out though it had become known that the sepoys disliked both the heat of Cyprus and more garrison work out of India. Wolseley professed to know of no sanitary problems, but Haines had pointed out that the sepoys were just as susceptible to malaria as the British troops and the sickness rate on the island was to prove disturbingly high. Indeed, between 50 and 75 per cent of men in some Indian units had been struck by fever after the first rain shower. More-over, it would be difficult to send the Indians back at this precise moment when they would encounter high temperatures in the Red Sea and, more than likely, the monsoon once in the open sea with all that entailed for men and animals. The special rations for the voyage could not be obtained in any case for at least three weeks and it was concluded, by the contingent's own officers, that such a voyage would be so damaging to morale as to undermine any future employment of Indian troops overseas.

Wolseley endorsed the views of his Indian subordinates but was still instructed to start preparations on 9 August, this persuading him that the real motive was neither political nor sanitary but economic. At least he managed to get agreement to dispatching vessels only two thirds full to spare men the worst of the heat and overcrowding. The Gurkhas and the 25th Madras Infantry went first as they were the most prepared to accept ordinary cooked rations on board. Advised that the monsoon might cause a 60 per cent death rate among the animals, Wolseley sent back the cavalry dismounted, and also kept hold of the sepoys' tents, which he felt were of better quality than those issued the British troops. Generally, however, Wolseley had not been impressed by the sepoys and fervently wished for the enrolment of Turks under British officers. There had also been something of a clash between Wolseley and Ross, who had anticipated commanding the troops on Cyprus as a whole. It was not altogether Wolseley's fault as it had been decided to send out Major-General William Payn to assume field command, which meant that Ross and Macpherson were largely redundant. Wolseley suggested, therefore, that they command districts, but Ross decided instead to take home leave. In fact, it hardly mattered since all the sepoys were away by 21 August, with the exception of the Madras Sappers and Miners, whom Wolseley retained until October.

By 16 September some units were already arriving back in India without the dire results anticipated, though the 2nd Gurkhas were delayed by their ship running aground in the Red Sea. Hodson's Horse, which had stayed on Malta, returned finally to Bombay on 24 October 1878. By this time, however, preparations were well advanced for the long anticipated operations in Afghanistan. Ross had returned to India to the command at Peshawar but was soon discredited in Lytton's eyes by his doubts as to the projected seizure of Ali Masjid. Ross, however, did lead a division in the second phase the war in both the Kabul and Kabul-Kandahar Field Forces. Ultimately, Ross became Commander-in-Chief in Canada. Watson, whom Wolseley rated most highly among the Indian contingent's commanders, was given command only of the princely contingents whose services were accepted for political reasons, for no one seriously intended that they should see action against the Afghans. Watson, however, did get a more active command in the second phase of the war in the Kurram and ended his career as Resident in Gwalior. Macpherson saw active service commanding a brigade under Sam Browne in the first phase of the war and continued in brigade command in the second. It was Macpherson who also took the Indian contingent to Egypt in 1882, subsequently dying shortly after assuming command of operations in the Third Burma War.

Naturally enough, the Second Afghan War soon eclipsed public memory of the expedition to Malta and Cyprus, while, during both the Afghan imbroglio and the Zulu War, military authorities in India and at home took equal pride in being able to sustain their respective major operations without calling upon each other's resources. Yet the use of sepoys well beyond their normal Asian sphere was an important precedent and the example of Malta was to be drawn upon in despatching expeditionary forces to Egypt and the Sudan, even if it was not for another thirty-six years that sepoys appeared on a European battlefield.

1. Ships in the harbour at Balaclava. Photograph by Roger Fenton.

2. Sir Colin Campbell advancing to relieve Henry Havelock at Lucknow. (*National Army Museum*)

3. Lundi Khana, a cave in the Khyber Pass. (*Illustrated London News*)

4. The meeting of Major Cavagnari and Amir Yakub Khan, 1879.

5. Bobbie, the pet of Sergeant Kelly, 66th Regiment, who was present at the battle of Maiwand, 1880. He was decorated with the Afghan Medal by Queen Victoria. (*Duke of Edinburgh's Royal Regiment Museum*)

6. Jellalabad, from Piper's Hill, 1879. (*Illustrated London News*)

7. Christmas at Jellalabad. (*Illustrated London News*)

8. The execution of a ghazi, Peshawar Gate, Jellalabad, 1879. (*Illustrated London News*)

9. A camel being loaded in Karachi, 1885, as part of the preparations for operations in the Sudan. (*National Army Museum*)

10. West Redoubt, Suakin. (*National Army Museum*)

11. Majuba. (*Ian F. C. Beckett*)

12. Burial trench, full of British dead, after the battle of Spion Kop, 24 January 1900.

Cavagnari's Coup de Main

One gets a distinctly odd feeling viewing British forces patrolling the streets of Kabul for the first time in over 120 years, though it is a just over eighty years since the third and last Afghan War fought by the British was waged along the frontiers of Afghanistan and what is now Pakistan. British experience of Afghanistan has few happy associations, the perennial British concern in the three wars being to secure a compliant administration in Kabul in order to create a buffer against possible Russian encroachment on India. To be sure, there were celebrated exploits: the defence of the 'illustrious garrison' at Jelalabad during the First Afghan War, or Frederick Roberts's march from Kabul to Kandahar during the Second Afghan War. But such exploits followed disaster: the destruction of the British-Indian army on its retreat from Kabul back to India in January 1842 during the First Afghan War, and the rout of another at Maiwand near Kandahar in July 1880 during the Second Afghan War, both characterised by 'last stands' – of the 44th Foot at Gandamak and the 66th at Maiwand. Involvement in the treacherous world of Afghan affairs also took its individual toll. One thinks of Alexander 'Bokhara' Burnes and William Macnaghten, butchered in Kabul in November 1841 and January 1842 respectively, or Louis Cavagnari, whose mission at Kabul was massacred in September 1879. As it happens, beyond their mistaken trust in Afghan good intentions and their deaths, there were other similarities between Burnes and Cavagnari.

Major Pierre Louis Napoleon Cavagnari, Deputy Commissioner at Peshawar, must always have seemed an exotic figure in British India, as befitted one with an Irish mother and an Italian father, Adolphe, who had served as a general in Napoleon's army. Cavagnari himself, however, had been brought up in England, naturalised in 1857, and passed through the East India Company's military seminary at Addiscombe before serving with the 1st Bengal Fusiliers in the latter stages of the Mutiny.

Transferring to the political service in 1861, Cavagnari had risen through administration of the Kohat district and had been posted to Peshawar in 1877. To some, Cavagnari was a *beau sabreur* in the mould of the giants of the frontier's past such as John Nicholson, who had died the hero of the storming of Delhi in September 1857. To others, Cavagnari was more reminiscent of the young, ambitious and supremely confident Alexander Burnes. Certainly, Cavagnari had the kind of charm to appeal to the Viceroy, Lord Lytton, becoming one of his principal advisers, but he was also clearly ambitious and confident of his abilities to handle the tribes.

There is a well-known photograph of Cavagnari meeting the Afghan Amir, Yakub Khan, at Gandamak in May 1879 – ironically the scene of the last stand of the remnants of the 44th Foot on the retreat from Kabul. Though still only thirty-eight, Cavagnari with full beard and curling moustache looks older and sits stiffly for all that his legs are crossed, left hand grasping the hilt of his sword, thumb and forefinger of the right hand holding what appears to be a pen, staring off to the side. It is a portrait of supreme self-assurance. Indeed, some said that Cavagnari conducted the negotiations with the Amir, which followed the first phase of the Second Afghan War, with scant regard for the latter's sensitivities. By the resulting Treaty of Gandamak, Cavagnari, now knighted in recognition of his services, was to head the small British mission in Kabul.

General Sir Neville Chamberlain, the Military Member of the Viceroy's Council, who had conducted an earlier mission towards Kabul with Cavagnari in September 1878, recognised the intellect and energy of one who had 'more of the Nicholson style than any man I know'. Writing just after the signing of the treaty, however, Chamberlain feared Cavagnari was also 'hasty and imperious', 'more the man for facing an emergency than one to entrust with a position requiring delicacy and very calm judgement'. Thus he foresaw Cavagnari 'not keeping us out of difficulties'.[1]

All this lay in the future when one of Cavagnari's schemes displayed not only his fertile brain and its attendant risks, but also the wider division between Lytton and his military advisers, and among those military advisers. As Deputy Commissioner at Peshawar, Cavagnari had personal control of a force drawn from the Corps of Guides and the 1st Sikhs with, according to the Commander-in-Chief in India,

General Sir Frederick Haines, 'no allegiance to the officer commanding the troops [at Peshawar], for the political officer seems to have a power of initiative absolutely independent of him'.[2] In October 1878, Cavagnari exercised that initiative by conceiving of a plan to seize the key to the Khyber, the fortress of Ali Masjid. The affair did much to reveal the poisonous state of civil-military affairs and internal military affairs that already existed in India on the eve of a major conflict.

Some background is necessary. Intended to exclude any Russian influence from Afghanistan, the mission to Kabul headed by Chamberlain, then Commander-in-Chief of the Madras army, had been refused entrance to the Khyber Pass by the then Amir, Yakub Khan's father, Sher Ali. It brought the prospect of war with Afghanistan much closer, but Lytton and Haines differed on the most appropriate strategy for such a war. Two years earlier, when the possibility of a wider war against Russia had been contemplated, Lytton and his Military (later Private) Secretary, Colonel George Colley, had selected the route through Peshawar and Balkh to Tashkent as the best line of offensive operations, since Tashkent seemed the real seat of Russian military power in Central Asia. Haines was no less an advocate of a 'forward policy' than Lytton or Colley, but regarded the route through Kandahar to Herat and Merv as the most suitable. His judgement was shared by his Quartermaster-General, Colonel (local Major-General) Frederick Roberts, though Roberts also appreciated the military significance of Tashkent.

With the more immediate prospect of a war limited to Afghanistan in the autumn of 1878, Haines responded to a request to suggest appropriate measures to secure the Kurram Pass from Thal, and to advance on Kandahar from Quetta, by additionally recommending a demonstration of force in the Khyber from Peshawar. Winter, however, was approaching and Lytton only wished to exert pressure on Sher Ali to accept the mission. Consequently, Lytton declined to authorise creating any reserve for the forces being gathered at Quetta, Thal and Peshawar. Solid and steady, Haines never quite grasped that Lytton wished to avoid an occupation of Afghanistan and that he wished to make further political points in proving to London that India could sustain operations without recourse to reinforcements from home, and in proving to St Petersburg that no threat to India would draw British forces out of Europe. Colley was to describe one conference as five hours of 'dull, stolid obstinacy such as I think I never witnessed before' as Haines continued to argue for what Colley subsequently suggested Haines envisaged as 'a great campaign on the Oxus and a peerage'.[3]

Arguably, few soldiers could avoid the lure of a campaign of conquest, especially when, like Haines, they had seen no action since the Crimea: he had been on the staff in Calcutta throughout the Mutiny. Indeed Haines, whom Lytton thought an unintelligent mediocrity, constantly tried to get to the front to direct operations personally once the war began, an officer being readied to intercept him and order him back to Simla when he set out for the frontier in November 1878. In the event, Haines unexpectedly returned and was fortuitously laid low by a fever for a month. Haines, however, was also felt to be under the influence of an even more ambitious headquarters staff. Much of the suspicion centred upon his Adjutant-General, Colonel Sir Peter Lumsden, whom Haines came to regard as his effective Chief of Staff. This was particularly so once Roberts was appointed to command the Punjab Frontier Force in March 1878, pending approval of further appointment as Chief Commissioner for the frontier, and subsequently to the command of the Kurram Field Force in September, leaving his berth at headquarters vacant. In fact, Haines had intended Lumsden both as Frontier Commissioner and commander in the Kurram, but Lytton vetoed it. Intensely jealous that his former friend, Roberts, should have secured both posts, it was said that Lumsden retaliated by doing his best to ensure Roberts's column lacked sufficient means of mobility.

Colley and Lieutenant-General Sir Arthur Hardinge, who commanded at Meerut until the autumn of 1878, undoubtedly fed Lytton's unfavourable perception of Haines and Lumsden, whom Lytton particularly disliked. Haines's frequent description of Colley as 'the finest theoretical soldier he had ever met' is capable of more than one interpretation, while Chamberlain noted that Colley, always present at meetings with Lytton, yet always silent, 'has given the Viceroy the key to the discourse and is his real military mentor'.[4] Haines had strongly deprecated Colley being sent in a supposedly private capacity to consult commanders on the Punjab frontier on ways of dealing with incursions by the Jowaki Afridis in September 1877, seeing this as intervening directly between him and his subordinates. As for Hardinge, his tenure at Meerut was coming to an end and he was singularly unsuccessful in securing an active field command. Together with Major-General Frederick Maude, who was displaced from the Peshawar Valley Field Force by the appointment of Lieutenant-General Sir Sam Browne in November 1878, Hardinge argued that, as Indian army officers, Haines and Lumsden were prejudiced against officers of the British establishment such as Maude and himself.

Haines and Lumsden were at pains to point out that, while all the principal field commands for the forthcoming operations were from the Indian army, the majority of staff appointments had gone to British officers. Yet there was clearly resentment on the part of Haines, if not Lumsden, that some officers exercised an independent role. The Punjab Frontier Force, for example, came under the control of the Lieutenant-Governor of the Punjab and not the Commander-in-Chief in Simla. And then there was Cavagnari.

Unknown to Haines in October 1878, since the Political Department had fallen behind in printing the official telegrams for circulation, Cavagnari had been negotiating with the Khyber tribes to persuade them to desert Sher Ali. Theoretically, Ali Masjid lay beyond the jurisdiction of the Amir, who had constructed and garrisoned it only under the sanction of the Khyberis. Cavagnari had extended pledges of protection to the tribes, which would be redeemed by handing the fortress back to them if the British seized it. It would also represent the kind of gesture Lytton had in mind by way of putting pressure on the Amir. Accordingly, a telegram from Cavagnari reached Lytton on the evening of Wednesday 2 October 1878, proposing immediate action against the fortress by the forces under his own control. It was a daring proposal, the sheer theatricality typical of its author. There was no actual necessity to consult Haines since Cavagnari could act at his own discretion, but Lytton felt it wise at least to alert Major-General John Ross, who commanded at Peshawar, to the possible need to assist Cavagnari. Colley managed to contact the Lieutenant-General of the Punjab and also Haines, but failed to contact Sam Browne, then acting as Military Member of the Council, who would normally have issued orders to Ross through the Military Department but who was somewhere out to dinner. As a consequence, the Secretary of the Foreign Department, Alfred Lyall, requested Haines to send orders to Ross, which was done in the early hours of Thursday 3 October. Haines, however, had not actually read Cavagnari's telegram and did not apparently have the opportunity to do so or to set down his considered views until after the despatch of orders to Ross.

Understandably, Haines was concerned that he had no information on the strength of the Afghan garrison in Ali Masjid and that the operation could only work if the Khyberis were fully committed to the British, a concern Lytton had also addressed in his reply to Cavagnari. Given the chance for further reflection, Haines warned that such a *coup de main* would be effectively the first act in a war and 'ought not to be undertaken without due deliberation and ample preparation for all its liabilities and consequences'.[5] In particular, Haines believed that, once the first shot had been fired, there should be the means to advance immediately beyond the Khyber to Jalalabad, for British action would be a provocation to the Afghan nation as a whole.

Haines had given his consent when first approached by Colley, as he was led to believe that Cavagnari's proposal had the backing of Ross and of Roberts, who was concentrating the Kurram Field Force at Kohat to the south west of Peshawar. Ross had anticipated some attempt to move against Ali Masjid and had a small force in readiness at Jamrud, but actually felt Cavagnari's scheme a wild one when the fortress was held by Afghan regulars rather than tribesmen. Moreover, he had no actual details of what Cavagnari proposed and, prompted by Haines, now queried orders which appeared to derive from the civil rather than the military authorities. In any case, the regiments at his disposal were reduced in strength by a combination of furloughs, sickness and absence on other duties. The support of Roberts for the plan also appeared somewhat equivocal: he did not consult Ross when first hearing of the scheme and, according to Hardinge at least, washed his hands of the whole affair from the beginning.

Lumsden suggested to Haines that furloughs be cancelled in order to reinforce Peshawar, but confusion now reigned and nothing was apparently done. Ordered, nonetheless, to continue preparations, Ross proposed to make a demonstration with about 400 British and 600 native infantry supported by three guns, while Cavagnari moved on the fortress with those troops under his direct control. Two days passed, with Lytton now pushing for action but others urging caution. Suffering from a dose of 'Peshawar Fever', Chamberlain had not yet left Simla for Madras and now tried to dissuade Lytton anew. Lytton remained unconvinced by Chamberlain's caution and Browne was summoned. Like Haines, Browne wanted some assurance of Khyberi support and saw little point in ejecting the Afghan garrison if it was able subsequently simply to reoccupy the fort. As Browne arrived to see Lytton, a new telegram from Cavagnari arrived indicating that three or four Afghan regular regiments and two batteries had just reinforced Ali Masjid. Lytton postponed the operation and telegrams were despatched to Cavagnari, Ross and Roberts for their views. Browne urged the reinforcement of Peshawar, slyly suggesting that this could best be done by reducing the strength of Roberts's column. Ross now strongly opposed any attack, as did Roberts. On 8 October, therefore, all preparations for Cavagnari's surprise attack were suspended.

Lytton was particularly aggrieved at the lost opportunity, making this abundantly clear to Haines that same day. He clearly believed Haines's objections had been motivated by jealousy of Cavagnari and that the Commander-in-Chief's claims that he had not been sufficiently consulted were encouraged by Lumsden, whose own motivation was resentment at Roberts's preferment in the Kurram. In the heated strategic debate that followed through October, as Lytton moved to despatching an ultimatum to the Amir to accept a mission at Kabul, it was agreed to establish the Peshawar Valley Field Force as a major field force, rather than a Peshawar force merely staging the diversion originally envisaged as a subsidiary to the operations of the Kurram and the Southern Afghanistan Field Forces. Lytton, however, insisted that Ross's lack of vigour over the Ali Masjid affair and his evident lack of what Lytton termed political capacity disqualified him from command. Equally, Lytton had little faith in Browne as an adviser and, indeed, Browne had only become Military Member in July 1878 when General Sir Edwin Johnson had suffered a stroke. Thus, the creation of the Peshawar force enabled Lytton to get rid of Browne into the field and replace him with Chamberlain, who, though he enjoyed poor health, had the great advantage for Lytton of displaying what Colley described as a 'wonderfully gentle and almost deferential manner'.[6]

As already indicated, however, these changes only served to alienate others such as Hardinge and Maude, while Browne badly mishandled the eventual attack on Ali Masjid in November 1878, conceivably because he was so conscious that Haines and Lumsden wanted to get to the front in his place themselves. Subsequently, after the end of the first phase of the war, Lytton refused to countenance Browne as divisional commander at Lucknow and, declining to work closely with Lumsden, intended bringing Donald Stewart back to fill Johnson's place on the Council since the latter was intended to replace Chamberlain in the Madras command. By that time, however, Cavagnari was already in Kabul and arrangements had to be reordered once more in the crisis following his murder.

All in all, the machinations surrounding Cavagnari's scheme to seize Ali Masjid were not the best background from which to embark upon a major war. In the event, Kandahar was occupied easily in January 1879 and, upon Sher Ali's death in the following month, his son agreed to receive a British mission in the fateful meeting at Gandamak. Possibly, in conceiving of his Ali Masjid scheme, Cavagnari had thought of the enduring fame of such a daring coup. Within four months of negotiating with Yakub Khan, however, he had suffered the fate not of Nicholson but of Burnes, his mission massacred and his body dragged through the streets of Kabul.

Cavagnari had arrived at Kabul on 24 July 1879, establishing his mission in the city's Bala Hissar. The following month, however, six regiments of Afghan regulars arrived from Herat. These regiments had not been engaged with or defeated by the British and greatly resented the British presence. Moreover, they had not been paid for some time. Gathering fruitlessly at the Bala Hissar on 3 September in the expectation that their arrears would be forthcoming, the regiments rushed to the British Residency when it was rumoured that money was to be had there. Cavagnari rebuffed the mob, shots were fired, and the Afghans, now swollen by the city mob, stormed the Residency. With the Amir refusing to intervene, Cavagnari and his small escort of three other Europeans and seventy-five members of the Corps of Guides were overwhelmed, the Guides fighting on to the last after Cavagnari and his colleagues had all been killed.

13

Chelmsford's Major-Generals

Instantaneous electronic communications are such a part of modern life that it is difficult to imagine a time when information took weeks to reach its destination. In one way, it did give statesmen the luxury of reflection on their response to events, although it could also mean that reaction time was too slow and that evens slipped beyond their control. Indeed, the outbreak of the Zulu War, an event not felt desirable in London, is a case in point for policy was driven by the High Commissioner in South Africa, Sir Bartle Frere, irrespective of Cabinet wishes. To be sure, maritime telegraph cables had revolutionised Victorian communications, as a visit to the fascinating museum at Porthcurno in Cornwall will amply illustrate. It has to be borne in mind in discussing decisions taken in London with respect to the campaign in South Africa, however, that there was no direct telegraphic communication until the Zulu War itself precipitated government subsidy for the extension of the cable from Aden through Zanzibar, Beira and Lourenço Marques: Cape Town was not linked directly with London until 1887 by extension of the cable from the Cape Verde Islands. Consequently, communications were slow, messages being conveyed to Cape Verde by ship and then telegraphed to London via Madeira, Lisbon and Porthcurno. Thus, the news of Isandlwana reached the War Office by telegraph only in the early hours of 11 February and did not reach Wolseley as High Commissioner and Governor-General on Cyprus for another four days, although the Commander-in-Chief in India, Sir Frederick Haines, received the news on the same day as the War Office. Letters, of course, took even longer, an illustration being one of Chelmsford's letters to the Commander-in-Chief at the Horse Guards, the Duke of Cambridge: completed on 25 May in reply to that of Cambridge of 16 April, which had only just arrived, it did not reach Cambridge until 17 July.

Given the dramatic events of the first invasion of Zululand in January

1879, it is not perhaps surprising that the second invasion in May has attracted rather less attention beyond the death of the Prince Imperial on 1 June and the culminating battle at Ulundi on 4 July. Similarly, the interval between the invasions is naturally enough dominated by Hlobane, Kambula, Ntombe and the siege and relief of Eshowe. Nonetheless, for an historian interested in the workings of command in the late Victorian Army, the period following the defeat at Isandlwana and embracing the preparations for the second invasion is just as instructive as the chaotic nature of Chelmsford's staff arrangements during the initial advance into Zululand or Chelmsford's subsequent supersession by Wolseley on 26 May, although Wolseley did not reach the Cape until 23 June. In particular, there is the matter of the four major-generals appointed to accompany reinforcements to South Africa in February 1879.

Once the news had reached London, the Secretary of State for War, Frederick Stanley, summoned both the Adjutant-General, Sir Charles Ellice, and the Quartermaster-General, Sir Daniel Lysons, to meet him and Cambridge later that morning – Stanley's note to Cambridge was written at 4.30 a.m. Stanley then requested the Prime Minister, Lord Beaconsfield, to call a Cabinet shortly after 1 p.m. Chelmsford's telegram to Stanley – not sent until 27 January – had called for immediate reinforcements of at least three battalions, two cavalry regiments and a company of engineers, while, in subsequent letters to Cambridge on 5 and 10 February, Chelmsford requested a designated second-in-command and an increase to six battalions. Lady Frere, acting under instructions from her husband absent in Pietermaritzburg, also communicated with Cambridge on 4 February, urging the appointment of a second-in-comand and suggesting the DQMG for Intelligence at the War Office, Sir Archibald Alison. The highly capable Brevet Colonel Evelyn Wood was commanding Chelmsford's No 4 Column in Zululand but he was low on the Colonel's list and, in Cambridge's view, already overrewarded for past services in the Ninth Kaffir (or Cape Frontier) War. Indeed, had Chelmsford been killed, the next senior officer was actually Colonel Fairfax Hassard, commanding Royal Engineers on Chelmsford's staff. Hassard had taken temporary command at Helpmekaar after Isandlwana but had not distinguished himself by his lack of activity and, after a nervous collapse, was sent back to the Cape:

meeting him there, Wolseley was later to remark that Hassard had no interest in his profession.

Accordingly, in deciding on 11 February to send out six battalions, two cavalry regiments, two artillery batteries and a company of engineers, Stanley and his military advisers resolved that three senior officers would accompany them. Since circumstances might arise in which the senior of the three would 'find the command has devolved on him', the Cabinet initially reserved its judgement on what were clearly Cambridge's personal selections, although as yet there were not considered to be any grounds for replacing Chelmsford in command. By 13 February the matter was settled with the three selections all accepted, namely Major-Generals Henry Hope Crealock, Edward Newdigate and Frederick Marshall. Subsequently, a fourth Major-General, the Hon. Henry Hugh Clifford VC, was added on 27 February 1879.

All four had served in the Crimea, Marshall having been ADC to Sir James Scarlett and Clifford having won his VC at Inkerman. Subsequently, Clifford had served in South Africa during the Seventh and Eight Kaffir (or Cape Frontier) Wars (1846–47 and 1850–53). Crealock and Clifford had also served in China, where the former had been Military Secretary to Lord Elgin. More to the point, however, all were well known to Cambridge, both Clifford and Marshall having been ADCs to the Commander-in-Chief, Marshall as recently as 1877. Clifford had also been an AAG at the War Office while Crealock had been Military Attaché at both St Petersburg and Vienna and, most recently, DQMG in Ireland. Newdigate had had a series of home staff appointments, most recently at the Rifle Brigade depot at Winchester. Curiously, both Clifford and Crealock were talented artists.

Opinions on the merits of the four varied. Naturally enough, Cambridge regarded his first three selections as men of energy and talent and, in nominating Newdigate once more to accompany Sir Frederick Roberts to South Africa in March 1881 after George Colley's death at Majuba, Cambridge again described him as good and reliable. By contrast, as might be expected, Wolseley was not over complimentary towards the commanders he inherited after his own appointment and was particularly acerbic with regard to Crealock, with whom he had served in the 90th Light Infantry, the regiment now commanded by Wood. Crealock had also been on Wolseley's Red River expedition in

Canada in 1870. While he regarded Crealock as clever, Wolseley did not believe him fitted for a field command in war and later wrote in the draft of his unpublished further memoirs that Crealock had been un-popular with officers, NCOs and men alike in the 90th. He also found Crealock as snobbish as his younger brother – the much detested Chief of Staff to Chelmsford, Lieutenant Colonel John North Crealock, incidentally another talented artist. Indeed, once in Zululand, Wolseley wrote that the elder Crealock's 'manner is so repulsive, that I hate even speaking to him'.[1]

Wolseley had not known Newdigate previously, although he had heard that he was 'sound', while he regarded Marshall as an 'idiot' sent out by Cambridge merely in order to earn a KCB. Wolseley took obvious pleasure in writing to Cambridge in July 1879 that even Chelmsford found both Newdigate and Marshall useless in the field. Although he found Marshall pleasant enough in person, Wolseley's view of the latter's capabilities was not improved by the rumour that Marshall, commanding the cavalry brigade attached to the 2nd Division, had 'fainted from excitement' when the adjutant of the 17th Lancers, Lieutenant Frederick Frith, had been killed at eZungeni on 5 June.[2] Certainly, the younger Crealock described Newdigate, when commanding the 2nd Division, as useless in a letter to Alison. The Queen's Private Secretary, Sir Henry Ponsonby, also noted in March 1881 that Wood had viewed Newdigate as no more than 'a steady old adjutant'. Equally, Marshall was relegated by Chelmsford to commanding the line of communications between the Natal frontier and the army in the field on 13 June, though Clifford for one believed that this had more to do with Chelmsford's own resentment against those sent out to the Cape. Chelmsford also kept Colonel Reilly, sent out to command the artillery, at a distance. There was general criticism of Crealock's performance in command of the 1st Division.

Wolseley suggested that Crealock had no dash while Clifford also referred to him as 'rather too easy going'. Clifford also delighted in sending to Cambridge a poem he had snipped from a local newspaper after Crealock had been unseated while on patrol when his horse was charged by a Zulu cow: 'The cloud passed off from his spirit, The shade passed off from his brow; For the horns of the Zulu army, Were the horns of a Zulu cow.' A relatively unbiased observer of the selections,

Lieutenant-General Arthur Herbert, wrote to Wood that he did not regard Crealock, Newdigate or Marshall as sensible choices: neither Newdigate or Marshall enjoyed good health, while Crealock also 'is not strong, and never was much on a horse' and, moreover, only excelled 'at long letters, and keeping an office in apple pie order'.[3]

The one choice, which did command considerable support, was that of Clifford, Cambridge regarding him as the most valuable of the four, particularly through his experience of South African warfare, although, of course, this had been twenty-five years previously and the difference between fighting on the Cape Frontier and in Zululand was pronounced. Wolseley thought Clifford 'zeal itself' and 'a bright object in the clouds of confusion that reign supreme in this military chaos' and even commended Cambridge on his choice. Similarly, Herbert believed that Clifford alone among the four was equal to rough campaigning and he was to receive general praise for his Herculean efforts to reorganise the transport system in South Africa as Inspector General of the Lines of Communication and Base.[4]

Reference to Clifford's appointment in South Africa raises the question generally of the purpose in adding him to Cambridge's original choices. Initially, as the senior from himself, Newdigate and Marshall, Crealock was clearly designated as Chelmsford's second-in-command, but there remained the problem of transport and supply arrangements with Brevet Colonel William Bellairs struggling to fill the posts of both DAG and QMG on Chelmford's inadequate headquarters staff. As Cambridge explained to Sir Bartle Frere on 27 February, Clifford would therefore take over responsibility for the lines of communication and the base of operations in Natal. However, Clifford was actually senior to Crealock. The rather clumsy solution adopted by Cambridge, therefore, was that, while Crealock would be second-in-command to Chelmsford in the field, it would be Clifford and not Crealock who would actually succeed to the command in the event of Chelmsford's death or break down. Clifford would also be available to replace Frere as High Commissioner. This was conveyed to both Chelmsford and Frere in letters on 27 February. A further complication was that, while Cambridge indicated that Chelmsford was free to place Crealock, Newdigate and Marshall in whatever commands were appropriate, he strongly suggested that one at least should be made Chief of Staff, but Chelmsford should also not interfere with the columns commanded by Evelyn Wood and Colonel Charles Pearson.

As already indicated, Chelmsford's solution to the surfeit of major-generals was to give divisional commands to Crealock and Newdigate with the most junior – Marshall – initially taking the cavalry brigade attached to Newdigate's division and Wood's former command becoming an autonomous flying column cooperating with Newdigate. Chelmsford himself accompanied Newdigate, giving Crealock, a free hand, while Pearson, after being given a brigade under Crealock was invalided home in June after the exertions of the siege of Eshowe. What was not resolved, however, was the respective seniority of Clifford and Crealock. Cambridge tried to clarify the situation by writing to Crealock on 27 March in the light of the receipt of Chelmsford's despatch of 9 February, in which he referred to the 'strain of prolonged anxiety & exertion, physical & mental' that had been telling on him even the year before.[5] Crealock was instructed that it was expected that he would be second-in-command in the field, although Chelmsford was still free to employ his major-generals as he wished. However, if Chelmsford broke down, Clifford would succeed with Crealock either remaining second-in-command or assuming Clifford's duties at base.

Nevertheless, both Crealock and Clifford remained confused as to their true responsibilities and not just due to the fact that Cambridge's letter did not reach Crealock until 9 May. Eight days previously Clifford had written to Cambridge requesting clarification of press reports he had read in South Africa that he would succeed to the command if anything happened to Chelmsford. Clifford had understood from conversations with both Cambridge and Stanley before he left London that Crealock had been promised command. It also transpired, from the letter Crealock sent to Cambridge, on receipt of that of 27 March from the latter, that he had spoken to Clifford at the Cape Verde Islands on the voyage out to South Africa and that both had assumed from the conversations with Cambridge and Stanley that Crealock would succeed Chelmsford. Apparently Chelmsford had also conveyed this impression, instructing Crealock to hand his division over to Pearson in the event of having to take overall command, although he must have received Cambridge's letter of 27 February well before Crealock received that of

27 March. It is interesting, however, that Cambridge also wrote to Chelmsford on 27 March spelling out the command arrangements as if it was sensed that confusion persisted.

The confusion hardly contributed to harmony among senior officers in South Africa, which, in any case, had been further damaged by Clifford's growing antipathy towards Chelmsford and Chelmsford's staff. In his first letter to Cambridge on reaching Durban on 17 April, Clifford reported on the evident dissension arising from John North Crealock's influence over Chelmsford and the poor relationship between the younger Crealock and Bellairs. Subsequent letters revealed Chelmsford's disagreements with the Lieutenant-Governor of Natal, Sir Henry Bulwer, and how Chelmsford 'moves in a very narrow world of his own, as I have told him, shut off by Crealock from many who would give him good sound advice'. Ultimately, indeed, Cambridge felt it necessary to reprimand Clifford for his constant criticism of Chelmsford: 'You cannot think what serious mischief must arise in an army where these sort of sentiments are entertained in the highest quarters – and whatever short-comings there may have been I had rather they had been less remarked upon than they have been. It is the tone and spirit of the service which must suffer in this way and I hope you will give such sentiments no encouragement in them.'[6]

Clifford resented the restriction of his authority to within the Natal frontiers and there was a particular dispute in June over Clifford altering one of Chelmsford's telegrams requesting additional reinforcements, John North Crealock accusing Clifford of backbiting and jealousy and deliberately making mischief. Crealock consoled himself that Clifford might 'have a fall from Colley' and, indeed, while Cambridge had urged Wolseley to appoint Clifford as his Chief of Staff and was determined to resist Colley, Wolseley was determined to secure the services of Colley, then private secretary to the Viceroy of India, Lord Lytton. Indeed, while recognising that Clifford was an 'indefatigable worker' as an adminis-trator, Wolseley felt Clifford had 'no brains & no scientific knowledge of his profession' and lacked a broader view.[7] Consequently, it was Colley who became Wolseley's Chief of Staff. Nonetheless, it was Clifford whom he had recommended should Colley not be available. He also recommended Clifford as his successor in South Africa, again should Colley not receive the command. Subsequently, Clifford was somewhat disappointed not to receive the appointment of High Commissioner of Natal in preference to Colley in 1880 and returned home rather than accept the less important command at the Cape, believing apparently that he had become fatally associated in Cambridge's mind with the Wolseley ring.

Wolseley had dispensed with the services of Crealock, Newdigate and Marshall as soon as possible, Crealock's division being broken up on 23 July and Newdigate's on 27 July. None commanded in the field again, Newdigate like the remainder of Roberts's reinforcements being re-embarked within twenty four hours of arriving in South Africa in March 1881. In fact, there had been general astonishment at Newdigate's appointment – extending to Roberts himself – when, as a major-general senior to both Roberts and Wood, who had only local rank, he was designated to command only a brigade under Roberts. But then the politics of command in the army were always complex.

14

Stanhope's Storehouses

Just behind the National Trust visitor centre and shop on Box Hill overlooking Dorking lies a now somewhat overgrown 'fort' originally constructed as part of the defences of London in 1888. Given the prominence of the town and its area in that great classic of invasion literature published in May 1871, George Chesney's *The Battle of Dorking*, it is an appropriate location. In reality, it is one of sixteen mobilisation centres – others also still survive – intended to be manned by brigades of the Volunteer Force in the event of an invasion and popularly known at the time as 'Stanhope Storehouses' after the then Secretary of State for War, Edward Stanhope. Rather similarly, Aldershot's South Camp once contained the Stanhope Lines. The latter, however, have long since disappeared beneath modern development. In that respect, they parallel the fate of Stanhope himself, despite the fact that he was the second longest serving incumbent of the War Office (after Richard Burdon Haldane) between the creation of the office in 1854 and its submergence in the Ministry of Defence in 1964.

Contemporaries not only regarded Stanhope as the greatest War Minister since Edward Cardwell but, subsequently, others in retrospect also saw him as the equal of Cardwell and Haldane. At one point, Stanhope was characterised as a likely rival of Arthur Balfour for the leadership of the Unionist Party in succession to Lord Salisbury. Yet Stanhope is virtually unknown today, his untimely death at the age of just fifty-three stifling any promise of a greater political future. Curiously, too, in an age of political hagiography, Stanhope attracted no biography beyond brief journalistic sketches by way of obituaries. To historians at least, he is known by association with the celebrated Stanhope Memorandum of 1888, but even that has sometimes been misunderstood as a statement of policy inappropriate to the circumstances pertaining at the time of its first circulation.

Why then did contemporaries see Stanhope's term of office as such a significant turning point and as an essential link between the reforms of Cardwell and Haldane? In part, it was because they recognised the achievements of his tenure of the War Office between January 1887 and August 1892 at a time of unremitting European tensions. Fears for the safety of Britain itself led to major reviews of defence capabilities – hence Stanhope's Storehouses – but at the price of exacerbating disputes between Eurocentric and Indocentric strategists within the military and political establishment. There were also fundamental administrative reforms within the War Office, the beginnings of a more organised system of imperial defence, and major enquiries such as those chaired by Lords Hartington and Wantage which heralded future developments in army and defence structures. That Stanhope achieved as much as he did was remarkable given the difficult issues he confronted upon assuming office and the concomitant problems involved in formulating military policy in the late Victorian age.

Born in 1840 and educated at Harrow and Christ Church, Oxford, Stanhope was the second son of the Fifth Earl of Stanhope. A Fellow of All Souls, Stanhope was called to the bar in 1865 but, after inheriting Revesby Abbey in Lincolnshire from his father's first cousin, he turned to politics. Elected Conservative MP for Mid-Lincolnshire at thirty-four, he was a Cabinet minister at forty-five, being promoted through junior posts at the Board of Trade and the India Office to enter Salisbury's first administration in 1885 as Vice-President of the Council of Education. Two months later, he was moved to the Board of Trade and, when Salisbury formed his second administration in July 1886, Stanhope was made Colonial Secretary. Upon the resignation of Lord Randolph Churchill as Chancellor of the Exchequer in January 1887, the reshuffle brought Stanhope to the War Office in succession to W. H. Smith.

Stanhope's appearance was hardly impressive, since he was small in stature and poor in physique, with one shoulder noticeably higher than the other. Reserved and sensitive, his dislike of publicity and occasional reticence in the face of parliamentary attack often suggested weakness, though he was an effective debater and a man of considerable intellectual ability. Dismissed by his military opponents, such as Wolseley and the Duke of Cambridge, as a 'prig', Stanhope could certainly appear obstinate, but his closest colleagues found him a man of charm, integrity and culture. Indeed, he was a trustee of the National Gallery and the avid collector of a unique collection of prints and caricatures of the younger Pitt. Moreover, he was a popular local squire in Lincolnshire.

Like other Secretaries of State at the War Office, Stanhope came to the task reluctantly and the burden certainly impaired his fragile health. His Financial Secretary of the War Office, St John Brodrick, recorded something of Stanhope's workload in the Parliamentary session of 1887–88, the Commons sitting until 2.30 a.m. on an average of four out of five 'Parliamentary Days' for eight months, with a total of 485 divisions which Cabinet ministers were expected to attend. In the same period, the Select Committee on Army Estimates, established as a result of Lord Randolph Churchill's allegations of military extravagance after his resignation, met two days a week from noon until 4 p.m. for much of the session, while a committee Stanhope himself convened on the defence of imperial coaling stations met on another two days a week. Rarely in bed before 4.30 a.m., Stanhope was invariably in his office by 11 a.m. to prepare Parliamentary answers for the day and make decisions on pressing issues. With the period between noon and 4 p.m. taken up by the various Parliamentary or War Office committees, Stanhope would work from 5 p.m. until 1 a.m. on routine departmental business including 'the long chapter of grievances, appeals against the decisions of his subordinates, and the like, which form the daily task of the War Minister'.[1]

One factor increasing the strain on Stanhope was his initial ignorance of military affairs. He needed to learn rapidly when the army was being subjected to the most detailed scrutiny through the increasing fears of French and Russian hostility threatening both Britain itself and India. Indeed, as recently as August 1886, the Director of Military Intelligence, Sir Henry Brackenbury, had produced the most pessimistic assessment of London lying undefended at the mercy of an invader. The two corps envisaged by Brackenbury's mobilisation scheme for home defence lacked artillery, transport and other supporting services, while the balance of regular battalions at home and abroad, as laid down by Cardwell's localisation scheme, had never been attained. Moreover, the short service system also introduced by Cardwell in 1870 was not providing sufficient recruits to sustain normal drafts to India and the colonies. The Royal Artillery still lacked modern breech-loading guns, while a committee on the new magazine rifle for the infantry had sat since 1883 without reaching any agreement. Meanwhile, the Gordon Relief Expedition of 1884–85 had shown up glaring equipment failures with defective cartridges, and swords and bayonets that had bent. As Stanhope took office, the Stephen Commission on 'warlike stores' was reaching the conclusion that there was excessive civilian control of the manufacturing and supply of military equipment, and a lack of political direction on what was actually required for national security. A separate committee under Lord Morley was investigating the organisation of the army's manufacturing departments and another commission chaired by Sir Matthew White Ridley examining the civil establishments of government departments including the War Office. Then, of course, the Churchill-inspired Select Committee, chaired by Churchill himself, began its work in June 1887.

There was little enough direction to assist Stanhope in his tasks. Every Minister had his own heavy departmental responsibilities and Salisbury was content to give each considerable latitude, provided they left him alone to conduct foreign policy. In turn, Stanhope's Cabinet colleagues depended upon him for all military advice, since there was no other formal access to professional military opinion. If the Cabinet as a whole, however, had little control over military policy pursued in its name, the most significant decisions were often taken by Cabinet committees or after ad hoc discussions involving relevant ministers. Thus, in his frequent battles with his military advisers, Stanhope sometimes attempted to bludgeon them into submission by recourse to the weight of Cabinet approval, a tactic not always as successful as he hoped. The Queen expressed her displeasure, for example, in July 1890 when Stanhope took refuge in Cabinet disapproval of her son, the Duke of Connaught, becoming Quartermaster-General at the War Office: 'It is unusual for the *Cabinet* to address the Queen on these *military* commands and it would appear scarcely desirable that *such* appointments sh'd *depend* on the decision of Cabinet *Councils.*' [2]

Stanhope's task was also made the more difficult by the lack of any higher forum for discussion of defence issues, the existing Colonial Defence Committee being little more than a postbox between the colonies and the departments responsible for defensive preparations. The absence of a coordinating body was particularly serious in view of the frequent disagreements between Admiralty and War Office. Neither knew readily of the other's plans, since the only formal communication was between the Permanent Under Secretary at the War Office and the Secretary of the Admiralty. Wolseley, indeed, assumed that matters were generally settled by private conversations between the Secretary of State and the First Lord without records being kept. In fact, neither Stanhope nor the First Lord, Lord George Hamilton, were anxious that the disputes between naval and military opinion should become public, as when Wolseley's maiden speech in the Lords on 14 May 1888 not only contributed significantly to the latest invasion 'panic', but also exposed the deep divisions with the Admiralty. Both Stanhope and Hamilton recognised the desirability of closer cooperation, however, and considered some kind of standing conference: at one point Stanhope also suggested a Council of State. In the event, a Joint Naval and Military Committee was established in 1891 to consider port defences and it proved something of a precursor for the future Committee of Imperial Defence in that it circulated agenda, papers and minutes, and had a secretariat.

Part of the difficulty was that the two departments were not only rivals in terms of strategic policy but for the allocation of the limited financial resources available for defence. Churchill's resignation had centred on the service estimates and the former Chancellor was determined to make the most of any apparent extravagance. In any case, War Office officials regularly complained of Treasury interference and even Salisbury once complained that Treasury officials were too apt 'not to impose their veto at the beginning of the policy, when they might prevent it, but at the tail of the policy, when they can only spoil it'.[3]

Churchill's successor, George Goschen, was somewhat more sympathetic, having previously served as First Lord in Gladstone's first administration, but was not about to issue any blank cheques. Stanhope, therefore, had to seek savings if he wished to secure sums for essential purposes, though he also argued on occasions that additional expenditure in the short term would lead to greater economy in the longer term. Thus, Goschen was persuaded to set aside funding for a new magazine rifle and for an enhanced barrack construction programme. The latter not only met urgent sanitary requirements, but also saved on repairs and lodging for troops who could not be accommodated in existing quarters. Goschen, however, refused to allocate more money for the War Office Intelligence Department on the grounds that the Admiralty already had one and that Brackenbury's argument that more money would render the department 'perfect' was merely an excuse for placing additional officers on the War Office establishment. Similarly, while Stanhope's Storehouses were funded, no provision could be made for actually enabling the Volunteers to train in these war stations.

Even within the War Office, Stanhope had manifold problems. In theory, the Cardwellian reorganisation between 1868 and 1872 had eliminated the former duality between the Secretary of State and the Commander-in-Chief, resolving the issue of responsibility in favour of the former. In practice, politicians were ill equipped to assume sole responsibility through their lack of technical knowledge of military affairs and the transitory nature of their tenure. Indeed, when appointed, Stanhope was the fourth War Minister in twelve months. The situation left the Secretary of State highly dependent upon receiving professional advice, but Cardwell had simultaneously undermined the very principle by taking all responsibility for the efficiency of the army out of the soldiers' hands. Military demands for resources were subjected to negotiation between the Secretary of State, the Financial Secretary to the War Office and the Treasury. Technically, soldiers were not then responsible for the result. Indeed, they refused either to answer for national security policies determined on political and financial grounds, or to state definitely what the army's actual requirements might be until such time as they had wrested back financial control from the politicians. There was a War Office Council of sorts, over which the Secretary of State occasionally presided, but this was invariably submerged in minutiae and was not actually required to come to any decisions. Mobilisation and Defence Committees also existed within the War Office, but Stanhope regarded them as all but useless, lamenting that, beyond his Military Secretary, there was 'as a rule no well-informed and capable adviser who looked at a question all round'.[4]

Stanhope's solution in February 1888 was to dispense with the civilian appointment of Surveyor General of the Ordnance established by Cardwell and reinvest the Commander-in-Chief with authority over all the principal departments of the War Office, with those transport and supply questions previously overseen by the Surveyor-General transferred to the jurisdiction of the Quartermaster-General. At face value, it seemed that the soldiers had regained a degree of control, but the Financial Secretary remained the key player and Stanhope could now chose to interpret the reorganisation as making the soldiers responsible for providing an efficient army. On the other hand, the soldiers believed that their responsibility now ended with the provision of an annual statement of the army's needs. The soldiers were understandably horrified, therefore, when Stanhope and Brodrick publicly declared the army responsible for its own failings, Cambridge demanding that it be placed on record 'that hitherto he has been more guided in his annual demands for men by what he thought he had some chance of getting than by what he knew to be the total military requirements of the country'.[5]

Moreover, the reorganisation of 1888 had not actually resolved the basic problem of providing professional advice, since the Commander in Chief was now considerably overburdened with additional duties. One government response to the invasion panic had been the establishment of the Hartington Commission on the day after Wolseley's provocative appearance in the Lords in May 1888, and it was Hartington and his colleagues who now addressed themselves to the problem of military advice. With three former Secretaries of State for War sitting on the commission, it was unlikely to challenge the principle of civilian control. A minority report by Lord Randolph Churchill favoured a single Minister of Defence. The majority, however, came down for the abolition of the post of Commander-in-Chief – though only after the Duke's retirement – and the creation of a War Office Council with a principal military adviser designated as a Chief of Staff presiding over a continental-style General Staff. Stanhope himself had favoured turning the Adjutant-General into a Chief of Staff responsible directly to the Secretary of State. Cambridge and Wolseley, however, would contemplate some kind of Chief of Staff only as a subordinate to the Commander-in-Chief, while the Queen was also implacably opposed to anything smacking of a dilution of the royal prerogative with respect to the command of the army. It might be added that Wolseley also opposed a recommendation, which he suspected had been orchestrated by one of the commission members, Brackenbury, as a means of securing the appointment for himself. In the face of such opposition, Hartington's report was effectively emasculated, though a rejuvenated War Office

Council was established in May 1890 in which decisions by the Secretary of State (but not the discussion) would be recorded.

Even if the Secretary of State had been exposed to a wider spectrum of military advice, it must be acknowledged that the rampant rivalries within the War Office would have resulted in little consensus. The quarrel between the Duke and Wolseley was of long standing by the time Stanhope came to the War Office. Though Wolseley was far from the radical depicted by the Duke, his views and the expression of those views undeniably undermined the military prerogatives of the Crown, which the Duke sought to preserve, as well as the authority of the office of Commander-in-Chief to which Wolseley himself aspired. The resulting situation was far from easy for Stanhope, especially when the Duke increasingly believed that Stanhope was more inclined to listen to Wolseley than himself. Indeed, the general lack of consultation between Secretary of State and Commander-in-Chief became increasingly marked. Yet Wolseley was equally critical of Stanhope if he did not get his own way, writing on one occasion of the Minister, 'I am sick of this class of official who born a gentleman sails as near the edge of the rocks and shallows of lying and misrepresentation as he can do without being denounced as a liar and a dishonest public servant'.[6] Stanhope, in turn, concluded on one occasion that Wolseley was too valuable as Adjutant-General to be given the Malta command, even though he could not 'help feeling that there are times when we ought to allow Lord Wolseley to be far out of reach'.[7]

While Wolseley frequently embarrassed Stanhope and the Duke by his public pronouncements, the Duke himself was not averse to making comments of his own which might be construed as attacks on government policy. Moreover, he had recourse to the Queen as an additional support. In the spring of 1887, for example, Cambridge approached the Queen to challenge the advice Stanhope had received from Wolseley and Brackenbury to keep to the previous policy of W. H. Smith to reduce the Royal Horse Artillery. Similarly, in March 1889 he prompted the Queen to question any possible reorganisation of the cavalry. The Queen, too, had her own agenda in promoting the career of Connaught, suggesting Stanhope's removal to Salisbury at least twice, while yet more pressure was exerted on Stanhope by the Prince of Wales to reinstate Valentine Baker.

Even if Stanhope could negotiate the pitfalls of organisational, financial, military and royal factors in the formulation of policy, there remained the political dimension in which those policies had to be applied. The soldiers were often justified in suspicions of political or party motivation behind policy decisions but they rarely appreciated political necessities. Thus, the decision to bring home Roberts from India to succeed Wolseley as Adjutant-General – in the event not actually implemented – was taken in June 1890 to head off criticism that the government had failed to carry through the Hartington recommendations. Connaught was similarly precluded from the appointment for political reasons. On another occasion Stanhope declined to press the conversion of the one remaining single battalion regiment in the army – the Cameron Highlanders – into a Guards battalion in December 1887 as it 'would be very prejudicial as a prelude to the other battles we may have to fight next session'.[8]

Naturally enough, not all opposition could be headed off, making Stanhope's experience at the hands of the Commons and the press often unpleasant. The proposed reduction of the Royal Horse Artillery was an early instance of concerted parliamentary opposition. The decision in December 1890 to reduce the General Officers' List from 140 to 100, with no promotion except to specific vacancies and then by merit, raised a storm of protest, not least from retired general officers in the Commons such as Sir Henry Havelock-Allan and Sir Edward Hamley. Even the selection of the new magazine rifle brought about 'a hornet's nest of disappointed inventors and promoters' in November 1890 with bitter attacks on the choice made in the columns of The Times.[9] Equally, Stanhope did more than any of his predecessors to assist the Volunteers; yet, he was defeated by the Volunteer 'interest' in the Commons on a vote in March 1890 on a motion demanding the government make good equipment deficiencies and cancel all Volunteer debts. It followed the failure of public appeals to raise sufficient funds for Volunteers to find those mobilisation items to be provided by themselves beyond what was granted by the government's reasonably generous mobilisation grant.

Under the circumstances, it is a matter of wonder that Stanhope should have accomplished what he did, but there is no doubt of the significance of his tenure of the War Office. Through the Imperial Defence Act of 1888 fortifications and armaments were provided for coaling stations and military ports. At the same time, the provision of that armament was reorganised: selection and inspection by the soldiers as consumers was separated from manufacturing vested in competent business experts. A civilian, William Anderson, became Director General of Ordnance Factories in 1889, while encouragement was given to private enterprise with contracts for firms such as Elswick, Whitworths and Vickers, the latter being introduced to armaments production for the first time. Stanhope also cut through years of bureaucratic delay to give the army an efficient modern magazine rifle and oversaw other supply improvements such as the creation of the Army Service Corps. There was an impressive barrack construction programme and adoption of some though not all recommendations on sanitation and soldiers' diets. Railway companies and some government departments were also persuaded to make better provision for the employment of reservists and veterans.

In terms of the higher organisation of defence, Stanhope at least began a process of a more systematic structure, embracing War Office and Admiralty while also resolving some of the problems of Cardwell's administrative legacy, albeit at the price of vesting more responsibility in an already overburdened Commander-in-Chief. In terms of national defence, the Volunteers became far more integrated into defence planning. Above all, through the Stanhope Memorandum, Stanhope finally gave the soldiers the definitive statement of purposes lacking for over twenty years, since they had argued that there was little point in reorganising the army without clear direction as to the purposes for which it existed. Wolseley and others had pressed for such a statement in the 1870s and the issue was once more revived in the wake of the invasion panic in May 1888. On 8 December 1888 Stanhope replied on behalf of the Cabinet with what became known as the Stanhope Memorandum. To a large extent, Stanhope merely recapitulated Wolseley's order of priorities, with the exception of laying down a standard of two army corps for all domestic and expeditionary purposes rather than three corps as Wolseley advocated. Aid to the civil power was placed first in priority, followed by the garrisoning of India and the colonies, the provision of two corps for home defence, and, finally, the possible but improbable employment of those corps for a European war.

At the time, Stanhope was frequently criticised for the financial retrenchments that had made his reforms possible. It is easy to castigate him in hindsight for failing to perceive a changing international and strategic environment, but he was heavily dependent upon soldiers who experienced the same failings. Certainly, he can be criticised for his hostility to the radical recommendations of the Wantage Commission, which he established in April 1891 to investigate the increasing failure to find sufficient drafts for India and the colonies. Many leading soldiers, however, also rejected such proposals by Wantage and his colleagues as increasing the army's pay, increasing its establishment, increasing soldiers' length of service, and introducing conscription. In any case, few of these represented practical politics. As it happened, before any decisions could be made, there was a general election, which swept the government from power. In other ways, constitutional problems militated against wider reforms such as the Hartington recommendations and little could be done until the Duke was persuaded to retire. Within the War Office, Stanhope also faced entrenched attitudes and the fundamental conservatism even of 'reformers' such as Wolseley and of permanent officials who remained wedded to Cardwellian principles. As Stanhope himself wrote in July 1892, 'it is impossible to avoid falling into collision with generals of a certain sort, and it is also impossible to act as freely as the heads of most departments can do'.[10]

Generally, Liberals found it easier than Conservatives to reform the War Office, but Stanhope achieved far more than most occupants of the office. Stanhope's health was never good and the price he paid for his successes was physical decline. He was already suffering from periodic attacks of gout by early 1889, getting through the parliamentary discussion of the estimates in 1891 only by dosing himself with colchium. The attacks became more serious in 1892, forcing him to spend most of May taking the waters at Aix-les-Bains. He attempted to play a full part in the election campaign but, as a result of his exertions, was unable to attend the laying of the foundation stone in the new church in the Stanhope Lines at Aldershot. He tried to work on in Opposition, devoting some attention to the Parish Council Bill, but died at Chevening, where he had gone for recuperation, in December 1893. He had come to regard the War Office as a thankless appointment and would certainly have agreed with Salisbury, who once remarked that a War Minister's only reward was to be found in his conscience or his salary. One suspects it would not have surprised Stanhope that his work at the War Office should be largely forgotten, nor that one of the only remaining physical monuments to his tenure should be largely overgrown.

15

One and a Half Battalions

As might be expected, much of the impact of the Australian War Memorial at Canberra derives from its commemoration of the Great War and the epic of Gallipoli, although, as it happens, the principal Australian overseas presence was actually in France and Flanders, with 87 per cent of Australia's war dead lost on battlefields other than those at Gallipoli. Even at Gallipoli, the Anzacs were a minority of the forces involved. To those interested primarily in the Victorian army, however, Australia's leading military museum has much to offer, not least Arthur Collingridge's fine and colourful painting, *The Departure of the Australian Contingent for the Sudan,* painted in 1885, marking the first real occasion on which an Australian expeditionary force – specifically, the New South Wales Contingent – went overseas. Admittedly, Australian militia had served in the Maori Wars from 1863 to 1866, but these 'Waikato' regiments were not strictly an expeditionary force. The Contingent did not serve at its destination long – only from 29 March to 18 May 1885 – and there were only 770 Australian infantrymen and artillerymen in a force of over 13,000 men, but the political and imperial significance of their presence was considerable. It created the precedent for those contingents that were to follow in the South African War and the Great War.

The Contingent's destination in the Sudan was Suakin. The Sudan is unlikely to feature on many tourists' itineraries and, even if it did, Suakin would not rate highly, since it was abandoned as a port in 1909 in favour of Port Sudan, and the latter also replaced Suakin as the administrative centre of the Red Sea Littoral in 1937. For all practical purposes, Suakin is derelict. Yet what a military legacy Suakin has bequeathed. It saw two major battles between the British army and the Dervishes of Osman Digna, at Tamai on 13 March 1884 and Tofrek on 22 March 1885. Together with Abu Klea (January 1885), they inspired Newbolt's famous poem, 'Vitae Lampada', the 'Fuzzy Wuzzies' breaking the British squares and, in the case of Tofrek, earning the Berkshire Regiment its 'Royal' title. Both battles are also recalled by more magnificent paintings, Godfrey Douglas Giles's three views of Tamai, two of which are displayed in London's National Army Museum, and Charles Fripp's version of Tofrek. Suakin was also the setting of Kipling's novel, *The Light That Failed*, the doomed war artist who is going blind, Dick Heldar, seeking and finding his own rendezvous with death there. Later in January 1888, when the main expeditionary force had long been withdrawn, Suakin continued to be held by the British-raised Egyptian army. The town's governor, the then Lieutenant-Colonel Herbert Kitchener, had the unusual experience of swallowing the bullet that struck him in the lower jaw, by way of his ear lobe, and lodged in his throat during a skirmish with Osman Digna's forces at Handub.

Suakin, however, has another significance in causing one of the most extraordinary upheavals in the history of British civil-military relations, all over the rather obscure issue of the despatch of just one and half British battalions. As indicated, Suakin had remained the one imperial garrison in the Sudan following the withdrawal of the Gordon Relief Expedition to the Egyptian frontier, the frontier itself secured by the defeat of the Mahdists at Ginnis – the last battle in which British soldiers fought in red coats – in December 1885. Since the Mahdi's successor, the Khalifa, had pursued territorial ambitions in Abyssinia, the British administration of Sir Evelyn Baring (later Lord Cromer) in Cairo had been able to concentrate on Egyptian financial recovery as a prerequisite of reform and stability. In turn, stability offered the hope of eventual evacuation of Egypt and smoother relations with the French, although it was increasingly clear that the British would probably have to remain indefinitely. Baring succeeded in recording a surplus on the Egyptian budget for the first time in 1887, but the parlous state of Egyptian finances could easily be jeopardised, necessitating in his view a reduction in both British and Egyptian military forces.

Reducing the British garrison in Egypt concerned both the army's Commander-in-Chief, the Duke of Cambridge, and the GOC in Cairo, General Sir Frederick Stephenson, but Stephenson was recalled in December 1887, as the size of the British forces now warranted only a major-general. Through 1888, however, Mahdist activity increased sufficiently to alarm the new GOC, Major-General the Hon. James Dormer, and the Sirdar of the Egyptian army, Major-General Sir Francis Grenfell. Both Grenfell and 'Jemmie' Dormer knew the Sudan well, having both been on the Gordon Relief Expedition. Grenfell had commanded a division at Ginnis while Dormer had earned the respect of the Dervishes in one skirmish by galloping forward and flinging his glass eye – he had lost his eye playing rackets – at them, crying, 'Can your Mahdi do better than this?'.[1] In 1891, and now Commander-in-Chief in Madras, Dormer's impetuosity led to a premature death. A wounded tiger he was foolishly stalking on foot through a *shola* (wood) mauled his leg badly. Dormer not only declined immediate first aid, but also subsequently ignored all medical advice, suffering a fatal heart attack nine days later.

In the case of Suakin, a virtual siege had developed and, while the two Egyptian and two Sudanese battalions in the garrison were thought more than capable of holding the defences, they were not strong enough to make any sorties. Grenfell was worried that the humiliation of not being able to attack an enemy only 500 yards from their positions would demoralise the garrison, commanded since Kitchener's wound by Lieutenant-Colonel Charles Holled-Smith. Accordingly, in November 1888, Grenfell proposed reinforcing the garrison to drive off Osman Digna's forces.

The idea was to transfer two more Sudanese battalions from their present station at Assouan (Aswan) to Suakin and to replace them at Assouan with British troops from Cairo. Some 500 men, or just over half, of the 1st Battalion, the Welsh Regiment were available. Dormer, who had never felt the garrison at Suakin really adequate, agreed and so did the Secretary of State for War in London, Edward Stanhope. Baring reckoned the proposed operation would be costly and strongly objected to the expenditure falling on the Egyptian government. He also feared that Grenfell's subordinates, especially Kitchener, now sufficiently recovered to command the Sudanese brigade to be sent to reinforce Suakin, would want to go beyond simply driving the Dervishes off. Indeed, without sufficient political control, the soldiers would want to seize Handub and embroil the British battalions in a lengthy campaign of 'useless blood letting'.[2] Grenfell had also asked for some mounted troops, having the locally-raised Aden Troop in mind, though it was only sixty-nine strong and not highly thought of. He settled instead for the offer of 110 mounted infantry from Cairo.

So far so good, but the War Office now began to have serious misgivings and, on 26 November 1888, the Quartermaster-General, Sir Redvers Buller, urged Stanhope to send at least one and half battalions of British troops to Suakin itself. Wolseley, the Adjutant-General, concurred. As a troopship, the *Serapis*, was due at Suez on 29 November with six hundred men of the 2nd Battalion, the East Yorkshire Regiment en route home from Aden, Buller proposed diverting them to Suakin, though it was a rather weak battalion. Another troopship with a Lancer regiment on board would be at Suez on 6 December, though it was not felt likely this would be required and, in any case, there were no horses available for them at Suakin. In the event, an attempt to intercept the *Serapis* at Aden failed. Rather than try to send out another ship to find it, it was proposed to send the 2nd Battalion, King's Own Scottish Borderers from Cairo, though this was a young and inexperienced battalion, many of whom were to fall sick at Suakin.

In Egypt, meanwhile, Grenfell was embarrassed by the whole affair, since he had complete confidence in his Egyptian and Sudanese battalions, felt the proposed operation to be a simple matter and had never considered asking for British troops until they were unexpectedly offered. He did now ask for a squadron of the 20th Hussars – 130 men with ninety-five horses – and Dormer reported to the War Office that Grenfell felt generally that, as so many troops were being offered him, he should not refuse them. It was a turn of events which persuaded Cambridge, Wolseley and Buller that their original advice had been correct and that Grenfell had needed more troops all along. Indeed, when it was agreed to send the Hussars, Dormer also proposed on 9 December sending with them three hundred men of the Welsh detachment from Assouan, replacing them at Assouan with half of the 2nd Battalion, Royal Irish Rifles from Alexandria.

Despite growing press speculation and claims that the proposed operation would fail from inadequate strength, Stanhope was reluctant to augment the force at Suakin with British troops when neither Grenfell nor Dormer had requested them, particularly as elements within the House of Commons would resolutely oppose any new involvement in the Sudan. The mounted infantry and the Borderers set out from Cairo on 3 December, the Welsh and the Hussars subsequently arriving at Suakin on 17 December. At least a few of the Royal Irish also ended up at Suakin. In all, Grenfell would now have some 4500 men, including 350 mounted men, to oppose an estimated three hundred Dervishes in the trenches opposite Suakin backed up by about 1500 at Handub. The intention was that the Borderers would act as the reserve and cover any retreat should the Egyptian and Sudanese battalions waver.

On 4 December 1888, however, the former Chancellor of the Exchequer, Lord Randolph Churchill, had sprung an adjournment debate, attacking both involvement in the Sudan and also any policy of partial reinforcement that might lead to disaster, raising the spectre of another Isandlwana. What concerned Stanhope and the government was not the motion itself, which was defeated by 231 votes to 189, but Churchill's claim in the debate that 'he knew the highest military authorities had expressed to me [Stanhope] the opinion that the British force prepared to be sent to Suakin was inadequate'.[3] Stanhope believed that the information could only have been leaked to Churchill and wrote to Cambridge as soon as the debate had ended, demanding that he be informed who had leaked confidential information on what had transpired between Stanhope and his military advisers. At the time, relations between Stanhope and the Duke and between Stanhope and Wolseley were at a low point through the various manoeuvrings over the succession to the Aldershot command. Despite his annoyance, however, Cambridge merely replied that, while he and others had initially regretted that Suakin was not be reinforced, particularly as the East Yorkshires were ready to hand, there had been no breach of confidence. Stanhope refused to accept this, accusing Cambridge 'after having tendered advice to the Secretary of State' of claiming 'the right publicly to criticise the action of the Government, if it is not in all respects in accordance with that advice'.[4] Complaining bitterly of Stanhope's rudeness, the Duke secured a declaration from Churchill that he had not been the source of the supposed leak.

On 20 December 1888 Grenfell, who had narrowly avoided being caught in the open by Dervish horsemen while on an early reconnaissance, attacked from Suakin with his six native battalions, the mounted infantry, the Hussar squadron and his one and half British battalions, comprising the Welsh and the Borderers. A noisy opening bombardment by artillery and Nordenfelt machine guns was staged to divert the attention of the Dervishes from the chosen point of attack. Grenfell's force advanced by successive rushes, opening fire only when they reached about 200 yards from the trenches, which were then carried at the point of the bayonet. In the space of an hour, the Dervishes were easily beaten off in what became known as the battle of Gemaizah, four zaribas being positioned on the former enemy trenches, two of them also having blockhouses constructed within.

Grenfell had taken personal command with Holled-Smith and Kitchener as his brigade commanders. Grenfell took with him two future minor celebrities. Major Robert George Kekewich, later the defender of Kimberley in the South African War, acted as his brigade-major. Ironically, Colonel Frank Rhodes, the brother of Kekewich's future antagonist at Kimberley, Cecil Rhodes, was Grenfell's staff officer. The elder Rhodes was subsequently cashiered as a result of his participation in the Jameson Raid in 1896, but regained his commission as a result of his services while a war correspondent in the Sudan in 1898, being wounded at Omdurman. The Scottish Borderers were commanded by Lieutenant-Colonel (later Major-General) John Talbot Coke, whose reputation was to be sullied at Spion Kop in January 1900. The Dervishes had over four hundred killed for the loss of two native and four British soldiers, the latter resulting from the 20th Hussars getting caught in a donga during a charge. The Borderers had done particularly well, in Grenfell's view, dispersing the enemy with 'excellent volley firing'.[5]

The mission accomplished, the British troops were recalled to Egypt, Grenfell himself leaving Suakin on 3 January 1889. For a small action, there were many who received awards, albeit that the majority were in the form of the (Turkish) Order of the Medjidieh. Rhodes, Kekewich and Coke together with Majors John Ross and Henry Dixon of the Borderers; Brevet Lieutenant-Colonel Charles Smyth and Captains James Sillem and William Giffard of the Welsh; and Captain William McWhinnie and Lieutenant Howard Brown of the Royal Irish were mentioned in despatches and received either the 3rd, 4th or 5th Class Order of the Medjidieh. Grenfell, Kitchener, Captain Montagu Wilkinson of the Borderers and Captain John Beech of the 20th Hussars were all mentioned in despatches. Holled Smith and Charles Barrow, who commanded the mounted troops as a whole, received brevet colonelcies and Major William Irwin of the 20th Hussars a brevet lieutenant-colonelcy. All those present were also to receive the 'Gemaizah' bar on the Egypt Medal. The dispute at home, however, was far from over.

The Prime Minister, Salisbury, accepted Cambridge's explanation that he had not personally leaked any information to Churchill but was still concerned at the constitutional issue surrounding the principle of confidentiality. In addition, Baring, who had earlier professed to see a plot by the military to embroil the government in the Sudan once more, now complained that he, Dormer and Grenfell had been treated as if they did not know their business. The Cabinet therefore resolved to draw up a formal reprimand to the War Office, copied for good measure to the Admiralty as well. Drawing attention to the inconvenience caused by the publicity accorded the supposed confidential advice given within the War Office, Salisbury warned officers that they were 'under the strictest obligation to observe silence with respect to all confidential matters coming to their knowledge, including, especially, their own opinion and those of their colleagues, upon the course which, on any military matters, Her Majesty's Government have decided to pursue'.6

Approved by the Cabinet on 7 January 1889, the letter, together with Baring's criticism of the War Office, was read out to the Duke, Wolseley and Buller by Stanhope in his room on 16 January in the presence of the Under Secretary of State, Lord Harris. According to his trusted confidante, Lady Geraldine Somerset, the Duke was furious: 'No War Minister he has ever yet had has *ever* assumed the insolence of tone towards him personally of this *beastly* little whippersnapper who might be his son, the Conservative! great Mr Edward Stanhope! Nasty filthy little prig!'7 Threatening to resign, Cambridge complained to Salisbury that he and his colleagues all refuted the allegation of a breach of confidence. The Duke was particularly annoyed that the letter should have been read out in the presence of a young man such as Harris when Stanhope could have conveyed the views to him privately to relate to Wolseley and Buller separately. Stanhope himself believed that neither Wolseley nor Buller were as perturbed as the Duke, though Buller had taken umbrage at Baring's comments.

The Duke, meanwhile, had promptly sent a copy of the government letter to the Queen. The Queen, however, was wary of any appeal against a Cabinet document and suggested Cambridge communicate privately with Salisbury. If Salisbury declined to act on such an approach she could then legitimately intervene. In the event, Salisbury was quite unrepentant in view of the continued leaks of information from the War Office:

> It is a matter of record that within thirty-six hours after the military advisers of the War Office had represented to Mr Stanhope that in their judgment the force at Suakin was insufficient, the fact that they had done so was stated by Lord Randolph Churchill in the House of Commons. A fact so secret, and so recent, that at the time he was stating it publicly, it was unknown even to me, could not have come to his knowledge except by indiscretion.[8]

Salisbury had also been told that one of Cambridge's 'distinguished officers' – presumably Salisbury meant Wolseley – had stated that he did not feel bound to conceal his opposition to the government's policy. Since the letter had been agreed unanimously by the Cabinet, it would not be withdrawn. What may have contributed to Salisbury's annoyance was that Wolseley had contributed an article to the *Fortnightly Review* reviewing Fredrick Maurice's entry on 'War' in the *Encyclopaedia Britannica* earlier that month, which though not controversial in itself was open to the interpretation that a senior officer was communicating his views to the public outside the legitimate channels. Despite their agreement on Suakin, Cambridge was also somewhat exercised by Wolseley's article as undermining his own authority. He had also heard that Wolseley planned a series of articles in *Harper's Magazine*, though, in the event, they were not to appear for another twelve months.

With this the Duke had to be content, though the Queen subsequently conveyed to Stanhope her belief that Salisbury did not understand military affairs and could not have intended Stanhope to use the letter as he had. Stanhope himself claimed that his relations with the Duke soon improved – once Cambridge had had a holiday in Gibraltar and the South of France to recover from the strain of events. Ironically, within twelve months of the Suakin episode, both Baring and Salisbury had been converted to the need to control not just Egypt but the Upper Nile, in view of Italian ambitions in Abyssinia and the southern Sudan. Thus, having repulsed a long expected Mahdist advance on Egypt in the summer of 1889, British and Egyptian forces retook Tokar from Suakin in February 1891, dispersing Osman Dinga's forces. A few months later, a substantial Dervish force was defeated at Toski in the Nile valley on 3 August 1891, and the leading Mahdist commander, Nejumi, killed. All was poised for the campaign of reconquest by way of Dongola, which Salisbury eventually authorised in his third administration.

16

The Improbable Probability

The Stanhope Memorandum is one of the most quoted documents in British military historiography. It clearly defined the purposes for which the army existed and placed those purposes in order of priority in a way neither previously stated nor subsequently repeated until the memorandum of Sir Thomas Inskip as Minister for the Coordination of Defence in December 1937. Yet Stanhope's memorandum has been widely misunderstood not only in terms of its background but also as to the ordering of its priorities.

The celebrated ordering of priorities was, first, aid to the civil power in the United Kingdom; secondly, the provision of reinforcing drafts for India; thirdly, the provision of garrisons for colonies and coaling stations; and, fourthly, the provision of two corps for home defence. Famously, the fifth priority was to prepare for the employment of one of the corps in a European war, but 'it will be distinctly understood that the probability of the employment of an Army Corps in the field in any European war is sufficiently improbable to make it the primary duty of the military authorities to organise our forces efficiently for the defence of this country'. In the past, the emphasis upon aid to the civil power has been condemned as outmoded in the context of the late nineteenth century, while, as a whole, the Memorandum ignored the realities of Britain's strategic position, stultifying wider imperial defence planning, and as of so little value that it was rejected by the Cabinet as having no real answer to the problems of Indian defence. Equally, there has been some confusion of dates since the Secretary of State for War, Edward Stanhope, wrote the original memorandum on 8 December 1888, but then reissued it on 1 June 1891. It did not become public knowledge until published as a parliamentary paper in 1901.

In reality, the circulation of Stanhope's memorandum in 1888 should be seen against the background of converging pressures on the Secretary of State for more political direction in the formulation of strategic and military policy. The effect of the Cardwellian reorganisation of the War Office had been to increase civilian control and to take the actual responsibility for the army's efficiency out of military hands. Consequently, soldiers were reluctant to answer for policies determined on political and financial rather than military grounds. In any case, there was little enough point in soldiers attempting to determine military requirements without knowing what contingencies they might be expected to meet, or the exact purposes for which they were supposed to prepare the army. The Mutiny Act alone had offered some albeit vague direction since 1689, in stating in its preamble that the army existed to preserve the balance of power in Europe. That clause, however, had been deleted in 1868. Garnet Wolseley had therefore demanded some kind of definitive statement of the army's role as early as 1871 and the demand had been repeated on several occasions since. In January 1888 and now Adjutant-General, Wolseley, together with the Director of Military Intelligence, Henry Brackenbury, once more urged a statement to be prepared. Indeed, Wolseley suggested an order of priorities very similar to that he had advocated seventeen years previously.

At the same time that there was some military pressure being exerted, Stanhope was also being urged to review the nature of civilian control in the War Office as a result of a number of official inquiries that had been undertaken during 1887. The most important was the Royal Commission on Warlike Stores, chaired by Sir James Stephen. The report memorably criticised a system of extravagance controlled by stinginess but, *inter alia,* also recommended that the soldiers be invited to submit an annual statement to Parliament of what was required for national security. Stanhope responded with a limited administrative reorganisation, vesting authority over all the principal departments in the hands of the Commander-in-Chief. In reality, while the public responsibility for the army's efficiency was now that of the soldiers, political and financial control remained firmly in the hands of the politicians. Yet the invasion scare in the summer of 1888 added weight to the military demands for real responsibility and a clearer definition of priorities. Thus, while the Cabinet debated the possibility of invasion, and another Royal Commission, chaired by Lord Hartington, was appointed to examine military and naval organisation, Stanhope turned his mind to Wolseley's reiteration of his list of priorities in June 1888. Brackenbury had probably prompted Wolseley. The formal reply to Wolseley on behalf of the Cabinet on 8 December became the Stanhope Memorandum.

In effect, Stanhope simply adopted Wolseley's list of priorities with the exception of laying down a two corps standard for all domestic and expeditionary purposes rather than the three corps scheme advocated by Wolseley. Stanhope had little military knowledge and was highly dependent upon military advice. While broadly satisfied with the list, therefore, many soldiers were unhappy with the two corps standard, which was modelled on the existing mobilisation scheme drawn up by Brackenbury in 1886. In turn, the mobilisation scheme had made organisational sense and use of the resources available rather than what might be thought actually necessary. Wolseley, indeed, was still advocating the three corps scheme as late as 1902, when he appeared before the Royal Commission on the War in South Africa. In June 1891 Stanhope was also forced to write to Lord Wantage, who was gathering evidence for a Select Committee on the terms and conditions of service in the army, to clarify the apparent belief of Wolseley's successor as Adjutant-General, Redvers Buller, that 'no instruction had been laid down as to the general objects for which an Army is maintained'.[1]

It seems strange that Buller should have been unaware of the existence of the Stanhope Memorandum, but the Commander-in-Chief, the Duke of Cambridge, also seemed to profess the same ignorance, hence the reissue of the document for Wantage's benefit. Stanhope offered to come personally to explain the policy to the commissioners, even though it went well beyond their terms of reference. Wantage replied that he was perfectly satisfied and that discussion of the document would be deleted from the minutes of evidence. Cambridge then objected, since Stanhope had given him to understand that he could refer to the memorandum if asked about the army's duties. Unfortunately, further surviving correspondence on this particular issue is lacking.

There is no mystery, however, with respect to the actual ordering of priorities. Almost as often quoted as the Stanhope Memorandum is the report of the Select Committee on the Employment of the Military in Cases of Disturbances of 1908, which indicated that British troops had been required to support the civil power in Britain on twenty-four occasions since 1869.[2] The figure is misleading in that it does not consider cases in which the use of troops was seriously contemplated as opposed to actually used. Nor does it take account of the considerable fears of social and political unrest that remained prevalent in government circles throughout this period. Stanhope's correspondence illustrates that aid to the civil power was constantly in mind at the time the Memorandum was first issued. After all, it was only some twenty years since Fenian activities had led to a widespread review of military security in Britain in 1866–67, and troops were still routinely employed in aid of the civil power in Ireland itself. Nor had Irish agitation ceased on the mainland, Irish-Americans beginning a bombing campaign with an attack on Salford barracks in January 1881, which continued sporadically in London, Liverpool and Glasgow until January 1885. A planned resumption to coincide with the Queen's Jubilee had been forestalled as recently as July 1887. Home Rule agitation also led to violence, culminating in the 'Bloody Sunday' riot in Trafalgar Square in November 1887, for which troops were called out. Troops had also been recently employed in the Welsh 'tithe war' and the Scottish 'Crofters' Land War'.

Aid to the civil power remained a live issue. In August 1889 troops were alerted in London during the dock strike and again during a police strike in July 1890, which coincided with the actual employment of Royal Engineers during a postal strike. The prevailing climate is well illustrated by a gas strike in London in September 1890. The Gas, Light and Coke Company applied for military assistance when its 11,000 strong work force threatened to cut off power to railway stations, parliamentary offices and 50,000 streetlights in the West End. Wolseley suggested reserving the entire London garrison for assistance to the police and drawing volunteers from the garrisons at Woolwich and Chatham as unskilled labour to maintain services. Worried that sufficient volunteers might not come forward, Cambridge had no doubt that troops should be actively used 'in order to prevent the entire collapse of society within its [London's] precincts and the endangering of the population from theft, murder and rapine in the darkness of the enormous number of streets which shelter their inmates'.[3] While there is some hint of panic in the old Duke's vision of the consequences for London if its inhabitants were let loose on darkened streets, it should perhaps be borne in mind that the Whitechapel murders were of very recent memory. Similarly, indeed, there was near panic reactions on the part of both Stanhope and the Home Secretary, Matthews, to the police strike in July 1890 and to the refusal of a company of the 2nd Battalion, Grenadier Guards to parade after what they regarded as excessive night duty that same month. The battalion was quickly shipped off to Bermuda and six men court martialled.

There was, then, logic to placing aid to the civil power as the first priority, while the second charge against the Memorandum, that it did not reflect Indian requirements, can also be refuted. To a great extent, this latter charge is reflected by the sympathies of some historians in the past for the arguments of Indocentric strategists in their long struggle with those serving in the home army. It would be something of a simplification to depict the strategic debate as essentially between Wolseley as representative of the home army and Roberts as representative of the Indian army. Nevertheless, Wolseley's strategic views held the field domestically in terms of envisaging any war against Russia as being primarily amphibious and fought at the peripheries – such as the Baltic, Black Sea or Caspian. It followed that any posture adopted by the Indian army should be primarily defensive. This latter aspect of Wolseley's strategy found its ultimate expression in a memorandum prepared by Brackenbury and Major-General Newmarch, the military representative on the Indian Home Council, in August 1889. It also involved, as far as the War Office was concerned, a search for appropriate allies such as Ottoman Turkey or Persia in order to facilitate amphibious operations. The first priority, however, was firmly home defence, the invasion scare in 1888 being regarded as justification for the ordering of the priorities.

The Indocentrists believed that the entire period since the early 1870s – if not since the Crimean War – demonstrated the intrinsic value of India as a great continental power in its own right. Consequently, any threat to India must be regarded as the first priority for the Empire and it would be in Afghanistan that the decisive battle would be fought against Russia. With the death of Charles MacGregor in 1887 the mantle of chief advocate of the Indian perspective on defence fell on Roberts. It has been argued that this was the more realistic strategic view and that, for this reason, the Stanhope Memorandum was effectively discarded by the Cabinet.

In reality, however, the Indian view did not have the support sometimes implied. Within the War Office, Roberts's leading informant, Sir
Charles Brownlow, recorded in December 1890 that, up the time he had
left for other duties in March 1889, he had never seen a 'single minute'
in favour of the massive reinforcements Roberts was calling for.[4] Brownlow also offered the considered opinion of one entirely favourable to
the Indian position that no British government would ever give Roberts
the answer he wanted. Cambridge may well have supported Roberts
rather than Wolseley in strategic terms (as well as much else), but he
was overruled on the crucial issue of Indian reinforcements in June 1887.
Moreover, the War Office Council was still insisting in July 1889 that
India must be defended from within its own resources. It was a position
Stanhope consistently supported. Even Salisbury, who largely approved
of Roberts's strategic ideas and rejected notions of alliance with Turkey
or Persia, recognised in March 1891 that India could not possibly be
reinforced to the extent Roberts wished. Thus Roberts's demand in 1892
for a front line reinforcement of 30,000 men in the event of war was
met by reiteration of the policy that India must rely on its own resources.
Lord Curzon was to make the same response eight years later. It was
simply beyond the bounds of possibility that enough men could be
found to supply Indian demands.

In terms of the acceptability of the Indian case, much has been made
of the transfer of posts in 1891 whereby Brackenbury became Military
Member on the Viceroy's Council and Major-General E. F. Chapman,
who had been Military Member, replaced Brackenbury as Director-
General of Military Intelligence. It is perfectly true that, once in India,
Brackenbury was converted to Roberts's views, but Chapman was equally
confined by the prevailing orthodoxy within the War Office and had
little chance to put over his point of view. The correspondence of one
of Wolseley's leading adherents intimately involved in mobilisation
planning, Sir John Ardagh, indicates the continuing War Office obsession with invasion. According to one of Ardagh's correspondents in
August 1889, for example, Stanhope's Military Secretary, Coleridge
Grove, was allegedly continually 'recasting the various schemes from the
point of view of our finding the French Army on our breakfast tables
with *The Times* tomorrow morning'.[5] When Colonel Gerald Ellison
joined the Mobilisation Section of the War Office in 1890, he, too, found

it engaged in the problems of the fortification of London to the exclusion of all else. Chapman himself stood by the two corps standard in January 1892 and his successor was Ardagh.

For all practical purposes the War Office was not converted to an Indian view of defence until Roberts became Commander-in-Chief in 1900. Even then his triumph was short-lived. The infant Committee of Imperial Defence may well have devoted fifty of its first eighty or so meetings between 1902 and 1905 partly or wholly to Indian defence, but attention was already moving towards acceptance of the likelihood of a German rather than a Russian enemy. Roberts himself resigned from the CID in November 1905 not over India but over his advocacy of a form of short-service conscription, which would have only served the needs of home rather than Indian defence. Stanhope, therefore, can hardly be castigated for failing to perceive the changing international environment when dependent on military advice that experienced the same failings, if failings they were.

The Stanhope Memorandum was thus a genuine response to the demands of the military for guidance as to the purposes for which the army existed, and the contingencies for which soldiers were expected to plan. Its ordering of priorities similarly reflected both contemporary fears in terms of aid to the civil power, and also the prevailing strategic orthodoxy of the majority of Stanhope's professional advisers. He had given the army the definitive statement it had lacked for over twenty years and, if the Memorandum failed to satisfy the soldiers entirely, it still provided 'more direction in the last third of the nineteenth century than at any previous period in British military history'.[6] Moreover, it resulted in the unprecedented and immensely successful mobilisation of the army between October 1899 and January 1900, even if that mobilisation was not actually sufficient for the demands of modern war. It is on these grounds that the Stanhope Memorandum should more properly be judged.

Part Three

Ways of War

.

17

The First Modern War?

In August 1894 Garnet Wolseley, Evelyn Wood and others returned to the Crimea for the war's fiftieth anniversary. What memories that now distant war held for them. Both Wolseley and Wood had been severely wounded before Sebastopol. Wood, then a midshipman from HMS *Queen* serving ashore with the Naval Brigade, had been hit on the left arm by case shot during the unsuccessful attempt to storm the Redan on 18 June 1855. Doctors had wanted to amputate, but Wood refused and thereby saved his arm. Some weeks later, Wolseley, who had also taken part in the failed assault, lost the sight of his right eye to stones kicked up by a shell burst while he was on duty in the trenches before Sebastopol on the night of 30 August 1855. Wood wrote reflections on the war as the result of his visit as articles in the *Fortnightly Review*, later published in book form. For Wood, 'the old sights and sounds lived again with almost startling reality',[1] for, in some areas, little had changed in fifty years. Sebastopol, much of which had been destroyed in 1855, had been largely reconstructed since 1879, but it was still possible to trace battery and camp sites and to find the locations where both he and Wolseley had been hit. Balaclava, too, was little changed, though there were now crops where there had once been only grass and wild flowers, and even more orchards and vineyards than there had been in 1854.

Much the same is still true today, though some rather ugly buildings now additionally straddle the North Valley over which the Light Brigade charged in October 1854. The panoramic view from the platform on the Sapouné Heights still gives a remarkable perspective over the North Valley from relatively close to where Lord Raglan viewed the scene, though the lower of the two platforms has been closed due to land slippage. Balaclava Harbour, with the Genoese castle seen in so many contemporary photographs presiding over it from the hillside, is also little changed for all that there is a rusting submarine in a dry dock as a monument to its later use as a Soviet base. Sebastopol, however, is much changed since it was again rebuilt after extensive destruction during the Second World War, the parapets of the defensive position of the Malakoff partly reconstructed in what is now a municipal park. Wood, however, would certainly be impressed by the atmospheric impact of the city's magnificent 360 degree panorama of the siege, painted by Franz Rubo and his assistants in Munich between 1901 and 1904 and opened for public display in Sebastopol in May 1905. It principally captures the Russian defence against the French assault on the Malakoff on 18 June 1855 (6 June in the Russian Julian calendar of the time), though the British assault on the Redan may be glimpsed in the background. In fact, the panorama is also a reconstruction of the original, the canvas having caught fire during the German bombardment of the city in June 1942. Though about two thirds was saved and the surviving pieces successfully evacuated from Sebastopol, it was in too poor a condition to restore, the reconstructed canvas being displayed to the public for the first time in October 1954.

The Crimean War of 1854–56, of course, is one of those conflicts of which we can remember much after some thought, though much that we can remember borders on the mythic. The Thin Red Line, the Lady with the Lamp, cardigans, Balaclava helmets, Raglan sleeves and, of course, the Charge of the Light Brigade as immortalised by the lines of Tennyson. Indeed, one sometimes gets that sinking feeling that, one of these days, a student will claim that, far from Cardigan leading the Charge of the Light Brigade on 'Ronald', Lord Lucan disappeared during it while riding 'Shergar'. There are other reminders around us. Parisians may be reminded of the Crimean War as they pass through Métro stations such as Pont de l'Alma, Malakoff, Sebastopol and, of course, Crimée. Equally, there are a large number of streets in Britain named after the Alma, Inkerman or Balaclava. In the case of the Alma, there are no less than 315 assorted avenues, cottages, closes, courts, crescents, drives, fields, gardens, greens, groves, heights, hills, houses, lanes, parades, parks, places, roads, rows, squares streets, terraces, vales, villas, walks and ways with Alma in the title.

All in all, however, it seems a very old-fashioned war. Indeed, it has been fashionable in the past to see it as the last of the old-style wars. The American Civil War of 1861–65 is seen as the first modern war in that it displayed many of the characteristics of what in the twentieth century is often described as total war, conveying the idea of a conflict fought on such a scale that every resource of the state had to be utilised, and in which the distinction between the front and the home front was eroded by the contribution of all elements of society to the war effort, and the exposure of all of society to the effects of war. But the Crimea should not be so readily dismissed, for it, too, invoked many aspects of modernity, and has equal claim to marking an important transitional stage in the evolution of at least what may be termed industrialised warfare. Moreover, as the only major war between the great powers between 1815 and 1914, it had significant consequences for the future of Europe.

It was much more than a war confined to the Crimean peninsula, which is why contemporaries tended to refer to it as the Russian War. While British and French forces did not arrive in the Crimea until September 1854, the war had actually begun a year earlier with the Turkish declaration of war in response to the earlier Russian demand to be able to protect Christians within the Ottoman Empire. In itself, the dispute simmering since the 1840s between France and Russia over the right of access to, and repair of, the 'Holy Places' in Jerusalem on behalf of the Catholic and Orthodox Churches respectively, of which this was the latest round, was merely a cloak for wider Russian strategic and economic ambitions. These related to the control of the Dardanelles and access to the Mediterranean, Turkish concessions to Austria in the Balkans having encouraged Tsar Nicholas I to force concessions from the Turks in turn. The Ottoman Empire was already being identified as decaying – 'the Sick Man of Europe' – and, therefore, ripe for exploitation by the great powers when it controlled such strategic routes between Europe and Asia as the Dardanelles, the Isthmus of Suez, Mesopotamia and the Persian Gulf. In July 1853, therefore, the Russians occupied the Turkish Danubian principalities of Wallachia and Moldavia (now Romania), Turkey declaring war on 4 October 1853. The Russians then destroyed the Turkish Black Sea squadron at Sinope (Sinop) on 30 November, an event commemorated by a small plaque on what appears to be a Turkish bathhouse in the unremarkable modern town.

Fearing Russian ambitions, the British and French had hastened to Turkey's support, already sending warships to Besika Bay to the south of the Dardanelles in June 1853. These passed through the Straits in October 1853, and Britain and France declared war on 27 and 28 March 1854, with the Tsar responding with a counter-declaration of war on 11 April. Ironically, the Turks had been reasonably successful in holding the Russians at Silistria on the Danube and, before the allies could act further, the Russians withdrew from the principalities in June 1854 under the threat of Austrian intervention, thus effectively complying with the original British and French ultimatum. Austria itself then occupied the principalities, with the Turks moving their army under Omar Pasha to the Crimea because British and French forces were already en route, the first British troops having left Southampton on 22 February. The allies concentrated at the Bulgarian port of Varna in May and June, from which it was originally intended they could relieve the Turks at Silistria. Subsequently, in January 1855, Britain, France and Turkey were joined by the kingdom of Sardinia, which was anxious to gain international recognition as a significant state, recognising that participation would give them a seat at the peace conference denied their rivals for control of Italy's destiny, Austria having remained neutral. Other European powers, which also remained neutral, had at least to consider whether to remain so. Moreover, a generally unremarked aspect of the war is the pro-Russian and anti-British feeling on the part of the United States, to the extent that some British politicians feared American intervention.

At the time, the commitment of an allied expeditionary force to the Crimea was seen as but the first stage in a wider struggle, which witnessed campaigning in Asia Minor, the Baltic and the Pacific, as a comprehensive assault upon the military and naval strength of a Tsarist Empire second only to Britain as a global power. The allied descent on the Crimea, which was actually opposed by all the British government's military advisers, though recommended by some of its naval ones, was really intended initially as no more than a large-scale raid against the main Russian fleet base of Sebastopol as an essential preliminary to wider operations in the Balkans. While this rapidly took on a momentum of its own, it should not divert us from the wider intentions of allied policy makers such as the First Lord of the Admiralty, Sir James Graham, who masterminded the British strategy as a whole.

The allies landed at Eupatoria on Calamita Bay twenty-five miles from Sebastopol on 14 September 1854, forcing the heights above the River Alma on 20 September and circling round the city to besiege it from its stronger, southern side because the French Commander-in-Chief, St-Arnaud, succumbing daily to an advanced cancer, declined to risk an assault on the city without formal siege preparations. Ironically, the main Russian field army under Prince Menshikov was retreating eastwards as the allies marched south and the city was virtually open to an approach from the north. Subsequently, the British developed an efficient intelligence system under the direction of Charles Cattley, the former British Consul at Kertch.

The Russian attempt to break the allied lines of communication between the new British base at Balaclava and the siege works before Sebastopol led to battles at Balaclava on 25 October and Inkerman on 5 November. Balaclava witnessed the repulse of Russian cavalry by the 'thin red line' of Colin Campbell's 93rd Highlanders, the routing of more Russian cavalry by Sir James Scarlett's Heavy Brigade, and the disaster that befell the Light Brigade. Inkerman became both the 'battle in the fog' and 'the soldier's battle', in which confusion reined supreme before the Russians were repulsed. After prolonged bombardment, the first major assault on Sebastopol in June 1855 – that in which Wood was so severely wounded – failed against the two major defensive works of the Redan and the Malakoff. A major Russian relief attempt led by Gorchakov, who was known to the British as 'Got such a Cough', was defeated by the French and Sardinians at Tchernaya on 16 August 1855 and, in a second major assault on 8 September 1855, the British failed again at the Redan but the French broke into the Malakoff, forcing the Russians to abandon Sebastopol.

Some events elsewhere in the Black Sea were linked directly to the Crimean campaign, the major allied expedition to seize the Straits of Kertch at the entrance to the Sea of Azov in May 1855 being intended to sever the Russian lines of communication to the Crimea. The naval bombardment of, and allied landing, at Kinburn on the confluence of the Dnieper and the Bug near Odessa, however, in October 1855 was part of a separate strategy to bring additional pressure to bear after Sebastopol had already fallen. There was every intention of undertaking further naval bombardments along the Black Sea coast in the following year and extending military operations to the northern Crimea and possibly Georgia. On the Russo-Turkish frontier in the Caucasus, the Russian advance swept all before it in 1854 and early 1855, only for the Russian army to be held up by a now long-forgotten defence of Kars in Armenia between June and November 1855 by a British officer, William Fenwick Williams, who inspired the Turkish defenders. The Russians had also been waging a war against the Chechen insurgents led by Shamil since 1834. French arms were channelled to him to cause the Russians further mischief. Much further afield, in the Pacific, British and French naval forces bombarded Petropavlovsk on the island of Kamchatka in August 1854 but were repulsed when attempting a landing, subsequently razing the now deserted town in June 1855.

There was some minor allied naval activity against Russian interests in the White Sea and the Barents Sea in the far north but, in some respects, it might be argued that the most important theatre of operations was actually the Baltic, into which an allied fleet moved in April 1854. It was intended to commence operations against Kronstadt and Sveaborg (Suomenlinna), the main seaward defences of St Petersburg and Helsingfors (Helsinki) respectively, and to impose a naval blockade on Russian trade. A French expedition seized Bomarsund on the Åland Islands off the Swedish coast in August 1854. With the new campaigning year, Sveaborg was bombarded in August 1855. Kronstadt was to be the next target, arousing Russian fears that St Petersburg itself was now vulnerable, especially as the Swedes had entered into negotiation with the allies to conclude an alliance. Over two hundred British warships were intended to enter the Baltic in 1856, the 'great armament' being reviewed by the Queen at Spithead in April 1856. Therefore, while the bombardments themselves were not especially effective, it was that threat to St Petersburg and additional pressure from the mobilisation of the Austrian army, coupled with the economic strains of the war, that convinced the Russians to accept terms, the Treaty of Paris being signed in March 1856.

It has often been maintained that the British army at the time of the Crimea was 'simply the Peninsular army brought out of its cupboard and dusted down'.[2] It is an image certainly seemingly supported by the despatches of W. H. Russell for *The Times* and by the proceedings of the radically-driven Select Committee on the Army before Sebastopol, the parliamentary motion for which in January 1855 led to the downfall of Lord Aberdeen's government. Other evidence might also suggest that the army had somehow been frozen in time at the moment of its victory at Waterloo, since Wellington had remained the dominant figure in the army until his death in 1852. The Military Secretary at the Horse Guards from 1827 to 1852 had been his former secretary in the Peninsula, Lord Raglan. Wellington's successor as Commander-in-Chief in 1852, Lord Hardinge, had also fought in the Peninsular War and four of the five divisional generals in the Crimea had also done so. Certainly, the army had remained marginalised within British society, mostly out of sight in overseas garrisons and largely ignored by civilian reformers, who were concerned only with economy. Much had changed in reality, however, because an increasing number of younger officers had embraced professionalism and generated internal reforms. Hardinge encouraged further change, an engineering school opening at Chatham, an artillery school at Shoeburyness in 1852 and a musketry school at Hythe in 1853, the same year in which a camp of exercise was held at Chobham with land also purchased for a more permanent site for manoeuvres at Aldershot. Chobham indeed allowed the largest concentration of troops in England since 1815 and attracted much public attention. As so often in British history, however, war caught the army at a moment of transition and it was not the limited colonial war for which the army was organised and prepared. Thus there were undoubted failures, not least in the supporting services of ordnance, commissariat, and medical organisation, the army's administration being bedevilled by the division of responsibility into thirteen separate and competing agencies originally designed to minimise any risk of military despotism.

These administrative failures, in particular, fuelled Russell's condemnation. Cholera, the cause of which was not understood at the time, struck the allies even before they had left Varna, killing perhaps five thousand men in three months, but the British troops then suffered mightily in the trenches before Sebastopol and from the seeming lack of medical provision. It did not help that the so-called Great Storm of November 1854 resulted in the loss of thirty-five allied ships, including one carrying most of the army's winter clothing and medical supplies. Transport difficulties then led to supplies, which had reached the

Crimea, simply rotting on the jetties of the overcrowded harbour of Balaclava or even rotting before they could be unloaded. To counter growing criticism, the Secretary at War, Sidney Herbert, asked his friend, thirty-four-year-old Florence Nightingale, then managing an 'establishment for gentlewomen during illness' in Harley Street, to go out to help. Miss Nightingale of course, established herself at Scutari hospital in Constantinople in November 1854. In fact, the death rate at Scutari was higher than in most other hospitals in the theatre until it was belatedly realised by the Sanitary Commission, which arrived in March 1855, that the drainage system was inadequate.

Miss Nightingale's time at Scutari was marked, too, by a bitter personal confrontation with the head of the Army Medical Department in the Crimea, Dr John Hall, who had not been informed by the government of the intention to introduce female nurses, and with the leader of a group of Irish nuns, the Rev. Mother Frances Bridgeman, whom Hall invited to send nurses to the Crimea itself. When Hall got the KCB, Miss Nightingale commented that it stood for 'Knight of the Crimean Burial Ground'.[3] Another rival was Mary Stanley, who also led a party of nurses to the East, and yet another was Margaret Weare, the Superintendent at the General Hospital at Balaclava. A complex and contradictory woman, Florence Nightingale received general superintendence of the female nursing establishment in March 1856. She was certainly not the founder of modern nursing, as she only exemplified a much broader movement, but clearly gave impetus to that movement. Other women also went out to assist, a West Indian woman, Mary 'Mother' Seacole, making her own way to the Crimea after being turned down for employment by Nightingale. Seacole's 'British Hotel', established at Spring Hill near Balaclava, dispensed much needed comfort to the troops.

Inevitably, as already indicated, the army's commanders were necessarily of an older generation than the young reformers, but they were not invariably useless simply because of age. Raglan, now sixty-six and who had lost his right arm at Waterloo, became Commander-in-Chief by virtue of his knowledge of the French language and his decency and tact, which would be invaluable for dealing with allies – even if he tended to refer to the enemy as the French. Raglan was undoubtedly brave. When he had had his arm amputated, he had called for them to bring it back so he could retrieve a ring his wife had given him. Sadly, however, Raglan seemed incapable of acting decisively, becoming a particular target of *The Times* and eventually dying of cholera in June 1855. The first man since Wellington to be appointed a field-marshal in the field, he remains the only one to have died on active service in the field though, technically, field-marshals never retire. Two other divisional commanders, Sir Richard England and Sir George Cathcart, had recent experience of operations in India and South Africa respectively, while Sir George de Lacy Evans had commanded the British Legion in the Carlist Wars in Spain. Sir George Brown was admittedly unpopular and old-fashioned but, though senior to Cathcart, he was pointedly not made second-in-command.

The cavalry division was inadequately led, but the fifty-four-year-old Lucan, recalled from retirement, had at least seen action and, moreover, had done so while accompanying the Russian army on campaign in the Balkans in the 1820s. Lucan, however, was very unpopular, quarrelsome and arrogant. Known as 'Lord Look-on' from his inactivity in the earliest engagements in the Crimea, Lucan was eventually made field-marshal in 1886 after having protested that one of his own staff officers had been promoted to that rank over him. It was rumoured that he had not been promoted because the War Office thought him already dead, but the reality was that he had not been forgiven for publicly challenging Raglan's Balaclava despatches. By contrast, the Hon. James Scarlett, commanding the Heavy Brigade, was both popular and capable. The Light Brigade was commanded by Lucan's fifty-seven-year-old brother-in-law, Lord Cardigan, who was notorious for the scandals that had accompanied his command of both the 15th Hussars and the 11th Hussars, and for the mutual hatred between himself and Lucan. No great advertisement for the system by which many commissions were still purchased, Cardigan refused to allow his troopers to wrap their cloaks around them at night for warmth because it was effeminate. He himself lived on his private yacht in Balaclava harbour, hence his nickname of 'The Noble Yachtsman'. The early historian of the war, Alexander Kinglake, remarked of Cardigan that he had no guile for 'of all false pretences contrived for the purpose of feigning an interest in others he was as innocent as a horse'.4

In some respects, what made it difficult for even the more competent commanders to adjust to conditions was the fact that the war did involve such innovation. It has to be said, moreover, that British, French and Russian commanders were equally poor. The British and French, for example, were armed with the new rifled musket firing the revolutionary cylindrical conoidal bullet known as the Minié ball, which, because it was hollow at the base, expanded when fired to fit the grooving in the barrel, thus dramatically increasing the range to perhaps a thousand yards. The Russians took particularly heavy casualties from the rifled musket at Inkerman. Even earlier than Inkerman, the products of Europe's increasing industrialisation had been illustrated by the dramatic demonstration of the power of modern explosive shell projectiles against wooden ships at Sinope, the Turks losing some three thousand dead to the Russian loss of but 38. The same shell projectiles also inflicted great damage on the allied fleets before Sebastopol in November 1854. French armour-plated floating batteries were used to bombard Kinburn, marking the real birth of the ironclad warship, and steam-powered gunboats and transports proved effective in both the Black Sea and the Baltic, the allied ability to supply their armies from the sea being of particular importance when the Russians had enormous difficulties supplying Sebastopol overland. The French army in the Crimea was also connected to Paris by electric telegraph and submarine cable by April 1855, instantly eradicating the two to three weeks it had taken previously to send messages. St Arnaud's successor as French Commander-in-Chief, Canrobert, did not welcome continual interference from Emperor Napoleon III over the wires and resigned as a result in May 1855.

Another product of industrialisation was the railway, the considerable difficulties faced by the British army in the trenches before Sebastopol being considerably eased by construction of the first ever field railway, from the harbour at Balaclava to the siege lines from February 1855 onwards. Seven miles of track were laid in seven weeks and eventually the line stretched fourteen miles with four locomotives and three stationary engines supplementing railway carriages drawn by baggage animals. By the end of the war some 248,000 shells alone had been conveyed to the siege batteries. The first ever hospital train was also operating on the line by April 1855. For that matter, it was the first campaign in which chloroform was used as an anaesthetic, though many doctors felt the knife was a more powerful stimulant to recovery. A prefabricated hospital was sent to the Black Sea in August 1855, and a floating brass foundry was established to maintain the dockyard at Balaclava in October 1855, a similar floating foundry accompanying the British fleet into the Baltic. Indeed, it was the first war in which the industrial capacity of one side played a significant part in military victory, the Russians failing to match the allied technological and manu-facturing challenge, and being forced to try and import technological expertise and products. As a whole, in fact, the war stimulated the introduction into Europe of American mass-production techniques for the manufacture of modern weapons, the British opening a new weapons plant with American machines at Enfield in 1855. William Armstrong of Newcastle was also motivated by reading of the difficulties experienced by British gunners trying to manhandle guns at Inkerman to develop new lighter artillery, producing sketches of the new breechloading ar-tillery he was to manufacture in 1857. Only three hundred patents for weapons were registered in Europe in the entire period between 1617 and 1850, but six hundred were registered in the 1850s as a direct result of the war's stimulus.

The Crimea was also the first war extensively covered for British readers by a new national popular press, Russell's first despatch for *The Times*, which he had sent from Malta as the allied contingents converged on the Black Sea, being published in April 1854. Earlier, *The Times* had also played a major role in whipping up public opinion in Britain against Russia, for this was an immensely popular war with the public already accustomed to anti-Russian rhetoric, not least after the Russian suppression of Hungary in 1848. There was a small peace movement but it proved entirely ineffective. The way in which Russell depicted the problems of the army to the detriment of the military authorities had encouraged the War Office to hope that the official war photographer they had despatched in June 1854, Richard Nicklin, would provide visual proof to the public that Russell's accounts were wrong. Nicklin and all his photographs, however, were lost when his ship sank en route for home in the 'Great Storm' of November 1854. Two subalterns also tried their hand but their efforts were of poor quality. The field was therefore open for a commercial photographer, Roger Fenton, who worked in the Crimea between March and June

1855 before returning home ill. Fenton's work was then continued by James Robertson, an amateur photographer, who was the chief engraver of the Ottoman Imperial Mint at Constantinople, and George Shaw-Lefevre, later a Liberal politician.

At least four French photographers were also active, while the Rumanian photographer Karol de Szathmari can also claim to be one of the first ever war photographers for his coverage of the Russian and Turkish armies in the Danubian principalities in the spring of 1854, all these men benefiting from the development of the wet-plate process in 1851. Though avoiding scenes of death, Fenton's photographs caused a sensation when exhibited in October 1855, although sales were not a great as anticipated and his stock was auctioned off at the end of the war by Thomas Agnew of Manchester, who also published the more traditional war sketches of William Simpson.

In addition to the press coverage and the work of artists, whose prints were sold widely, there were theatrical performances in many British cities and towns depicting episodes from the war. By the end of 1854 in London you could visit a panorama of the battle of the Alma in Leicester Square, a model of Sebastopol at a second establishment in the square, a diorama of Balaclava in Regent Street, effigies and tableaux of allied generals at Madame Tussaud's, a representation of the Alma at Astley's Amphitheatre, and a Turkish exhibition at Hyde Park Corner. Later, there were various displays at the Crystal Palace, and yet further panoramas, re-enactments and other war-related amusements. Interest continued into 1856 but then rapidly waned with the outbreak of the Indian Mutiny in 1857.

Some twenty years later, however, Elizabeth, Lady Butler made her name with a painting, *The Roll Call*, in 1874, depicting the Guards in the Crimea. In Liverpool alone it was seen by 20,000 people on a national tour, touching the nation's heart as William Holman Hunt expressed it 'as few pictures have done'.[5] The *Roll Call* was commissioned by Charles Galloway, a Manchester industrialist, who refused all offers until Queen Victoria expressed an interest and to whom he eventually ceded it. It marked the upsurge of interest in the war amid the introduction of the Cardwell army reforms, the first Balaclava reunion being held in 1875, though noticeably only for veterans of the Light Brigade, with a Balaclava Commemoration Society formed in 1877. Lady Butler's own subsequent painting, *Balaclava*, was seen by an estimated 50,000 people in London before going on its national tour in 1876. Survivors were specially invited to view the Queen's Jubilee in 1897, prompting the establishment of the Roberts Relief Fund by a London publisher, Harrison Roberts, which raised sufficient funds to pay weekly sums to the forty most deserving veterans until the last died in 1920. Kipling, too, had been moved by the plight of some to pen 'The Last of the Light Brigade' in 1891. The last survivor of the charge, incidentally, died only in 1927.

The Crimea was depicted to the public in an entirely new way and in the process ordinary British soldiers were cast in an heroic mould by Russell to the ultimate improvement of their status, for now they were no longer oppressors of the poor in Britain itself but fighting Tsarist tyranny. Vast amounts of clothing and supplies were gifted to the Crimean War Fund organised by *The Times*, one regimental doctor describing the material sent by well wishers reaching the Crimea in February 1855 as 'fit only for a polar expedition or a fancy dress party'.[6] The soldier's new status was also confirmed by the institution of the Victoria Cross in January 1856, though the first awards were not gazetted until February 1857 and the first bestowed by the Queen in Hyde Park to sixty-two individuals in June 1857. The first award was to Mate (later Rear-Admiral) Charles Lucas for throwing a live Russian shell off HMS *Hecla* during the bombardment of Bomarsund in the Baltic on 21 June 1854. Technically, the most awarded for a single engagement was not for Rorke's Drift in the Zulu War, as most people assume, but the twenty-one awarded for Inkerman, though this was a battle fought over a very large area and some argue that the twenty won for the unsuccessful British assault on the Redan at Sebastopol on 18 June 1855 should more properly be considered the most for a single action.

Russell's despatches also provoked a considerable challenge to authority and raised serious questions as relevant then as now as to the control of the press in wartime, *The Times* being held to have published information of use to the enemy between November 1854 and March 1855, at which time a more effective censorship was introduced. It was also thought that such disclosures weakened British morale in the Crimea and British prestige abroad, a point made among others by the French commentator Alexander de Tocqueville. The influence of *The Times*, whose circulation increased by 50 per cent during the war, also persuaded the government to abandon stamp duty in March 1855 in the hope of encouraging competition from rival newspapers such as the *Daily News* and *Daily Telegraph*, but the circulation of *The Times* ran at about 61,000 daily by 1855 compared to a combined 3000 to 6000 for all its rivals put together. In the event, therefore, this did not lessen press criticism, which was reinforced by some officers' letters. Moreover, with its celebrated declaration that the 'noblest army ever sent from these shores has been sacrificed to the grossest mismanagement', the paper took up the cause of administrative reform, attacking the 'incompetency, lethargy, aristocratic hauteur, official indifference, favour, routine, perverseness, and stupidity' which, it claimed 'reign, revel and riot' in the Crimea, at Scutari and 'how much nearer home we do not venture to say'.[7] It had not helped that Raglan, and virtually all his staff and senior commanders, had ignored Russell. Raglan also declined to make scapegoats of his leading staff officers, Richard Airey and James Estcourt, refusing requests by the government to dismiss them. It should be borne in mind, however, that Russell and his editor, John Delane, had a political agenda and that a great many soldiers who experienced the Crimea believed the reports exaggerated.

Overall, class-consciousness is thought to have increased markedly in Britain as the middle classes now attacked vulnerable aristocratic institutions. The Trevelyan/Northcote proposals for civil service competitive examinations were first aired in 1854, while an Administrative Reform Association emerged in May 1855. Moreover, many of the technological developments in the Crimea were the products of middle-class initiative. It was Brunel who sent out the prefabricated hospital, while the railway was first proposed in October 1854 by Samuel Morton Peto, an MP but also a railway contractor, who together with Thomas Brassey and Edward Betts (with whom he had earlier constructed the Eastern Counties Railway and the Victoria Docks) established a corps of civil engineers to go out to the Crimea. The floating brass foundry was the initiative of a Tyneside engineer, Robert Frazer, in October 1855, while Sir Joseph Paxton sent navvies from his workforce on the Crystal Palace to build huts and roads. The chef at the Reform Club, Alexis Sayer, went out to the Crimea in February 1855 at his own expense to supervise an overhaul of the army's catering. Sayer's portable cooking stove remains the basic design still used by the British army to this day. Another wartime initiative came, perhaps surprisingly, from Charles Dickens, who commissioned a prefabricated clothes drying machine sent out to Scutari in March 1855. As *Punch* expressed it in May 1855 :[8]

> No more will we be ruled by men
> Whose sole qualification
> Is not ability and ken;
> But lies in rank and station:
> None shall this land
> Henceforth command
> No men will we submit to,
> But those who business understand;
> Practical men of ditto.

Certainly the war fuelled radical ideas for constitutional change, although much of the legislation passed during the war years was relatively minor, and, in the case of army reform, interest was not maintained much beyond the fall of Sebastopol. The office of Secretary of State for War had already been separated from the Colonial Office in June 1854 before the army reached the Crimea, partly in response to the campaign of *The Times*. The motion proposed by a radical MP, John Roebuck, to establish a Select Committee on the Army before Sebastopol then led to the fall of Aberdeen's government in January 1855. At that point Palmerston's new administration merged the posts of Secretary of State for War and Secretary at War and abolished the Board of Ordnance. The latter change left army administration much simplified as a duality between a Secretary of State for War at the War Office and a Commander-in-Chief at the Horse Guards. New organisations were also formed including the Land Transport Corps and the Sanitary Commission despatched to the East. In the longer term, however, as conditions in the Crimea improved, the impetus was lost. The report of the Select Committee was effectively shelved in June 1855 and the highly critical McNeill/Tulloch report on the commissariat in January 1856 led to a commission of enquiry into the conduct of leading officers such as Cardigan and Lucan, which duly exonerated them all in July 1856.

In other ways there were no dramatic departures from past methods of waging war, financial policy continuing along lines established in the Napoleonic Wars of heavy government borrowing and lending to its allies abroad. However, it was necessary to raise income tax from 7*d.* to 1*s.* 2*d.* and then 1*s.* 4*d.* in the pound, a level it did not exceed again until 1915. In April 1854 there was an attempt to stop exports of strategic goods to eastern Europe while enabling imports to reach Britain as normal, though goods previously obtained from Russian had to be replaced. Wool, for example, was brought in from the colonies, oilseed from India and hemp from Italy. Amid the tentative beginnings of an allied economic offensive directed against Russia through naval blockade of the Baltic and Black Sea, the Russians tried to circumvent it through imports by way of Belgium and Prussia. Russian exports fell to a quarter of their pre-war volume but imports only by about a third.

What was different, however, was the realisation by politicians that they had to reconcile themselves to competing demands for manpower between the armed forces and industry. Rural depopulation and large-scale emigration had already reduced the army's ability to recruit in Scotland and Ireland, but there was also now competition from high wages offered by manufacturing industry and even agriculture facing labour shortages. Thus, while the number of males of military age had doubled between 1815 and 1854 as the British population grew, the army was chronically short of men. Politicians still shied away from increasing pay and conscription was an impossibility, the popular opposition to that for the home defence militia having led to its abandonment in 1831. Raising civilian labour was one solution as in the case of the Land Transport Corps. Another solution was the employment of mercenary formations recruited from Poland, Switzerland, Turkey, Italy and the German states, a course favoured by British business on the grounds that it would not denude the domestic labour force, for they regarded continuing economic competitiveness as a major factor assisting the achievement of victory. In all, Britain sent some 98,000 men to the Crimea over the course of the war as a whole, but its army's strength at any one time was rarely more than 30,000 men. France sent perhaps 309,000 men over the war as a whole but, again, rarely had more than 120,000 in the field. Curiously, therefore, the victors had far fewer men than the vanquished, Russia mobilising perhaps two million men by the end of the war, though the Russian army was divided between the

Balkans, Caucasus, Poland and the Baltic, with perhaps only 60,000 men or so in the Crimea at the start of the war.

The war resulted in more casualties than the American Civil War, costing somewhere between 485,000 and 640,000 dead, of which Britain's share was some 22,000. This does not appear a large figure in the case of the British army, but it represented an average loss of 35 per cent of its field strength between October 1854 and April 1855, largely from disease brought on by overwork, exposure, poor food, insufficient clothing and insufficient shelter. The international results of such suffering were seemingly small. The Crimea remained a limited conflict in terms of its geographical extent, the ways in which diplomatic control was largely maintained, and the mobilisation of resources. Moreover, Russia sued for peace before the opening of the 1856 campaign, in which Britain for one had intended to widen the war by drawing in the Scandinavian powers and encouraging insurrections among non-Russian subjects of the Tsar. The Treaty of Paris did, however, neutralise the Black Sea, and the Dardanelles was made an international waterway. Russian turned eastwards but was also induced to begin a reform process, culminating in the abolition of serfdom in 1861. Russia, however, then repudiated the Black Sea clauses without penalty in 1870.

Turkey proclaimed equality of all citizens before the law to avoid further possibility of outside intervention on behalf of religious minorities. This, however, merely preserved Turkey for another future crisis, since the issue of reform was to open up the question of nationalism within the European part of the empire with all that that meant for the future peace of the Balkans. The first of the new Balkan states to emerge from the Ottoman Empire was to be Romania in 1862, the Paris treaty having guaranteed the autonomy of the Danubian principalities and Russia having ceded Bessarabia to them, though Romania did not become formally independent until 1877. The war may also have had a direct impact on the Indian Mutiny since Azimullah Khan, secretary to the notorious Nana Sahib of Bithur, visited the Crimea and formed a low opinion of the British army, which contributed to his master throwing in his lot with the mutineers at Cawnpore. Above all, the war had ended forty years of peace between the great powers and had broken the concert of Europe established in 1815. Prussia had noted that Austria had threatened intervention not from strength but weakness.

Sardinia, too, was poised to challenge Austrian control of Italy. War was to become a much more frequent instrument of policy thereafter. In many ways, therefore, the Crimean War was a modern conflict. Certainly, it has as much claim as the American Civil War to be a highly significant step on the road to total war.

18

War, Technology and Change

The Victoria and Albert Museum in South Kensington hosted a major exhibition, 'Inventing New Britain: The Victorian Vision' in 2001, while the Science Museum hosted an accompanying major conference, 'Locating the Victorians'. The inclusion of some military exhibits such as a Maxim machine gun was entirely appropriate given the cooperation between the two museums, the Science Museum being housed in a building designed and begun by a Royal Engineer, Captain Francis Fowke. Born in 1823, Fowke designed some collapsible pontoons, which were shown at Paris Exhibition in 1855. As a result, Fowke met another Royal Engineer, Colonel Owen, who involved him in the Machinery Department of the Exhibition and he became its secretary when Owen was despatched to the Crimea. As well as working on the new home for the Exhibition's Science and Art Department at Marlborough House in South Kensington, Fowke also designed the interiors of both the Dublin National Gallery and Edinburgh's Museum of Science and Art before designing the South Kensington (later the Science) Museum and the Prince Consort's Library in Aldershot. It is appropriate to recall Fowke's achievements because it is a corrective to a particularly persistent image of the Victorian army as a conservative institution notoriously resistant to embracing technological change, and in which anti-intellectual currents ran deep.

It is all too easy to call to mind some oft-repeated stock quotations. Famously, Frederick Maurice, later Professor of Military Art and History at the Staff College from 1885 to 1892, wrote in 1872 that 'the British army officer hates ... literary work even in the form of writing letters'. Similarly, Wolseley while Commander-in-Chief wrote in 1897 that he hoped officers 'may never degenerate into bookworms. There is happily at present no tendency in that direction ...'[1] Equally, from the earlier period of the Queen's reign, one can find Sir Charles Napier supporting the retention of the smoothbore musket over the adoption of the rifle in 1851 and the Marquess of Anglesey, as Master-General of the Ordnance in 1847, saying he would prefer railways levelled and steam 'exploded'. It is not therefore surprising that the military radical J. F. C. Fuller, who fought in the South African War as a subaltern and was later a pioneer of armoured warfare in the 1920s and 1930s, suggested that the army of his youth collectively possessed a 'Brown Bess' mind.

Fuller had his own agenda in wishing to highlight his own contribution to modernisation and, in fact, such quotations can be taken out of context. Wolseley was a leading military reformer and Anglesey was particularly open-minded as Master-General, the quotation reflecting his concern with the potential invasion threat identified as arising from the application of steam to transport by land and sea. Clearly, there was a strong preference in some quarters for character over intellect, but other leading soldiers such as Sir John Ardagh were utterly contemptuous of the idea that 'the athletic "duffer", who is useful in a football team, must necessarily be a better soldier than the man who comes first in any examination'.[2]

Napier's support for the retention of the smoothbore musket was on the grounds that the rifle would 'destroy that intrepid spirit which makes the British soldier always dash at his enemy', reflecting not so much blinkered conservatism as a continuing concern with the ability of men to meet the psychological challenge posed by modern firepower.[3] Similarly, in recognising the implications of what he called the 'second tactical revolution' introduced by the appearance in the 1880s and 1890s of magazine rifles, quick-firing guns and smokeless powder, arguably one of the most significant military theorists in the Victorian army, G. F. R. Henderson, subscribed to the Social Darwinist emphasis so common in European military circles at the turn of the century that it was necessary, and possible, sufficiently to enhance the psychological preparation of soldiers in order to overcome firepower. In fact, the increasing concern with morale represented something of a reversion to an older tradition, compared to the positive British military interest in scientific and technological innovation readily apparent between the 1830s and the 1860s.

In fact, there are innumerable examples of new technology being applied to the army's colonial campaigns, technology substituting for manpower given the army's difficulty in recruiting and retaining men under a system of voluntary enlistment. It was a necessity given both the small army's lack of manpower and its need to meet the physical challenges of warfare conducted, as Charles Callwell noted in his celebrated manual *Small Wars: Their Principles and Practice* in 1896, as much against nature as indigenous opponents.

Imperial needs drove the introduction of technology. Significantly, although the first Atlantic submarine cable failed just three months after its inauguration in 1858, it had already been used to transmit orders to British battalions in Canada. Similarly, the annexation of the Transvaal in 1877 and the outbreak of the Zulu War two years later hastened the extension of the cable from London to Durban via Aden in December 1879. Strategic concerns subsequently created a global cable network under effective British control, just as the introduction of steam had itself necessitated the acquisition of a string of coaling stations such as Aden. The strategic use of railways for the defence of India was appreciated at an early stage with the first line begun between Bombay and Kalyan in 1852. The importance of the railway was soon borne out by the experience of the Indian Mutiny in 1857–58. Five thousand miles of track had been laid by 1870. Subsequently, with the Russian threat to Afghanistan, the Indian government constructed a new 133 miles-long strategic railway from the Indus to the Bolan Pass in just 101 days during the Second Afghan War (1878–81).

According to John Lawrence, however, it was another technological innovation that saved India for the British during the Mutiny, namely the electric telegraph. In passing it can be noted that the Mutiny itself was in part triggered by another new technology in terms of the issue to sepoys of the greased cartridges of the new Enfield rifle musket. Consequently, the length of telegraph line in India had increased from just over 4250 miles in 1856 to over 17,600 miles by 1865. The Royal Engineers formed its first telegraph company in 1870 and deployed it to Ashanti in 1873. Equally, the deployment of steam gunboats was crucial to British success in the First and Second Burma Wars (1824–26 and 1852–53), the First and Third China Wars (1839–42 and 1856–60), and the Third Maori War (1863–66). Military railways were equally crucial to success in the Egyptian campaign of 1882 and to the reconquest of the Sudan in 1896–98, where over 630 miles of track were laid.

The reconquest of the Sudan likewise demonstrated the significance of modern artillery, magazine rifles and machine guns. Churchill wrote that the battle of Omdurman on 2 September 1898, in which some 11,000 dervishes were killed for the loss of just forty-eight British, Egyptian and Sudanese dead, represented the 'most signal triumph ever gained by the arms of science over barbarians'.[4] A year earlier, a similarly equipped force of thirty-two whites and 507 African troops of the Royal Niger Company had beaten off an army of 31,000 men at Sokoto. The new Enfield rifle musket, firing the revolutionary Minié bullet, had first been used in the Eighth Cape Frontier (Kaffir) War in 1851, while the explosive soft-nosed bullet developed by Captain N. S. Bertie-Clay at the Dum Dum arsenal in India was first used during the great tribal rising on the North-West Frontier in 1897–98, when it was judged that more stopping power was required against fanatics. The machine gun had first been used by the British in Ashanti in 1873, though largely for demonstration purposes, proving its value for the first time in action in the Zulu War.

Nor was it the case that the army was blind to the application of technology in European warfare. In fact, it was not so much a case of the adoption of new technology, but how to employ it in the means best suited to the British system and in such a way that it conserved precious manpower. Thus the lively discussion concerning machine guns was primarily whether it should be regarded as an infantry or an artillery weapon: machine guns were attached to every brigade in 1893 when they did not form a permanent part of any other army. Similarly, Britain had actually led the way in introducing breech-loading artillery in 1868, though subsequently reverting to rifled muzzle-loaders between 1870 and 1885. Technical difficulties determined the artillery debate and this apparent reversion to older technology, much as technical difficulties had also delayed the adoption of both rifled muskets and breech-loading rifles in the 1830s and 1840s. It can also be noted that the British army introduced magazine rifles only a matter of months after the German army.

Indeed, it cannot be said that the army lagged that much behind its continental counterparts at any point. A whole series of military periodicals were founded in the very period of the 1820s and 1830s when the army has been traditionally regarded as simply stagnating, with the growing professionalism marked by the establishment of the United Service Institution, the Royal Engineers Institution and the Royal Artillery Institution. Railways had been extensively used to move troops around to combat the Chartist threat between 1839 and 1842, and the value of railways for the defence of the United Kingdom against possible invasion was a matter of some debate in the 1840s and 1850s. Between 1855 and 1859, the government arms factories at Enfield and Woolwich had also taken on board the automated mass-production techniques of American arms manufacturers, importing American semi-automatic milling machines, though subsequently they were unable to compete with the greater flexibility of private manufacturers such as Armstrong, Whitworth and Vickers. Indeed, it has been argued that even the expeditionary force sent to the Crimea was neither technologically nor tactically inferior to its opponents.[5]

Not surprisingly, Royal Engineers were constantly at the forefront of innovation. In terms of the science of fortification, the great defensive works constructed around naval ports and arsenals such as Portsmouth, Plymouth, Pembroke, Portland, Dover, Cork, the Thames and the Medway in the 1860s showed continuous modification to meet the challenge posed by developments in artillery. Submarine mining, which the Royal Engineers also undertook between 1863 and 1905, meant that they were 'constantly having to cope with the expanding demands of new technology in the field as much as in the laboratory, and a technology that was simultaneously both physically onerous and mentally taxing, as well as potentially dangerous'.[6] In the process, they developed the electro-contact mine.

Colonial experience and a degree of hostility to continental ideas did hinder innovation in the 1870s and 1880s, but artillery practice camps such as that established at Okehampton in 1875 proved important testing grounds for new ideas.

If, then, the army used and appreciated the value of technology in colonial campaigning and was not unreceptive to its application at home, why has the conservative image persisted? Similarly, why is it that, when many officers of the Royal Navy clearly possessed attitudes in common with their military counterparts, the same charge has not tended to be directed towards them to anything like the same extent?

In part, of course, the difference lies in the fact that Britain was first and foremost a global maritime power, whose naval mastery depended on maintaining a technological lead over its immediate rivals, France and Russia. The invasion panics that periodically affected the Victorians, as in the 1840s, 1850s and 1880s, were predicated upon the perceived loss, albeit temporarily, of technological superiority. Thus Palmerston had spoken in June 1845 of the Channel being bridged by steam, reflecting French progress towards the construction of a modern fleet and the preparation of Cherbourg as a potential invasion port through modern rail and telegraph links with Paris. Much as the Admiralty disliked the way in which steam had entered strategic calculations, it had still commissioned its first steamers in 1827 and had over seventy by 1840. Following trials in 1844, its first screw frigate, HMS *Amphion*, was launched in 1846. HMS *Prince Regent*, as rebuilt between 1845 and 1847, was the first ship with a full battery of guns firing shells. Similarly, when the French launched *La Gloire* in November 1859, thus bringing together steam power, the screw propeller, rifled ordnance and armour plate in a seagoing ironclad, the British riposte in 1860 was HMS *Warrior*. Wooden ships were rendered obsolete; though, due to the lack of sustained cruising range; the first true steam capital ship, HMS *Dread-nought*, was only launched in 1875. It could be argued that the 'steam tactics' resulting from the ability to centralise naval movements in ways not possible under sail actually had a stultifying effect on naval initiative, but in any case the Royal Navy never lost its working superiority in battleships and steamers.

Naval supremacy required a massive and ever more costly investment in evolving technology. Between 1859 and 1864 alone, for example, there were seven distinct evolutionary changes in ironclad design. Though iron and steel was far more durable than wood, qualitative improvements in propulsion, armour, gunnery and projectiles, or entirely new weapons such as the torpedo, also carried the risk of near instant obsolescence while costs escalated. *Warrior* cost six times more than an eighteenth-century ship of the line and, by 1888, the newest generation of warship, HMS *Nile*, cost twice as much again as had *Warrior*. As a result, new naval building programmes prompted by renewed fears of French and Russian challenges saw naval expenditure increase by £5,500,000 in the period 1884–88, and from £15,800,000 in 1889–90 to £23,700,000 in 1896–97. In effect, it was also the needs of the Royal Navy that brought increasing partnership between government and privately-owned arms manufacturing concerns, the army remaining generally more satisfied than the navy with the ordnance produced at the Royal Arsenal at Woolwich.[7]

By contrast, an army dispersed on the imperial periphery, and distanced from continental strategic culture both by British maritime power and its imperial duties, had no real need to lead Europe in technological terms. Indeed, as Henderson was to write in 1900, in view of the varied nature of the practical challenges facing an imperial constabulary, 'it is as useless to anticipate in what quarter of the globe our troops may be next employed as to guess at the tactics, the armament and even the colour ... of our next enemy. Each new expedition demands special equipment, special methods of supply and special tactical devices, and sometimes special armament'.[8] More often than not, obsolete methods such as rallying squares worked perfectly well against indigenous opponents, though most soldiers assumed that European opponents would not be as susceptible to the application of technology in warfare.

The lessons of modern conflict were also often distinctly ambiguous, irrespective of a lively tactical debate between those within the army who might be termed 'continentalists' and those who might be characterised as 'imperialists' as to the likely conditions prevailing in a future conflict. The lessons of the South African War, for example, were affected by climate and terrain and were to be contradicted in many instances by those of the next war to which the British and the other European powers sent observers, the Russo-Japanese War of 1904–5. To give but one illustration, the Royal Artillery successfully agitated for re-equipment with quick-firing guns on the back of the South African War when, in fact, the Boers did not use them and their use by British naval brigades accounted for only an estimated 2 per cent of the shells fired by the British during the war.

The army was also compelled to operate within the context of crippling economic and political limitations. Lack of proper practice facilities in Britain, for example, was acute. The line of fire on the artillery ranges at Plumstead in the 1830s and 1840s crossed the Thames so that firing had to be halted each time a vessel moved up or down river. Shoeburyness was not fully authorised as an alternative until 1862.

An innovative camp of exercise was held at Chobham in 1853, and Aldershot was purchased between 1854 and 1861, but there were then no more manoeuvres in Britain between 1853 and 1871, or between 1875 and 1890. Similarly, it has been argued that the constant financial restrictions encouraged the army to introduce tactical reforms that did not require new technology.[9]

In any case, technology was not always the answer to the problems encountered in colonial warfare. There was no substitute for sweat in Wolseley's Red River expedition, confronted with forty-seven separate unnavigable sections of water or portages in the Canadian North West in 1870; or in Ashanti, when Wolseley was faced with the need to bridge 237 water courses in 1873–74. Nor was there any real substitute for oxen in either Zululand in 1879 or in South Africa generally in 1899, especially as the Boers seized 875 miles of the 5050 miles of the railway lines existing at the very outset of the South African War. The existence of the railway lines themselves predicated the British line of advance on the two Boer republics and the subsequent protection of the railways during the guerrilla phase of the war proved an enduring problem.

Equally, while the expedition to Suakin on the Red Sea coast in 1885 'brought together all the significant technical developments – steamship, railway, electric telegraph, balloon, machine gun, breechloader, tinned food, distilled water, anaesthetics, even the humbler sunglasses',[10] it was of little strategic value since the government determined to abandon the Sudan as a whole within a month of the expedition landing. As with the line in Abyssinia and the improvisation accompanying the use of railways in Egypt in 1882, the Suakin railway also left much to be desired, its eighteen and a half miles costing £865,000.

Nor was technology always the answer on the battlefield itself. Those well-known lines from Belloc's 'The Modern Traveller' – 'Whatever happens, we have got the Maxim Gun, and they have not' – need to be balanced by those equally well known lines from Newbolt's 'Vitae Lampada' – 'The Gatling's jammed and the Colonel dead'. Wolseley's demonstration for the Ashanti chiefs in 1873 was spoiled by one of his Gatlings jamming and he chose not to take them on his advance to Kumasi. The fabled square was indeed broken at Abu Klea in the Sudan in 1885, despite the presence of Gardner machine guns, while the Jameson raiders did not have sufficient water available to cool their

Maxims when surrounded by the Boers at Dornkop in 1896. The Boers, of course, were themselves armed with modern weapons and it needs to be recalled that even less advanced opponents did not always lack modern weapons. Those British soldiers proceeding to South Africa from India in 1899 had already faced and learned much from tribesmen armed with magazine rifles on the North-West Frontier in 1897–98.

Some apparent advances eagerly assimilated were also false dawns. An example is the bicycle, first used by the army on manoeuvres in 1887 and described by Lieutenant-Colonel A. R. Savile, the Professor of Tactics at the Royal Military College, Sandhurst, as a 'machine capable of great possibilities in the future of actual warfare'. It was pointed out by one military periodical in 1890, however, that 'a cyclist with perhaps two cavalrymen behind him in pursuit would, except on a good road, be surely hard pressed'.[11] In much the same way the sheer weight of the traction engines, with which the Royal Engineers had first experimented in 1859, used in South Africa led to such damage to metalled roads that they were only a supplementary to baggage animals.

One should not push the traditional image of the Victorian army altogether into the background. Political limitations also played their part. These derived from the resistance on the part of British politicians to any effective machinery by which military advice could be systematically offered to them, with the concomitant stimulus that would have been offered to military and strategic thought generally. It was only in 1901 that professional advice was officially recorded and there was no General Staff until September 1906, although a Chief of the General Staff had existed since February 1904. Prior to this, military advice was taken on an entirely ad hoc basis. In 1854 the Cabinet ignored the advice of soldiers in selecting its Sebastopol strategy, although the Secretary of State, Newcastle, did subsequently seek the advice of the elderly Inspector-General of Fortifications, Sir John Burgoyne. During the war scare during the Franco-Prussian War in 1870, Gladstone took advice solely from Captain Evelyn Baring. Disraeli, or Lord Beaconsfield as he had become, ignored the Duke of Cambridge during the Eastern Crisis of 1876–78 to take advice from one of Burgoyne's successors, Lintorn Simmons, and Colonel Robert Home of the War Office Intelligence Department, which had been founded only in 1875. Subsequently, Simmons and John Ardagh accompanied the Prime Minister to the

Congress of Berlin. Nevertheless, the fact that politicians could at least find officers capable of advising them is indicative of a profession not of unremitting intellectual bleakness.

The curricula of Sandhurst and the Staff College were undemanding, while it took a long time for attendance at the latter to become fully accepted as a sine qua non for professional advancement. Professionalism, however, increased markedly through the late nineteenth century. By its end, there was a ready market available to many officers aspiring to be authors, in the sense that publishers were offering series such as the 'Wolseley Series' from Kegan Paul, Trench, Trubner & Co. from 1897 onwards. Throughout the period, too, there had been military periodicals such as the *United Service Journal* (later *the United Services Magazine*), founded in 1827; the *Naval and Military Gazette* from 1833; the *United Service Gazette* of the same year; and the *Journal of the United Service Institution* from 1857, the institution itself being founded in 1829. There were also the rigorously professional journals of the Royal Artillery Institution, which published its first volume of proceedings in 1857, and the Royal Engineers Institution, which had done so twenty years earlier. Soldiers could also choose to contribute to commercial periodicals such as the significant series of articles by the Chaplain-General and Inspector-General of Army Schools, G. R. Gleig, in the *Quarterly Review* between 1845 and 1852, or the contributions by men like Wolseley and Sir Edward Hamley to *Blackwood's Edinburgh Magazine*.

It is admittedly difficult to judge the extent to which any of these publications or major works on tactics or strategy were read or otherwise disseminated. Both Maurice and Henderson complained that military books did not sell sufficiently well because their purchase was usually left to Mess Secretaries as if they were cases of wine. In his characteristically malicious way, James Edmonds, the official historian of the Great War, always maintained that Sir John French had only ever borrowed one book from the War Office Library – a copy of Hamley's celebrated *Operations of War*, published in 1866 – had failed to understand it, and had never borrowed another. As it happened, French was to claim that he did not commit the British Expeditionary Force to the fortress of Mauberge in August 1914 during the retreat from Mons precisely because he had read Hamley. Certainly, officers could get by comfortably enough with digests of required reading. Evelyn Wood recalled of his Staff College days in 1863–4 that one fellow student, to whom he recommended some reading on Marlborough's campaigns, told him he would rely entirely on Hamley's lecture notes, Hamley being Professor of Military History at the college from 1859 to 1865 and then Commandant from 1870 to 1877.

Then, again, books might merely represent a consensus view held by many contemporaries or be a synthesis of other sources such as foreign treatises, and lack all originality. Hamley and Henderson at various times both criticised the tendency to pay slavish attention to German authors though Hamley's *Operations of War*, which remained required reading for Staff College entrance until 1894, was almost purely based on the rather rigid theoretical approach to war favoured by Henri Jomini, the Swiss-born military theorist. Sir Patrick MacDougall's *Modern Warfare as Influenced by Modern Artillery* from 1864 was also heavily influenced by Jomini, while two popular digests, Robert Home's *Precis of Modern Tactics* of 1873 and C. F. Clery's *Minor Tactics* in 1875, were heavily continental in influence. Curiously, despite their influence in terms of the posts they held at Camberley and Woolwich respectively, neither Frederick Maurice nor Henry Brackenbury ever wrote a major theoretical work between them.

In many ways, however, the one distinctively British contribution to military theory was displayed in terms of the concept of small wars and, supremely, Charles Callwell's work. Yet even the great strategic debate over the appropriate means of defending India, and the relative importance of fighting Russian expansion on the North-West Frontier or of amphibious operations in peripheral areas like the Balkans, was conducted largely in terms of the circulation of official or unofficial memoranda, with the exception of the polemics of Charles MacGregor. Success or failure in the debate by the distinctive 'Imperial' and 'Indian' schools of military thought, moreover, was measured not in publications but by successful lobbying for senior appointments.

Mention of individual appointments leads to the point that any reform or change within or affecting the army might itself derive from the real but unwritten influence of individuals. These perhaps included soldiers such as Sir John Sutherland, Alexander Tulloch, J. H. Lefroy and E. F. DuCane, who were influential in the 1860s in areas such as the health, education and the discipline of the army. Others were not soldiers but politicians such as Sidney Herbert or Edward Cardwell, though soldiers might influence them in turn. Evelyn Baring, John Adye, Archibald Alison and George Balfour, for example, advised Cardwell. There were also leading civil servants within the War Office such as Ralph Knox, Ralph Thompson and Arthur Haliburton, who at the very least were powerful institutional defenders of the Cardwell legacy after 1872. Civilians, too, could be important, such as the retired soldier, Sir George De Lacy Evans, who contributed to the debate on reform and the abolition of purchase in the late 1850s and early 1860s. Similarly, the trio of Sir Charles Dilke, H. O. Arnold-Forster and Henry Spenser Wilkinson were of considerable importance as exponents of the 'Blue Water' school, which, in assuming the supremacy of the Royal Navy, openly challenged the War Office's obsession with invasion in the 1880s and 1890s. They, too, might publish powerful polemics, such as Spenser Wilkinson's *The Brain of an Army*, but again much depended upon the readership.

The problem was that there were all too many distractions for officers, not least social and sporting, while the dispersal of the army, and its customary divisions between regiments and arms of service, also militated against both a greater sense of professionalism and the emergence of any common military doctrine. Nonetheless, in reviewing the sometimes paradoxical relationship between the late Victorian army and technological change, it is important to look beyond the traditional view that soldiers resisted technological change and were unprepared for modern war. Far from it being a case of the fog of peace as opposed to the fog of war, the Victorian period was not one of prolonged peace for the British army, but one of constant and varying military challenges in the expanding Empire actually served only to complicate matters. Militarily, however, the *Pax Britannica* conveyed both advantages and disadvantages.

19

'Troopin'

Some years ago, Donald Headrick identified technological advances in areas such as medicine, modern weapons and communications as 'tools of Empire', which had made European expansion possible in the mid to late nineteenth century. In terms of communications, he had in mind railways, steam navigation, the electric telegraph and the submarine telegraph cable, all of which enabled imperial governments and colonial administrations alike to react more quickly to events. Apart from opening up river routes into the interior of Africa and Asia, steam navigation shrank the time taken to reach distant colonies, so that India could be reached from Britain in something between thirty and forty-five days by 1852 using the overland route across Egypt, the time dropping by about a third after the opening of the Suez Canal in 1869. For the British, in particular, this was highly significant given the sheer extent of the Empire, the periodic need to relieve regiments in far-flung imperial posts, and the likely occurrence of colonial wars necessitating hasty reinforcement.

Transport, or logistics in modern military parlance, is one of those unglamorous subjects rarely mentioned in historical accounts. Yet it was and is vital to the success or failure of operations and of grand strategy. As Winston Churchill wrote in his contemporary account of the reconquest of the Sudan in 1898, *The River War*, 'Victory is the beautiful, bright-coloured flower. Transport is the stem without which it could never have blossomed.'[1] One particularly neglected aspect of British military logistics is sea transport. Indeed, the only museum display devoted to it appears to be the imaginative section of a reconstructed troopship in Fort Siloso, the former fortification built to defend Singapore's Keppel Harbour in 1885. On Blakang Mati Island, it forms part of the Sentosa leisure entertainment complex, also incorporating the Images of Singapore Museum in the former British military hospital as well as less martial attractions such as 'Volcano Land'. By contrast, visitors to the Maritime Museum in Southampton will find no mention of the port's significance for military transportation, unless they notice that three of the forty-five ships represented on the large-scale model of the port, originally made for the New York World Fair in 1939 and depicting the port as it was in 1933–36, carry the unexplained designation 'HMT' (His Majesty's Transport).

The practice of regular trooping in peacetime was as old as the Empire itself, certainly dating back to the acquisition of Tangier in 1661, while expeditionary forces had long been sent overseas, not least in the wars of the eighteenth century and early nineteenth century, by which the 'First Empire' had been won and lost and a second established. The first large-scale transportation of an expeditionary force was arguably that of the 8000 men sent to Cartagena during the War of Jenkins's Ear in 1740, though Cromwell had dispatched a force of perhaps 9000 men to the West Indies in 1654–65. Both expeditions sailed from Portsmouth. Merchant ships including 'East Indiamen', converted warships and ships of the line were used as required for both trooping and expeditions. For much of the Victorian period, Portsmouth was the principal port for routine trooping, the Royal Navy operating its own five-strong transport fleet for the Indian Troop Service based on Portsmouth from 1860 until 1894. The trooping season extended from September to March, with two of the ships running between Portsmouth and Suez, and three operating between Suez and Bombay. To give an indication of the scale of the routine logistics of Empire, the pre-season estimate for 1868–69 was that the service would carry approximately 11,798 officers and men to India and 11,983 back from India between September 1868 and March 1869.[2] Inevitably, Kipling captured the essence of the service in 'Troopin':

> They'll turn us out at Portsmouth wharf in cold an' wet an' rain,
> All wearin' Injian cotton kit, but we will not complain.
> They'll kill us of pneumonia – for that's their little way –
> But damn the chills and fever, men, we're goin' 'ome to-day![3]

Commercial firms, however, were also involved in Indian trooping before 1860 and continued to be involved in trooping elsewhere after 1860. Trooping continued to Canada until 1871 and to the West Indies and southern Africa throughout the Victorian period. Notably involved from the commercial sector were the Bibby Line of Liverpool; the British India Line of Calcutta; Peninsular & Oriental, originally formed in Dublin in 1823; and the Union Line, which began as the Southampton Steam Shipping Company in 1853. In addition to Bibby, British India and P & O, and the Union Line, Donald Currie's Castle Line also started carrying troops in 1872, competing with the Union Line on the Cape route until the two lines merged as the Union Castle Line in March 1900, the raising of the new line's flag on the *Dunottar Castle* being cheered by troops leaving Southampton for South Africa on the Union Line's former ship, *Gaika*.

Moreover, commercial vessels still took military personnel to the East even after the navy acquired its own. Such hired transports were frequently berthed at Southampton rather than Portsmouth. Thus the future Field-Marshal Lord Roberts first sailed to India in February 1852 on the P & O steamer, *Ripon*, en route to Alexandria, crossing Egypt by the land route and continuing on the *Oriental* from Suez. Similarly, the future General Sir Richard Harrison saw off his brother's regiment to Jamaica from Southampton in June 1861, and the future General Sir Archibald Hunter also sailed from Southampton in 1875 to join his new regiment at Gibraltar.

Hired transports were preferable to the Admiralty ships, but trooping was rarely comfortable and, on occasions, also hazardous. As late as 1889 the future General Sir Hubert Gough, en route to India, recalled men, women and younger officers confined to the bowels of the ship with no port holes, the women on board having little privacy, and bathrooms shared by all the officers and their wives. Moreover, 'to reach the bathrooms we had to walk through two or three inches of very dirty water, as that deck – on which some horses were stalled – was also being swabbed down'.[4] A number of disasters occurred, the most celebrated being the loss of the *Birkenhead* on 24 February 1852 off the South African coast. With 630 on board and only three lifeboats that could be launched, the troops – drafts from a variety of different regiments – were assembled on the deck while the twenty women and children were placed on the boats. In all, 438 men drowned, their example in standing fast doing much to portray the army in a new and more favourable light in Victorian Britain. Moreover, the King of Prussia ordered the story to be read at the head of every Prussian regiment.

There were, however, other equally commendable examples of discipline in adverse circumstances such as that of 54th Foot (later the 2nd Battalion, the Dorset Regiment) on the *Sarah Sands* off Mauritius on 11 November 1857. When a fire broke out and the crew abandoned the troops and their families, the men threw powder kegs overboard to prevent any explosion, the crew then returning. Sarah Sands Day is still commemorated in the regiment's lineal descendant, the Devonshire and Dorset Regiment. Some years earlier, in 1842, men of the 64th Foot (later the 1st Battalion, the North Staffordshire Regiment) were assembled in ranks below decks and up to their knees in water to keep the *Alert* stable after it struck a rock off Nova Scotia. Curiously, two regiments retained a silver snuff-box as the only surviving pieces of mess silver from shipwrecks, the 17th Foot (later the Leicestershire Regiment) having lost the remainder in the wreck of the *Hannah* in 1840 and, somewhat earlier than our period, the 31st Foot (later the 1st Battalion, the East Surrey Regiment) in the East Indiaman *Kent* in 1825.

When the navy's own transports began to reach the end of their useful service life in the 1890s, it was decided not to replace them but to hire from the shipping companies and to relieve the pressure on Portsmouth by switching the operation of the Indian Troop Service to Southampton. Accordingly, in February 1894, no. 25 Berth in the Empress Dock was hired from the London and South West Railway Company annually from September to March at a cost of £100 per berthing vessel, this particular berth drawing twenty-five feet of water, and being chosen due to its proximity to a large shed, its railway line, and its accessibility at all stages of the tide. The storage space cost an additional £50 per annum for 2000 square feet. Additional advantages over Portsmouth was that ships would not need to be moved from the berth to coal, and it was closer to the large military hospital at Netley for the transfer of invalids.

The first ship to use the new berth was the last of the ageing naval transports, the *Jumna*, in January 1895, followed immediately by P & O's *Britannia*, which was contracted, together with the same company's *Victoria*, for six months to cover the trooping season of 1894–95. Indeed, as both ships ended up in port together, the *Britannia* had to be berthed temporarily at an additional cost of £50, a practice that became fairly frequent with either a berth at South West Quay or the

No. 3 Extension to Empress Dock being used. On a few occasions, a ship was moved to meet the convenience of the dock company as in January 1895, September 1896, March 1898, and March 1901. A reberthing scheme in 1905 saw the Indian Troop Service moved to No. 34 berth at Ocean Quay.[5]

Some indication of the usual routine for peacetime trooping from Southampton can be gauged from examples drawn from the 1898–99 season. The British India Line's *Dunera*, for example, arrived from Bombay and Queenstown on 1 December 1898, disembarking returning troops at the second berth and commencing coaling. Fresh provisions were taken on board on 5 December and the ship cleaned. It moved to the trooping berth on 7 December; embarked horses, women and children on 9 December; embarked troops on 10 December; and sailed for Queenstown on 11 December before going on to Bombay. The Admiralty's Transport Department had made innumerable adjustments to the passenger list through November and December, with more troops getting on at Queenstown and Malta, and others leaving the ship in Egypt. In addition, it carried a thousand of the new 'Burma' pattern water bottles in cases of two hundred supplied by John Pound & Co. of London on the order of Colonel Eaton Travers of the 2nd Gurkhas.

P & O's *Simla* had sailed a few days before bound for Bombay via Port Said and Aden, its outward voyage having been delayed by a late arrival in Southampton due to bad weather. It carried twenty-three officers, five wives, one child and one female servant in first class; two warrant officers – one a schoolmaster – and four children in second class; and thirty-eight NCOs, 1160 other ranks, forty-one wives and eight children in third class, the officers and men drawn from thirteen different regiments and corps. As Southampton was its last port in home waters before sailing, whereas the *Dunera* called in at Queenstown, the *Simla* was given its inspection at Southampton as required by the regulations specifying the attendance of one or two naval officers, an army officer of field rank, a second army officer, an army doctor and, if appropriate, an army vet.[6]

If Southampton only emerged as the main peacetime trooping port in 1894, it had played a significant role in the despatch of troops in wartime much earlier. In the Crimean War, for example, Portsmouth and Southampton together saw the despatch of 20,000 men for the East

by November 1854, the future Lieutenant-General Sir Gerald Graham VC
sailing from Southampton with his Royal Engineers company on P & O's
Himalaya in February 1854. P & O sold the *Himalaya* to the government
and another eleven of their ships were taken up, while the Bibby Line
provided two and the Cunard Company also provided eleven ships.
The Crimea was also the first occasion on which the new Union Line
carried troops, all five of its ships being taken up. Indeed, the first
shipment of new prefabricated wooden huts to accommodate troops
through the Crimean winter went out through Southampton in the
Line's ship, *Norman.* Similarly, some 33,166 officers and men were sent
to India as reinforcements during the Mutiny of 1857–58, 21,406 of them
between receipt of the news in England in June 1857 and November
1857.[7] One memorial to the hasty despatch of reinforcements are two
fine paintings, *Eastward Ho!* and *Home Again*, by Henry Nelson O'Neil,
the first depicting women seeing off a regiment on board a troopship
bound for the East in August 1857, the second the return. It seems,
however, that most troops left from Portsmouth.

During the Zulu War, Southampton was used for the despatch of
cavalry reinforcements to the Cape following the disaster at Isandlwana.
Alexander Tulloch, who was responsible for the embarkation arrangements as a staff officer in Southern District, recalled later that this was
especially difficult since cavalry officers 'as a rule disappeared below
deck as soon as their regiment arrived, doubtless to look after the
berthing of their men', compelling him to requisition naval personnel
to help. Using brows and lifts, Tulloch devised a method of embarking
three hundred horses in just four hours.[8] In all, eight of the twenty-one
vessels used to send reinforcements to South Africa sailed from Southampton between February and May 1879, carrying 3443 officers and men
and 955 horses, principally from the 1st Dragoon Guards, 17th Lancers,
Royal Artillery, and 90th, 91st and 94th Foot. It represented 37 per cent
of the total troops despatched and 51 per cent of the horses. Indeed, the
very first ship to sail was the Union Line's *Pretoria*, leaving Southampton
with the 91st on 19 February, having been taken up immediately on its
return from its maiden voyage, and reaching the Cape on 13 March in
record time.[9] All four of the major-generals sent out to assist Lieutenant-
General Lord Chelmsford left from Southampton, as did the Emperor
Napoleon III's son and heir, the Prince Imperial, on the Union Line's

Danube, being enthusiastically cheered on his arrival at the rail terminus and then seen off by his mother, Empress Eugénie. Subsequently, his body was brought back through Woolwich, but the Empress left from Southampton when going out to visit the death site in March 1880.

For the Egyptian campaign of 1882, Southampton despatched eleven ships between 7 and 10 August carrying 3451 officers and men and 2001 horses, principally from the 4th and 7th Dragoon Guards, 19th Hussars, Royal Artillery, Royal Engineers and 1st Royal Irish Fusiliers, representing 21 per cent of the troops and 36 per cent of the horses sent from British or Irish ports.[10] Unfortunately, while the overall figures of troops and ships are available for the two Suakin expeditions of 1884 and 1885 and the Gordon Relief Expedition of 1884–85, there is no detailed breakdown of the ports of embarkation. It would seem that of over a hundred vessels used, of which eighteen carried troops, few went from South-ampton to Suakin in 1885, though the Union Line's *Arab* did sail for Suakin from the port in February 1885, carrying command, artillery and medical staffs together with carts, wagons and ambulances. Similarly, and sadly, it is difficult to discover if any ships sailed from Southampton in the attempt to rescue its most famous military son, Charles Gordon, whose family home, to which he frequently returned, was at 5 Rockstone Place, now containing luxury apartments with but a small plaque to record its celebrated resident. It would seem that most went from Portsmouth, Liverpool, Glasgow and Woolwich.

Undoubtedly, Southampton's finest hours as an imperial port in wartime came in the South African War and the Great War. It is customarily believed that the British army performed badly in the opening months of the South African War, but the actual process of mobilisation, once the government had finally and belatedly agreed to it, was an outstanding success. To put ten thousand fighting men and all their support services into Egypt within forty days of the expedition being authorised in 1882 was remarkable enough, but the mobilisation and despatch of 112,000 regulars to South Africa between 7 October 1899 and 30 January 1900 has been characterised as an unprecedented achievement for Britain.[11] Moreover, Britain sustained a war six thou-sand miles from the home base at a time when the French had to rent shipping from Britain to invade Madagascar in 1895, the Germans were unable to contribute even a battalion to an international peacekeeping operation on Crete in 1897, and the United States experienced extreme difficulties in invading Cuba only ninety miles from its coast in 1898. Some confusion ensued as a result of the decision to break up the army corps and send some to Natal rather than concentrate all at the Cape, necessitating re-embarkation at Cape Town. Similarly, the loading of freight had been done too hastily in some cases, but it was still a remarkable achievement.

Military and naval, if not political, preparation had begun in April 1899, with meetings between the Admiralty's Transport Department headed by Rear-Admiral Sir Bouverie Clark and the Transport Division of the Quartermaster-General's Department of the War Office headed by Major John Cowans, later Quartermaster-General during the Great War, as DAQMG. The first meeting of the War Office Confidential Mobilisation Committee was held on 17 June, being reconstituted as the Army Board for Mobilisation on 8 September. New fittings for horse stalls were deemed necessary and ordered in July, but the government only authorised expenditure on such equipment on 23 September. Some thirty-five leading ship owners were then contacted confidentially on 28 September, though the Admiralty had already requisitioned two cargo vessels. The principal firms used were the Union Castle, White Star, Cunard, Allan, Leyland, Anchor and North Atlantic Lines, including such well-known large ships as the White Star's *Majestic*, the Allan Line's *Bavarian* and the Castle Line's *Kildonan Castle*. Generally, though, it was felt better to use medium-sized vessels of around 5000 tons. It should be noted, of course, that those vessels taken up required fitting out for troops and/or animals, which was carried out either by government contractors or the companies themselves. In most cases, provision was also made for more coal to enable the ships to make faster passages.

Mobilisation was finally ordered on 5 October, with the royal proclamation signed on 7 October and the War Office sending the first official requisition to the Admiralty on 9 October, requesting transport for 46,000 men and 8600 horses, representing an army corps and a cavalry division, specifying numbers to be sent to each port. The Admiralty then allocated vessels and indicated their size and the date they would become available, the allocation being made on the basis of every man having a space of eighteen inches at a mess table, though later twenty-four inches was allocated to the Imperial Yeomanry, and tonnage calculated as four tons for a man, eleven and half for a horse and three for a mule. Units were then specified and orders issued to units and railway companies accordingly, so that units could be embarked in the morning and the ship sail in the afternoon. Subsequently, there was an attempt in 1900 to persuade officers to arrive at the docks earlier so that ships could leave promptly, pilots being concerned about navigating the Needles in winter mists and darkness.

The embarkation of supporting units from the Army Service Corps and Army Ordnance Corps began on 7 October, two days before the War Office sent the formal requisition to the Admiralty. The main embarkation began on 20 October with twenty-five trains running into Southampton that day. Some 5000 men left on 20 October, followed by another 5615 on 21 October, 4864 on 22 October, and 6335 on 23 October. Approximately, 20,000 men were despatched in the first week, transports leaving at the rate of five a day. Wolseley, the Commander-in-Chief at the War Office, saw off the 2nd Brigade of 1st Division from Southampton, writing to the Queen: 'I never saw five finer Battalions, not one man under the influence of drink. When the five ships carrying those 5000 men had pushed off from the quays, the men crowding every possible part of the upper decks, sang "God Save the Queen".' [12] The first ship to leave Southampton on that day was the Castle Line's *Roslin Castle*, which reached the Cape on 9 November 1899.

Primarily, Southampton was used for infantry since, despite the experience of the Zulu War, it was felt the rise and fall of the tide not best suited to the embarkation of horses. Consequently, cavalry went mostly from Liverpool and Birkenhead, though some units also went from the Tilbury and Royal Albert Docks in London. By 17 November when mobilisation was completed, 47,081 officers and men had been despatched, comprising four infantry divisions and a cavalry division. Another four infantry divisions and a cavalry brigade, however, were embarked between 24 November 1899 and 17 February 1900, together with auxiliaries such as the City Imperial Volunteers, the Imperial Yeomanry, volunteers service companies joining regular battalions, militia and reinforcing drafts. The 6th Division, for example, was embarked between 16 December and 1 January in five ships, of which three sailed from Southampton, namely the *Gascon*, the *Tintagel Castle* and the *Gaika*. By June 1900, some 12,000 men had gone out through Southampton with over 150 vessels employed in their transport and without disrupting the port's ordinary dock work under the able direction of the Admiralty's Divisional Transport Officer, Captain Graham White, assisted by five naval officers, and the dock superintendent, John Dixon. White specially commended the American-owned Richardson, Spence & Co. for putting its plant and coal stocks at the Admiralty's disposal. Temporary stands were also erected for the handling of officers' baggage by a number of baggage agents including Thomas Cook & Son, the Army and Navy Co-operative Society and two Southampton firms, A. W. White & Co. and Hickie, Barman & Co.[13]

Among the troops were the commanders, General Sir Redvers Buller embarking at Southampton on the Castle Line's *Dunottar Castle* on 14 October, amid much rejoicing, the scene recorded by the movie cameras of the Biograph Company. Buller, in mufti, declined the civic reception offered him by the mayor but made a short speech of thanks at the head of the gangplank. As the ship sailed to the sound of 'Rule Britannia', 'For He's A Jolly Good Fellow' and 'God Save the Queen', he stood on the navigation bridge, waving his hat as the ship disappeared into a mist. Still widely popular despite his early defeats, Buller returned to Southampton to an equally enthusiastic reception on 9 November 1900, receiving the freedom of the borough from the corporation. When sent out to supersede Buller, Field-Marshal Lord Roberts also sailed from Southampton on the *Dunottar Castle*, on 23 December 1899, ultimately returning to Southampton on 3 January 1901 by way of the hospital ship *Canada*, the Isle of Wight and a visit to the Queen at Osborne. The defender of Ladysmith, Lieutenant-General Sir George White, returned to Southampton on the *Dunvegan Castle* on 14 April 1900, the town clerk reading a welcome address on behalf of the Mayor and Aldermen. Kitchener, who succeeded Roberts in the South African command, returned to Southampton on the *Orotova* on 12 July 1902 to a rapturous reception, being driven through decorated streets to the Hartley Institute, where he received the freedom of the Southampton before catching a special train to London.

By 31 May 1902, indeed, 224,394 individuals had been sent to South Africa from the United Kingdom out of a total of 423,373 landed there during the war, but there were also the remounts and stores required to sustain the campaign, a total of 459,663 animals and 1.3 million tons of stores being sent to South Africa. Most of the ships used for the carriage of remounts were chartered through Messrs Houlder Brothers, and it is clear that, despite the previous concerns over the tide, South-ampton was used for this purpose along with Queenstown and the London docks. At the end of the war, of course, the troops had to be brought home, 148,000 officers and men being brought back to England between May and October 1902, many by freighters in the course of their normal work. Not a single life was lost in terms of wartime sea transport and loss of animals was restricted to 4 per cent of horses and 1.9 per cent of mules.[14] In some respects, of course, the sea transport of the army to South Africa was purely a logistical exercise in that the Boers possessed no warships to challenge the Royal Navy's control of the sea lanes and there was no need to seize hostile shores. Thus, as suggested by Leo Amery, it was 'of the same character as troopship work in peace, but carried out on a gigantic scale'.[15]

Of a different nature entirely, therefore, was the despatch of the British Expeditionary Force to France in August 1914 and the subsequent war-time use of Southampton as the officially designated Port Number One, since there was always the risk of German submarine or surface attack on troop convoys. In the Second World War, Southampton again served as an embarkation port for the BEF in 1939–40, but the fall of France rendered it inoperable for subsequent troop convoys until the late autumn of 1944. With peace restored once more, trooping resumed from Southampton until the advent of large-scale air transport in the 1950s, the last troop ship to enter Southampton on its last voyage from the Far East being the Bibby Line's *Oxfordshire* on 18 November 1962.

It seemed unlikely that the port would ever again be used for military embarkation of any kind. Yet twenty years later, in April 1982, the unexpected occurred and a British expeditionary force sailed once more for the Falklands. Most of the Naval Task Force, including the two carriers, sailed from Portsmouth, but passenger vessels were also taken up, the *Canberra*, which sailed on 9 April, and the North Sea ferry, *Norland*, taking troops and the *Uganda* serving as a hospital ship. Moreover, the *QE2* took 5 Brigade to South Georgia to be transferred to *Canberra* and *Norland* in May. There had been no crowds at South-ampton in 1914 or 1939–40. Thus when *Canberra* returned to

Southampton, her welcome certainly rivalled anything seen at the port during the South African War. That moment serves perhaps as an appropriate epitaph to all servicemen those who have embarked or disembarked at Southampton in peace and war.

20

A Frenchman's Horse

The village green at Latimer, near Chesham, in Buckinghamshire contains a war memorial and a grave. There is nothing unusual in a war memorial on a village green, though it is not to the Great War, but to the South African War, the first war in which the deaths of ordinary British soldiers were routinely commemorated. The county as a whole raised a large and impressive obelisk on Coombe Hill, one of the highest points of the Chilterns, to its war dead in 1904. To be sure, there are some earlier Victorian monuments, such as the lion monument to the men of the 66th Foot who fell at Maiwand in 1880, erected in Reading's Forbury Gardens, or the obelisk to those of the 24th Foot who fell at Chillianwallah in January 1849 during the First Sikh War, which was erected in Chelsea's Royal Hospital Gardens in 1853. These, however, are isolated commemorative occurrences and it was only with the wider military participation which ensued during the South African War that such commemoration became routine. Indeed, the fate of many of those who fell on European battlefields such as Leipzig in 1813 and Waterloo in 1815 was to have their bones swept up in the 1820s for importation by Yorkshire-based bone grinders through Hull for the production of fertiliser.

To return to Latimer, the grave even more unusually contains the heart and ceremonial trappings of a horse which, according to the description, 'was ridden by General de Villebois-Mareuil at the Battle of Boshof, South Africa, 5 April 1900, in which the General was killed and the horse wounded'. A second inscription notes that the horse, Villebois, was brought to England by Lord Chesham in 1901 and died in February 1911. Since the memorial honours all those from the village who went to South Africa rather than just those who died, Chesham's name heads the list, but his eldest son, Charles Cavendish, is also commemorated, having been killed in action at Diamond Hill in

June 1900 with the 17th Lancers. Chesham is also remembered by a fine statue in Aylesbury Market Place, as are John Hampden and Benjamin Disraeli. There is a chance that some passers-by may recognise Hampden or Disraeli, or at least know who they were. As elusive as Graham Greene's 'Third Man', there is nothing to suggest what Chesham did to stand with Hampden and Disraeli, and it is doubtful if more than a few who attend the market will have ever heard of him. Yet, like the memorial and the grave at Latimer, the statue in Aylesbury reflects the moment when the degree of military participation in Britain itself became a harbinger of the far greater totality just a few years in the future. Of that greater participation, Chesham may stand representative.

Charles Compton William Cavendish, Third Baron Chesham, was born in 1850 and educated at Eton before being commissioned into the Coldstream Guards as an ensign-lieutenant in March 1870, transferring to the 10th Hussars three years later. An accomplished horseman, Chesham became regimental adjutant in 1876 and receive promotion to captain before transferring once more to the 16th Lancers in 1877. That same year he married Lady Beatrice Grosvenor, second daughter of the First Duke of Westminster, before retiring from the army in 1879 and succeeding his father to the title in 1882. This particular cadet branch of the family of the Dukes of Devonshire had been established at Latimer since 1615. William Cavendish had been Whig MP for Aylesbury from 1804 until killed in the Peninsular War in 1809. His brother, Charles, unsuccessfully contested Aylesbury in 1814, but was then returned for a number of other constituencies before being elected for Buckinghamshire in 1847. Elevated to the peerage in 1857 as the First Baron Chesham, he was succeeded as MP for the county by his son, William. In turn, William Cavendish succeeded as Second Baron in 1863.

The Third Lord Chesham appears to have had no interest in politics and retired from his military career to manage the family estates, extending to 12,000 acres, as well as property in London. However, he also fulfilled those duties to be expected of his rank, as magistrate, deputy lieutenant and yeomanry officer, joining the 2nd Royal Bucks Regiment of Yeomanry Cavalry in the rank of captain in July 1879. On the retirement of the commanding officer in April 1889, Chesham succeeded, though he had only been promoted to major as recently as February 1889. There were more senior officers, but one other former regular,

James Poynter, was not from the county and had accepted his majority at the same time as Chesham on the understanding that in the yeomanry 'a big man in the County will be promoted over less men and quite acquiesced in'.[1] Another out-county captain, R. Purefoy Fitzgerald, was less accommodating and, as a result of his complaints, was also promoted to major on the strict understanding he resign within one month of being gazetted. Once installed, Chesham was instrumental in having the regimental title changed to the Royal Buckinghamshire Hussar Yeomanry.

The yeomanry was one part of the auxiliary forces for home defence – the militia, yeomanry and volunteers – to escape unscathed the Cardwell reforms between 1868 and 1872. Moreover, after the passing of the Volunteer Act of 1863, the yeomanry alone remained subject to the provisions of the Volunteer Consolidation Act of 1804. As a result, few changes were effected in the yeomanry's organisation, with even minimum strengths not laid down for troops, squadrons or regiments until 1875. Artillery troops attached to some regiments, including the Bucks, were removed in 1875–76, but the now traditional eight days training a year – inclusive of two days for travel to and from the specified location – remained as the annual permanent training requirement. Often, however, the annual training was dispensed with altogether on the grounds that the force had been judged effective previously, as was the case in 1849, 1851, 1857, 1860, 1861 and 1879. Indeed, it was only in 1888 that the National Defence Act made the yeomanry liable to serve anywhere in Britain upon the embodiment of the militia.

An annual capitation grant of £1 was introduced in 1892 and, from January 1893, yeomanry regiments were paired in brigades in the expectation that brigade training would occur every three years. Brigading, however, came at the price of individual regiments losing their regular adjutants, who were now attached only to brigades, but the idea of brigade camps was then abandoned in 1898. Moreover, training was rarely realistic and the yeomanry proved highly resistant to the introduction of musketry requirements, and very much wedded to cold steel. Its strength also gradually declined to just under 12,000 officers and men in 1899. But, in many ways, the yeomanry retained its significance in local county society, so much so that it was a recognised entrée to that society. The Royal Bucks Hussars, indeed, acquired the nickname of the 'Flying Foreskins' from the number of emerging Jewish families such as the Rothschilds associated with it, though, as late as 1893, the Colonel of the Cheshire Yeomanry gave one of his tenants notice to quit on the grounds that he required them to be both Anglicans and yeomen.

When war broke out between Britain and the Boer republics in October 1899, there was little expectation that there would be any need to call on the auxiliary forces. Confidence was high and offers made by the auxiliaries to serve overseas were declined. In fact, legal difficulties prevented easy acceptance of such offers, but it is also clear that most regulars did not believe that the auxiliary forces would be of any utility. Militia battalions including the Royal Bucks King's Own Militia, more correctly the 3rd Battalion, Oxfordshire Light Infantry, were embodied in November 1899, but purely with the intention of releasing more regulars for South Africa by replacing them in garrison. What changed the situation was the shock of 'Black Week' when British forces suffered three successive defeats at Stormberg (10 December), Magersfontein (11 December) and Colenso (15 December). In addition, three British garrisons were by now besieged at Ladysmith, Kimberley and Mafeking.

The defeats renewed earlier agitation from the auxiliaries and on 16 December the Commander-in-Chief, Wolseley, accepted an offer by the Lord Mayor of London to raise what became the City Imperial Volunteers. Legislation was rushed through to enable the militia to go to South Africa as well as foreign garrison, while on 2 January 1900 the volunteer force was also invited to provide special service companies to be attached to the regular battalions of their regiments in South Africa. In the event the Royal Bucks King's Own Militia undertook garrison duty only in Ireland, but a service company drawn from the 1st Bucks Rifle Volunteers was attached to the 1st Battalion, Oxfordshire Light Infantry in South Africa.

One particular requirement identified by Sir Redvers Buller, commanding in South Africa, after his initial defeats, was the need for mounted infantry and riflemen. In October 1899 Lieutenant-Colonel A. G. Lucas of the Loyal Suffolk Hussars had suggested drawing on the yeomanry and he did so again on 14 November. Once more, the War Office rejected the idea. Following the publication of Buller's appeal for 8000 mounted men after Colenso, however, Lord Lonsdale of the Westmoreland and Cumberland Yeomanry and Chesham offered to raise 2300 yeomen. Wolseley, whose auxiliary forces staff officer was the Hon. T. F. Fremantle of the Bucks Rifle Volunteers, still opposed the suggestion, but the Under Secretary of State for War, George Wyndham, himself a Wiltshire yeoman and a friend of Chesham, took up the offer on behalf of the government.

On 19 December, therefore, Wyndham established the Imperial Yeomanry Committee consisting of Chesham, Lucas, Lonsdale, Viscount Valentia of the Oxfordshire Hussars, Ernest Beckett of the Yorkshire Hussars, Lord Harris of the Royal East Kent Yeomanry, and two retired officers. The creation of the force was announced on 24 December; formal approval by Royal Warrant following on 2 January 1900. Wyndham does not seem to have expected any more than the 2300 men first suggested by Chesham and Lonsdale, but the response proved far greater. Indeed yeomen represented only about a third of the Imperial Yeomanry as a whole, which was organised, as befitted mounted riflemen, in companies and battalions rather than squadrons and regiments. Wyndham gave the committee a free hand and a capitation grant of £25 (later £35) per man to provide clothing and equipment, and £40 to provide a horse.

Large sums were contributed by individuals. The Bucks County Fund, for example, was started by the Lord Lieutenant, Lord Rothschild, to equip all Bucks auxiliaries. By 4 January it had already raised £3047 3s. 0d. for the Imperial Yeomanry and £673 for the Volunteer Service Company, though, in reality, Rothschild had contributed £1000, other Rothschilds another £1000 and Waldorf Astor a further £1000. Lionel Walter Rothschild, who served in the Royal Bucks Hussars, purchased a machine gun and one of the Miss Rothschilds provided each man with a pipe and a pound of tobacco.

Two companies were raised in Bucks for the 10th Battalion, Imperial Yeomanry, the other two being from Berkshire and Oxfordshire. The 37th Company was raised at Buckingham and the 38th at High Wycombe, commanded respectively by Captain Walter de Winton of the Royal Bucks Hussars and Captain the Hon. William Lawson, later Third Baron Burnham, and then serving in the Scots Guards. Two subsequent companies were also raised for the 15th Battalion – the 56th and 57th Companies – though neither were commanded by local men and they were more diverse in composition than the 37th and 38th. By 30 December 1899, 101 yeomen from the Bucks Hussars and forty-three others had given in their names at Buckingham or Northampton alone, the regiment having a squadron in Northamptonshire from 1892 to 1902. Chesham set rigorous standards, testing claimed riding skills, before attesting seventy-eight men at Buckingham and seventy-one at Wycombe on 1 January 1900. H. S. Gaskell, a medical student from Peterborough, described his fellow recruits as 'the better sort of farmers, horse dealers, etc., many of whom already belonged to the existing corps of Bucks Yeomanry, with one or two tradesmen and grooms and a sprinkling of public school and University men'.[2] The largest occupational group – sixty-eight men across the two companies – comprised farmers. A total of fifty-one men were from the Royals Bucks Hussars and eighty-two were from Buckinghamshire.

The composition of the Bucks companies fits well with the national pattern of the first contingent of the Imperial Yeomanry drawn from traditional yeomanry sources or the professional middle classes. In all, 10,242 men were raised between the ages of twenty and thirty-five, and of good character, to serve for one year or the duration. It was still anticipated that the war would not last longer than a year, but it dragged on as a guerrilla conflict despite the surrender of the main Boer field army at Paardeburg in February 1900 and the capture of the capitals of both republics by June. Consequently, it was felt undesirable to hold yeomen to serving beyond a year, and a second contingent was duly raised in 1901 with the added incentive of daily pay of 5s. 0d. compared to the 1s. 3d. received by the first contingent, few of whom stayed on. The second contingent of 16,597 was not trained until it reached South Africa and proved less than satisfactory, being contemptuously referred to by the first contingent as 'yeomanry militia'.[3]

Chesham claimed 75 per cent of the second contingent had never sat a horse before they reached the Cape. Indeed, he recounted the story of seeing one man leading a horse on consecutive days. Assuming the horse must have a sore back, Chesham congratulated its cockney owner on his care. The man replied that he had simply lost his left-hand stirrup. Astonished, Chesham told him to mount on the other side, receiving an incredulous retort: 'Get along with you! Why, if I did that I'd be facing the wrong way!'.[4] As the middle class left the Imperial Yeomanry, so the working class took their place, not simply because the former declined but also partly due to an increase in domestic unemployment over the war period. A third and last contingent of 7239 men was raised in January 1902, and trained at large centres in Britain and Ireland, but the war ended before they could take any active part.

To return to the first contingent, it arrived in South Africa only after Paardeburg, the 10th Battalion having embarked at Southampton on 10 February 1900. Arriving at the Cape on 28 February, it transferred to East London, and entrained for Kimberley, where it was concentrated in March 1900. It became one of four battalions employed with Lord Methuen's column, covering the western flank of the main British advance northwards towards Bloemfontein. The four battalions were placed under Chesham's command, command of the 10th passing to the one-armed Eric Smith of the Berkshire Yeomanry. On 5 April 1900 Chesham's men became the first of the Imperial Yeomanry to see action, defeating the International Legion, fighting for the Boers under the leadership of the flamboyant Frenchman Georges Henri Anne-Marie Victor, Comte de Villebois-Mareuil, at Boshof in the Free State. Villebois-Mareuil had resigned from the French army as a colonel in 1895. Though due to be promoted to general, he wished to stay with his regiment, now the 1st Foreign Legion, and believed he was being side-lined into a provincial command for political reasons. He was given general's rank by the Boers in March 1900 and command of their International Legion.

In truth, the action at Boshof was a small affair. Trying to cut the railway line south of Kimberley, Villebois-Mareuil made the mistake of holding two kopjes at Tweefontein, some five miles outside Boshof, when his presence was discovered, whereas a Boer commander would have used his mounted mobility to retreat long before. The British dismounted attack at about 6 p.m. was directed by Chesham, who had some 750 yeomen available from the 3rd and 10th Battalions, with an additional 250 men of the Kimberley Mounted Corps. For fear of the Boers slipping away in semi-darkness, a converging attack was mounted, by which the yeomen actually risked shooting each other. There is some confusion as to whether Villebois-Mareuil was killed by a shell splinter or by a bullet, his force surrendering as the yeomen prepared to close with the bayonet. A total of ten Boers were killed, eleven wounded and a further fifty-one taken prisoner, including twenty-two Frenchmen, several Dutchmen (including Comte Pierre de Bréda), and the Russian

Prince Bagratian of Tiflis, whom Lawson claimed was really a Polish Jew from Hornditch! Another twenty or so Boers escaped. In all, British casualties amounted to just three dead and ten wounded, including the Hon. Lionel Walter Rothschild, hit in the finger by a shell splinter. One of the dead was the thirty-four-year-old Sergeant Patrick Campbell, who had enlisted in the 37th Company on 6 January 1900. His estranged wife was the celebrated actress and reputed mistress of George Bernard Shaw, Mrs Patrick Campbell.

Like Campbell, Villebois-Mareuil and his men, the names of only six of whom were known, were buried in the cemetery at Boshof on 6 April with full military honours. Regarded by the Boers and the French as something of a martyr for the cause, Villebois-Mareuil's body was reinterred at the Burgher Monument at Magersfontein in 1971. His original gravestone, for which Methuen paid, however, is still preserved in the cemetery, a lonely and dusty enclave without shade, enclosed by a wall off a side road of the town, which itself consists of little more than the main street on the road between Bloemfontein and Kimberley. It does not really seem to have changed since the Hon. Sidney Peel, serving with the 40th Company, described it as consisting of 'low, flat-roofed, whitewashed houses' dominated by a large church.[5]

Alongside Campbell and the Frenchmen lie the other two British dead, Captain Cecil Boyle of the Oxfordshire Hussars, shot through the head at the height of the action, and Second Lieutenant Arthur 'Jeb' Williams of the Sherwood Rangers, serving with the 3rd Battalion and shot through the heart just as the Boers raised the white flag. Most of the 120 graves in the cemetery are later war burials, the kind of simple plain, and rather grim, metal crosses encountered all over South Africa. The dead of the Boshof action are commemorated differently by stone headstones or monuments, though the polished marble of Campbell's looks too modern to date from the battle. The inscription on Boyle's monument is still reasonably clear but that on Williams's has all but disappeared. Another of the monuments is to Sergeant Edwin Mason Brett Bennett of the 37th Company, who died at Boshof of enteric (typhoid) on 16 May 1900. A twenty-eight year old farmer born at Beachampton, he had been working for his father at Heathencote near Towcester when he enlisted from the Royal Bucks Hussars on 1 January 1900. It is a reminder that this was the last major conflict involving

British soldiers in which far more men died from disease than battle.* Of Britain's 20,721 war dead, 13,139 (63 per cent) were victims of disease.

Following Boshof, the Bucks companies of the Imperial Yeomanry remained in the Orange Free State, operating on the flank of the British advance into the Transvaal. Time was spent on convoy work or chasing the Boer commandos of skilled opponents like Christiaan De Wet across the veldt as the war degenerated into a guerrilla conflict. In June 1900, the 10th undertook a forty-eight hour forced march to try and relieve the 13th Battalion trapped at Lindley but failed to get there in time. When sent in June to relieve another beleaguered force at Heilbron, the 10th became the 'Beecham's Pill Column', since they 'relieved without pain'.6 In August 1900, they spent nine days in pursuit of De Wet from Potchefstroom to Oliphant's Nek, only for the commandos to slip over the Nek to safety when others failed to block it. With just one day's halt, they covered an average of twenty-three miles a day on the other eight, being engaged on four days with a four-hour running fight on one of those days. When they arrived at Mafeking soon after, 40 per cent of the men were on foot, as their mounts had died or been destroyed. Their hardest action was at Hartebeestefontein in February 1901, with four dead and sixteen wounded, though most of the casualties were in the 40th Company. Not surprisingly, thoughts had turned increasingly to home and the Bucks companies returned to England in June 1901 to an elaborate county reception.

Chesham, meanwhile, had moved to Johannesburg when his brigade was broken up in November 1900 to become Inspector-General of the Imperial Yeomanry in South Africa as a whole. Lady Chesham had accompanied her husband to South Africa and, together with Lady Georgina Curzon, launched an appeal for an Imperial Yeomanry Hospital. It opened at Deelfontein in Cape Colony in March 1900 with four others subsequently established elsewhere. At Deelfontein, a total of 6057 officers and men were treated during the war, of whom 2937 were

---

* In 2000 the author was privileged to be invited to give the address at a service for the rededication of a fine bronze plaque in Maids Moreton Church near Buckingham in memory of another Bucks Hussar who died of enteric in South Africa. Fred Dancer, whose family still farms Upper Farm, was just twenty-one when he died at Mafeking in November 1900.

Imperial Yeomen. Lady Chesham raised over £174,000 and Chesham himself was also active in organising a South African Imperial Yeomanry Fund for those Bucks Hussars in distress from sickness or other causes as a result of war service. On his return from South Africa, Chesham was knighted, promoted to Major-General and made Inspector–General of Imperial Yeomanry in Britain in April 1902, the force at home having also been confusingly renamed Imperial Yeomanry in April 1901. The change in nomenclature was part of a series of reforms, which included extending its training to eighteen days a year, of which fourteen were obligatory, and imposing a three year minimum term of enlistment, and a new squadron establishment. Now all yeomen were to be converted to a mounted infantry role, though in the event, many resisted the change and the sword was restored for war service in 1913. The yeomanry, however, was to enter the Great War in much healthier shape. It had often been accused of being an aristocratic sham prior to the South African War, but it had done as well as the many colonial contingents that also served in large numbers, as Chesham had always believed it would.

Chesham was the first member of the auxiliary forces to achieve general rank. Some regulars had criticised Chesham for his lack of military expertise in South Africa and Lawson also found him 'rather an old woman about the soldiers, fussy and faddy'.[7] That care, however, was much appreciated by his men, one writing home: 'His Lordship seems to possess every quality that a good soldier wants and it is a real pleasure to all ranks to carry out his orders, because it is felt that he knows exactly how to handle men and get the best out of them without that bustling which is so irritating. We all recognise that we could not serve under a better chief.'[8] Indeed, on returning to Buckingham, where his health was proposed at yet another celebration banquet, Chesham characteristically insisted that all those yeomen present should also stand, for it was only with them and as one of them that he would accept the honour. Given the nature of the man, it was not therefore strange that he should have brought Villebois-Mareuil's horse back to England and, presumably, to leave instructions that its remains be interred at Latimer. By that time, however, Chesham himself was dead, his neck broken in a hunting accident in November 1907. He may now be all but unknown, but he deserves his statue in Aylesbury – unveiled in 1910 by Lord Roberts – no less than Hampden and Disraeli.

21

A Question of Totality

How many followers of Liverpool Football Club, one wonders, know why their most celebrated stand is called 'The Kop'? It is named after Spion Kop, the battle in Natal in January 1900 during Redvers Buller's attempt to relieve Ladysmith, in which Lancashire regiments in particular took heavy casualties. The naming of a football stand conveys something of the popular impact of a war which was truly the forerunner of the far greater conflict to come in 1914.

Over the last twenty years, historians have come increasingly to recognise the often pivotal role played by war and conflict in historical development, a theme characterised by Leon Trotsky's observation that war was the 'locomotive of history'. In particular, the concept of 'total war' has become generally familiar as a means of describing the nature of the two world wars of the twentieth century, and also as a means of differentiating them from other conflicts. The term itself originated towards the end of the First World War, being associated primarily with the German First Quartermaster-General, Erich Ludendorff; the French Prime Minister, Georges Clemenceau; the French writer, Léon Daudet; the German combat veteran, Ernst Jünger; and the Italian theorist of airpower, Giulio Douhet.

In its modern sense, total war conveys a linkage between war and social change, and is most associated with the analytical framework postulated by Arthur Marwick in the 1960s and early 1970s. The concept of total war as a determinant of major change had a profound histo-riographical impact. The interpretation of the two world wars as marking a significant discontinuity with the past, however, has been frequently challenged. So, too, has Marwick's apparent contention that, even where change might have been attributable to longer-term evolutionary trends, total war was likely to accelerate the pace of changes already occurring. It is clear, of course, that total war is a relative concept since, as an absolute akin to Karl von Clausewitz's concept of absolute war, it was unrealisable until the development of an instantaneously destructive weapon at the very end of the Second World War. In any case, no state has yet been able totally to subordinate all civilian needs to those of the military. Like universal conscription, wartime mobilisation is invariably partial.

It is also the case that historians of earlier conflicts have suggested that warfare prior to 1914 was not limited, either in terms of the means available to belligerents or of the perceived erosion of the often fragile barrier separating soldiers from civilians. The period of incipient European warfare between 1648 and 1789 could be regarded as limited only when compared with the Thirty Years War which preceded it, and the 'new totality' of the Napoleonic Wars that followed it. Compared to the twelve years of total war in the twentieth century, France was involved in major wars for a total of sixty-four years in the seventeenth century, fifty-two years in the eighteenth, and thirty-two years in the nineteenth. In the case of the subjects of the Habsburgs, it was seventy-seven years of warfare in the seventeenth century, fifty-nine years in the eighteenth, and twenty-five years in the nineteenth.[1]

Nor was it the case that these supposed 'limited' wars were confined to Europe. Both the French Revolutionary and Napoleonic Wars and the Seven Years War have been characterised as the 'real' First World War. Certainly, prior to 1914, the British had used the term 'The Great War' to describe the great struggle with France between February 1793 and June 1815, a period of twenty-two years of warfare with just two short intervals – the fourteen months of the Peace of Amiens, and the eleven months between Napoleon's abdication and his return from Elba. Indeed, it is almost certainly the case that there was a higher proportion of the British male population under arms during the Napoleonic Wars than in either world war, and that British losses were higher in terms of the proportion of men under arms.

American historians, as one might expect, have also pushed back the notion of total war to embrace not only the American Civil War but even the American War of Independence. More recently, there has been a tendency to recast this particular debate in terms of 'people's war' rather than total war, thus embracing both the War of Independence and the French Revolutionary and Napoleonic Wars. Starting with the elder Moltke's declaration in 1890 that 'The age of cabinet's war is behind us, now we only have people's war', a recent collaboration between American and German historians has further refined the American Civil War and the Franco-Prussian War as 'industrialised people's war'. In this way some of the undoubted difficulties of describing the Franco-Prussian War in the same terms as the Civil War are apparently solved.[2]

Without arriving at any greater acceptance of an agreed definition of total war, this collaboration has usefully focused attention on the varying ways in which limitation of military violence has broken down as a departure point for the analysis of totality. The process has now been taken a stage further by a second American-German collaboration focusing on the period between 1871 and 1914, in which particular consideration is given to the German campaigns in their African colonies between 1904 and 1908, and to the bitter guerrilla war which followed American occupation of the Philippines between 1898 and 1902. A concept emerges of 'unlimited wars of pacification', which incorporated elements of totality, but which represented only a variation in methods applied previously elsewhere. Significantly, the examples cited are the Spanish campaign on Cuba between 1896 and 1898 and, of course, the British campaign in South Africa during the guerrilla phase of the conflict following the fall of Pretoria. Collectively, the results of such colonial campaigns are interpreted as preparing nations psychologically for dehumanising the enemy. Indeed, it has now been argued that 'total war' in the twentieth century was no more than 'colonial warfare writ large'.[3]

The context of this comparison between colonial warfare and total war is that of the degree of violence involved in pacification rather than the extent of industrial mobilisation. Nonetheless, it is worth considering how the South African War fits into the pattern, not only of the British experience of war, but also of the emergence of totality in modern war. While criticised and, indeed, subsequently modified by its own author, Marwick's celebrated 'four-tier model' of total war is at least a useful starting-point for such an analysis. This suggested that a total war was one in which there was enhanced destruction and disruption on an unprecedented scale; the emergence of a testing challenge to the existing social and political structures of states and societies; greater participation in the context of the total mobilisation of the state's resources; and a cataclysmic socio-psychological impact upon existing attitudes and values. The focus here being purely on the British experience, the impact of the war upon either Afrikaner or African society will not be considered.

Turning first to the scale of the war and the nature of the challenge faced, as well as being the greatest conflict ever waged in southern Africa, the South African War was by far the largest conflict involving Britain between 1815 and 1914. Between October 1899 and January 1900, Britain despatched some 112,000 regulars to South Africa. By the end of the war, Britain had deployed over 448,000 men from Britain and the Empire, and also employed perhaps 120,000 blacks and coloureds in auxiliary roles. In contemporary context, this was still not that great a scale of mobilisation. Yet, for Britain, it was clearly far more than simply the 226th colonial campaign fought since the Queen's accession.

Rather than costing the British government no more than £10,000,000 for a three or four month campaign utilising a maximum of 75,000 men, as originally expected, the war lasted thirty-two months and cost £230,000,000. In 1902 this represented 14.4 per cent of net national income, a proportionate cost exceeding that of the first eight months of the Great War, which represented only 12.6 per cent of net national income. The war contributed significantly to government expenditure as a proportion of GNP, rising from 9 per cent in 1890 to 15 per cent during the war, before declining to 13 per cent by 1910. The National Debt increased by £160,000,000, reaching its highest point since 1867. This was far more costly than any of the other wars during the Queen's reign. Both the Zulu War and the First Boer War had cost about £5,000,000 and even the Crimean War only about £68,000,000, while the recent reconquest of the Sudan between 1896 and 1898 had been the cheapest campaign on record at a cost to the British Treasury of under 800,000 Egyptian pounds.

It must be recognised, however, that the unexpected war costs did not create a fiscal crisis, although adding considerably to steadily rising national expenditure. The market could be sensitive to events in South Africa. Thus the news that Buller had withdrawn from Spion Kop in January 1900 resulted in the London markets becoming 'flat' and the Manchester Stock Exchange being plunged into depression. Nonetheless, while it is a little difficult to disentangle the recouping of the cost of war from subsequent expenditure on Liberal social reforms after 1906, it was met largely from revenue and short-term loans. This still involved the largest increase in direct taxation prior to 1914, with income tax rising from 8*d*. in the pound to 1*s*. 3*d*. in the pound, although this did not involve a substantial increase in the numbers paying tax as was to be the case during the Great War. Duties were increased on tobacco and tea and a new duty imposed upon imported grain. The loans raised were also sufficient to damage British credit, with the addition of a temporary adjustment in the Bank Rate from 3 to 6 per cent to compensate for the potential loss of gold supplies from the Rand. The Sinking Fund was also suspended. In the longer term, both the Unionist government and its Liberal successor sought not only to reduce military expenditure but also defence commitments through securing new international arrangements. Britain entered into an alliance with Japan in 1902, and reached rapprochement with France in 1904 and Russia in 1907, though these agreements also reflected wider security concerns than simply the difficulties encountered in South Africa.[4]

While the financial cost of the war could be accommodated, a degree of economic mobilisation was required in order to meet the severe shortages of shells and heavy guns experienced by the British army in South Africa. Already by 20 November 1899 there was only eight weeks' supply of .303 ammunition left and the supply of shells had been exhausted even before that. British firms were capable of producing only 2,500,000 rounds of .303 ammunition a week when the demand exceeded three million rounds. Sir Henry Brackenbury threatened to resign as Director-General of Ordnance in December 1899 unless there was a rapid improvement in the provision for artillery and shells, remarking in his memorandum of 15 December 1899 that Britain was 'attempting to maintain the largest Empire the world has ever seen with armament and reserves that would be insufficient for a third class military power'.[5]

The programme finally agreed with the Treasury fell short of Brackenbury's requirements, but it was still the case that in 1900 the Director of Army Contracts was purchasing in a month supplies which would have been regarded previously as sufficient for twenty years. In some cases, the arms manufacturing companies were still two years behind completion of orders by May 1901. Not only were the government-owned ordnance factories severely stretched but private manufacturing concerns in Britain were also pushed to the limit of their capacity. Moreover, firms like Vickers and Armstrong's were regarded as the leading technological concerns of the day. Unfortunately, since the war ended before an even greater economic mobilisation became necessary, the lessons were not absorbed. Thus the Murray Committee of 1906–7 concluded, in a spirit of continued economy, that government ordnance factories should be cut back and that the private sector could supply any wartime needs in the future.

Instead of the modest casualties anticipated, the British and imperial forces suffered almost 22,000 dead, the majority from disease. To place the loss of British lives in context, F. W. Hirst, a Pro-Boer opponent of the war prominent in the League of Liberals against Aggression and Militarism, used figures produced by the *Manchester Guardian* to point out after the First World War that, compared to the 5774 actual combat deaths in South Africa, a total of 7125 Britons had died in road accidents in 1933 alone, with a further 216,401 injured.[6] Of course, this was not how it appeared at the time when such casualties were unprecedented within recent memory. The British army had lost over a hundred men killed in a single action only twice since 1857: at Isandlwana and Maiwand. The numbers killed or died of wounds totalled 102 at the Modder River, 205 at Magersfontein, 171 at Colenso, 348 at Paardeburg, and 383 at Spion Kop. Such, indeed, was the effort and cost required to subdue no more than 78,000 Boers that contemporaries feared for the very future of the British race amid the apparent evidence of national physical deterioration.

More will be said of the issue of national deterioration later, but it suitably illustrates the sense in which the war was regarded as necessary to the survival of the Empire. It is apparent that most of the Cabinet believed, at least until August 1899, that British aims could be achieved without war. There was a clear reluctance to undertake the most elementary of military preparations until absolutely necessary. Faced with the unwelcome news on 12 August that it would take £1,000,000 to reduce the timescale for mobilising the army corps from four months to three, the Cabinet declined to spend money, which as the Colonial Secretary, Joseph Chamberlain, explained, could not be recovered without war. The reinforcement of Natal by ten thousand men was not agreed until 8 September and mobilisation only finally commenced on 7 October, four days before the Boers invaded Natal. Similarly, the City was confident that war was not imminent when Parliament broke up for its summer recess on 9 August. Parliament itself was not recalled until 17 October.

Yet, whatever the unwillingness to confront the possibility of actual hostilities in the summer and autumn of 1899, the risk of conflict was never entirely ruled out. Moreover, there was an overriding totality of aim in terms of achieving the supremacy in southern Africa deemed essential – by those like Chamberlain and Milner – for the consolidation of British imperial unity and power, the frustration of the efforts of European rivals to infiltrate the region, and the safeguarding of the route to India. This aim did not require actual annexation of the Transvaal, merely the certainty of a cooperative government. In the longer term, this is what the post-war settlement achieved with the restoration of self-government in 1907.

In the shorter term, however, the hostility of Kruger precluded such a solution and, once the war began, a policy of annexation was adopted. Moreover, once the war became prolonged, the Boers were increasingly cast in the role of 'the other' with a new intensity given to the already prevailing image of Afrikaner society as backward and uncivilised. The controversies over alleged Boer abuse of white flags and use of dum-dum bullets, which the British government refused to allow to be used by British troops in South Africa, accentuated the process of dehumanisation. In such circumstances, it became easier to adopt what Campbell-Bannerman memorably characterised as 'methods of barbarism', though these were no more than standard pacification techniques as applied to uncivilised opponents. It also became easier to view the death rates in detention camps as resulting primarily from the Boers' own insanitary habits. In effect, the Boers became viewed as just another native opponent.

There is the paradox that, at the same time that they frequently despised the conduct and character of their enemy, British soldiers could also find much to praise in a rural society which accorded with many of their own values. Indeed, many leading soldiers not only displayed a distaste for a war conceivably being fought to benefit Jewish capitalists, but also increasingly advocated a compromise peace. Some were uneasy with the methods being used against Boer guerrillas. Kitchener was hardly squeamish in his prosecution of the war, but he and his closest advisers, such as Ian Hamilton, were instrumental in forcing through a far more magnanimous peace than Milner would have imposed. At the same time, Milner himself feared the long-term political consequences of the application of martial law by the military authorities in Cape Colony.

In fact, the opponents were, of course, white. Consequently, though there were mixed views on the potential employment of Indian troops, they were not deployed because, as Chamberlain made clear to the Commons in August 1901, it was regarded as 'bad policy' in the circumstances of South Africa. Indeed, one justification for the concentration camps was to protect Boer women from native depredations. Though a convenient cover for what was regarded as military necessity, this perhaps gives a slightly different complexion to J. F. C. Fuller's well-known and improbable description of the conflict as the 'last of the gentleman's wars'. Subsequently, Fuller was to characterise the war as one of the 'roots of armageddon'.

Conceivably as many as 30,000 of the 120,000 Africans used by the British army were armed. Fear of the very kind of social revolution Chamberlain and others wished to avoid, but which was provoked by the active encouragement of African resistance to the Boers, played a role in the erosion of Boer morale. The methods employed by Roberts and Kitchener in the guerrilla phase of the war, while a violation of the accepted conventions of war as recently codified at The Hague in July 1899, but not signed by the Boer republics, fell short of the total destruction of the enemy implied by total war. They were certainly not new. Not only do they bear comparison with Cuba and the Philippines, but also with Union measures against Confederate guerrillas in the American Civil War and German measures against *francs-tireurs* in the closing stage of the Franco-Prussian War.

There are similar paradoxes in purely military terms. There were certainly many modern elements to the war with the use of railways, steam tractors, aerial reconnaissance by balloon, the telegraph, electric illumination, breech-loaders, smokeless powder, blockhouses, wire entanglements, and entrenchment. Indeed, as Sir Frederick Maurice was later to write, the British army 'was dealing, as no European army has yet done, with the new conditions of war' amid what G. F. R. Henderson characterised as the 'second tactical revolution' induced by smokeless powder, repeating rifles and quick-firing artillery.[7] Equally, there was still a reliance upon horses, mules and oxen for transport. Similarly, while the army was prepared to embrace X-rays, the handling of the outbreak of bubonic plague in Cape Town in 1901 demonstrated that it was not yet prepared to adopt what has been described as the 'talisman of modernity', namely bacteriology, or inoculation.[8] It is at least some defence of the conditions in the concentration camps to acknowledge that the British army was no better at preserving the lives of its own men from disease.

Rather like the First World War, the South African War is best regarded as a transitional military conflict. The war did seem to suggest that firepower was the most decisive factor in warfare and that man-oeuvre was required to avoid the destructive defensive power of modern weapons. Through the perceived reluctance of officers and men to face modern firepower on occasions in South Africa, however, there was also a new emphasis upon morale and the offensive spirit. The success of manoeuvre, moreover, would equally rely upon the offensive power of modern weapons. Even for the cavalry, the lessons were not as clear-cut as often supposed since, in many instances, sword and lance had been just as effective as carbine. Indeed, the military lessons were ambiguous, particularly when viewed alongside those of the Russo-Japanese War, enabling different commentators to pick and choose examples to fit their own perceptions.

Turning to the question of participation, if the scale and intensity of the war did not require the kind of economic and industrial mobilisation associated with total war, the mobilisation of manpower was still sig-nificant. It needs to be borne in mind that this was the first large-scale war Britain experienced within the context of the emergence of a mass urban-based industrial society. Since the Reform and Redistribution Act of 1884, some 60 per cent of adult males enjoyed the franchise. Moreover, it was a relatively literate society exposed to a modern mass media characterised by the launching in 1896 of Harmsworth's *Daily Mail* as the first half-penny daily newspaper, the first demonstration of the moving film image by the Lumière brothers in the same year, and the introduction of the pocket Kodak in 1897.

It was also a militaristic society, saturated, 'with the images, advertising and propaganda of Empire'.⁹ School, popular literature, the illustrated periodicals and music hall all contributed to the process. By 1898, moreover, conceivably 22.4 per cent of the entire male population of the United Kingdom and Ireland aged between seventeen and forty had some current or previous military or quasi-military experience in youth organisations, auxiliary forces or the army itself.

Despite the conclusions expressed by J. A. Hobson concerning working-class enthusiasm for the war, modern historians of the left have invariably questioned the extent to which imperialism penetrated the British working class, portraying the 'jingo crowd' as essentially lower middle-class youths. In these terms, the excessive reactions of Mafeking Night on 18 May 1900 become a simple exercise in collective relief, in which the working class acquiesced in recognition of the opportunity for having a good time. Similarly, wartime recruitment into the army and into special wartime creations such as the City Imperial Volunteers and the Imperial Yeomanry are portrayed initially as middle-class responses with a subsequent larger working-class presence due not to growing war enthusiasm among the latter, but to difficulties in the labour market. It has been argued that the displacement of the middle-class by working-class elements in the second and third contingents of the Imperial Yeomanry as a result of trade depression.

The logic of such an interpretation is that the Unionist triumph in the 'Khaki Election' in September 1900 was also due more to divisions among the Liberals, who did not even contest 143 seats, than to the appeal of jingoism and a popular patriotic war. Indeed, it is argued that the election was marked by voter apathy, the only real passion being experienced in the sixty-four seats with pro-Boer candidates, of which the Unionists took only twelve. This interpretation of the war, however, as unpopular among the working class has been largely discredited.¹⁰

It is true that public interest in the war fluctuated, the peril facing the European legations in Peking taking the war off the front pages in the summer of 1900. If, however, there was less of note after the fall of the Boer capitals, the national press still returned to the war in December 1900, the *Daily Mail* urging one of its correspondents to increase his coverage due to the public demand. Soldiers' letters were an increasingly important supplement to correspondents' despatches, and the regional press had never lost its interest in the activities of local regiments, volunteer service companies and Imperial Yeomanry companies.

Recruitment into the regular army brought in a higher number of working-class recruits than would have been normal, with a 'massive rise in enlistment in 1900 from those groups that had traditionally filled the ranks in peacetime'. Additional working-class recruitment over the war years may have reached over 72,000 men. The overwhelmingly working-class militia also largely volunteered for overseas service, fifty-nine battalions serving in South Africa, six in the Mediterranean, three on St Helena and the remainder in garrison in Britain and Ireland. Those accepted for the volunteer service companies and the Imperial Yeomanry were more a reflection of the physical fitness of the middle class than an unwillingness on the part of the working class to enlist.

The City of London Volunteers was unrepresentative of the volunteer movement as a whole in that the so-called 'class corps' of the metropolis, from which the City of London Volunteers was largely raised, had continued to reflect the original middle-class composition of the volunteers from the 1860s rather than the dependence upon artisans that now characterised the majority of the volunteer units in the country. On the other hand, the composition of the volunteer service companies did reflect the bias towards artisans in the volunteer force as a whole. To dwell upon the nature of working-class participation in the volunteer units that went to South Africa, however, is to miss the point that the volunteer movement was far more representative of society than the regular army precisely because it did embrace elements of the middle classes, together with those artisans who, because they were in receipt of regular wages, would never have contemplated service in either the regular army or the militia.

The response to the call for volunteer service companies and the Imperial Yeomanry was very significant given the unrepresentative nature of the regular army, and what might be regarded as the non-active participation of the middle classes and artisans in the defence of empire. Indeed, there was a resurgence of middle-class enthusiasm for the volunteers. The volunteer force at home increased its strength by over 58,000 men in 1900 and 1901 and the home yeomanry also raised fifteen new regiments before the end of the war, some in counties which had not previously had a yeomanry presence. Bearing in mind that volunteers were men in regular employment, it is remarkable that over 19,000 served in South Africa with the active service companies (inclusive of the City of London Volunteers) while the Imperial Yeomanry raised 34,078 men for South Africa in the three contingents. In fact, the social composition of the active service companies was so mixed as to suggest that class is not very relevant to a universally popular response to the war.

New, quasi-military youth organisations also emerged, including the Lads' Drill Association and the Boys Empire League. National Rifle Clubs were also stimulated by the war, Salisbury leading the call for their establishment in May 1900. At the end of the war, however, there was a predictable loss of men from the volunteers, 1902 being the worst year in the history of the volunteer force with a net decrease of almost 20,000 men. In all, it is estimated that 14.2 per cent of the male population of the United Kingdom between the age of eighteen and forty was in uniform during the war. Again, to place this in context, during the First World War, some 22.1 per cent of the male population of the United Kingdom passed through the ranks of the British army.[11]

Other historians have cast doubt on whether it was possible for the working class to be in any sense immunised from the prevalence of imperial propaganda and the creation of a genuine sense of national unity during the war. Contemporary commentators like Hobson could hardly have misinterpreted the everyday evidence of their eyes. Thus the founder of the Social Democratic Federation, H. M. Hyndman, commented that poor districts of London displayed far more patriotic bunting and decorations than the West End during the war.

In addition, of course, the war generated new propaganda in terms of music hall songs, commemorative pottery and other souvenirs, cigarette cards, board games, patriotic buttons, plays and picture postcards. Some ten million patriotic buttons had been sold by June 1900 alone: the most popular pictured Baden Powell, of which four million were sold; followed by 1,200,000 of Redvers Buller; a million of George White; and 750,000 of Roberts. War featured significantly in new boys' journals such as *Boys' War News* and *Boys' Realm*, while the existing *Chums*, first published in 1892, also became particularly associated with war themes. Of the boys' journals, indeed, only the *Boys' Own Paper* ignored the war, the Religious Tract Society which had founded it in 1879 being influenced by Baptists' anti-war sentiment. Alongside the new journals and the new youth movements, new imperial propaganda agencies also appeared such as the Victoria League and the Imperial South Africa Association.

There was, too, the infant cinema. The war gave the cinema its 'first great opportunity to prove its value in presenting "actuality" material'. Fr example, British Biograph's film of Buller arriving at Cape Town, filmed on 31 October 1899, was shown in London's Palace Theatre on 21 November, dramatically increasing the audience. The company itself increased its profits by 52 per cent over the first six months of 1900. There were also, of course, a great many faked films, often shot on Hampstead Heath, and even a faked newsreel of the signing of the peace at Vereeniging, but these are still significant in terms of their propaganda value and their evidence of the demands of the viewing public.

At Madame Tussaud's there were tableaux of such events as Cronje's surrender at Paardeburg, while the entertainment entrepreneur, Imrie Kiralfy, staged 'Briton, Boer and Black in South Africa' at Olympia in December 1899 and Joseph Poole's new myriorama displayed panoramic battle paintings in a show entitled 'Greater Britain – Savage South Africa'. Also under the title of 'Savage South Africa', another show, created by Frank Fillis and promoted by Kiralfy, which included ten Boer families, toured northern England in 1900. Manchester's Free Trade Hall enjoyed a photographic exhibition billed as 'The War Boerograph' and the siege of Ladysmith and the battle of Paardeburg featured in George Jennison's 'pyrodramas' at Manchester's Belle Vue Gardens in 1900 and 1902 respectively, with the siege of Mafeking featuring in 1908. The annual Royal Tournament began a celebrated field gun competition, which endured until becoming a victim of New Labour's disdain for tradition in its very centenary year.

War charities are also significant with the numerous funds for the equipping of local military units, but also offering more general assistance for veterans. The existing Soldiers and Sailors Families Association, founded in 1883, raised £1,000,000 for the relief of dependants of men serving in South Africa, while over two thousand disabled veterans were assisted by the Soldiers and Sailors Help Society, founded in 1899 by Princess Christian, whose son was a noted victim of wartime disease. The celebrated Absent Minded Beggars Fund begun by the *Daily Mail* in October 1899 raised at least £250,000, funding a hospital at Alton in Hampshire. The *Daily Telegraph* had its own fund, while others included the Lord Mayor's Fund, to which many regional newspapers subscribed their own collections. At a local level in Buckinghamshire, war charities included the Darktown Charity Organisation at Wolverton, and the *Buckingham Express* Relief Fund for the north of the county. Villagers at Whitchurch contributed £11 0s. 3d. to the national Transvaal War Fund. Perhaps the best-known gift to wartime servicemen was the Queen's Chocolate Box.

The role of the press, to which reference has already been made, in creating and sustaining war enthusiasm was, of course, considerable. In some respects, the public had been prepared for war by the careful manipulation of the press by Milner, a former journalist on the very title, the *Pall Mall Gazette*, which had pioneered in Britain many of the techniques of the new American tabloid-style journalism. Chamberlain was also well aware of the significance of cultivating public opinion, foreign and imperial policy having been an issue of abiding public interest at since at least the late 1870s. A total of 140 correspondents representing forty-seven different newspapers and periodicals from Britain and the Empire were theoretically entitled to the Queen's South Africa Medal. Of these, twenty-two represented Reuters; thirteen the *Morning Post*; eleven *The Times*; and ten the *Daily News*. Edgar Wallace of the *Daily Mail* did not receive the medal after his critical reports on the conduct of the war. At one point, *The Times* had twenty correspondents in South Africa.

Three entirely new illustrated weekly periodicals appeared in January 1900 – the first to be launched since 1842 – including the *Sphere*. A whole series of popular illustrated histories began to appear during the war itself such as H. W. Wilson's *With the Flag to Pretoria*, originally a weekly part-work from Harmsworth commencing in March 1900. Others included *Khaki in South Africa*, *The Transvaal War Album*, *Cassell's History of the Boer War* and Louis Creswicke's *South Africa and the Transvaal War*. The celebrated American naval historian Alfred Thayer Mahan concluded his *The Story of the War in South Africa* in July 1900, while the analysis of an equally distinguished military commentator, Spenser Wilkinson's *Lessons of the War*, appeared even earlier in March 1900. In 1900, indeed, the *United Service Magazine* had already reviewed twenty-seven books on the war and reviewed a further seventy-one before the war's end. Over 1100 artists, sculptors, medallists and engravers produced work related to the war world-wide. Over sixty of them exhibited at the Royal Academy alone and there were almost continuous exhibitions of work in galleries run by the illustrated press.

Anti-war demonstrations were less likely to be broken up in 1901 and 1902, but this fate still befell David Lloyd George's meeting in Birmingham in December 1901. Moreover, the tide in favour of Unionist candidates was still evident in municipal elections throughout the war, the swing to the Unionists being essentially an urban phenomenon of the unskilled and semi-skilled. The anti-war movement, by contrast, had little coherence, with only the Baptists really showing a united front, although it has been argued that Methodism turned against imperialism as a result of the war. Most leading clerics supported the war, as did most leading intellectuals in the universities. Most feminists opposed the war, but again, in a precursor of the Great War, many British women took on a humanitarian role in nursing or in the concentration camps. The Pro-Boers were effectively marginalised.

An assumption that the war was largely a popular one is reinforced in many respects by its social and psychological impact. Clearly, this was not a war which altered the status within British society of the labouring classes or of women. It had been anticipated that at least 15,000 officers and men might be induced to stay in South Africa after the war in the constabulary, civil service and railways, and that a further 140,000 men might be needed as settlers or mine workers. In the event, fewer than two thousand men could be persuaded either to stay or to move to South Africa, since capital was not made available. The settlement scheme was bedevilled by slow administration, and unforeseen drought and cattle fever.

Nor did the war have the same resonance for British nationalism and identity as it did for Australian, Canadian and even Afrikaner identity. It did, however, have a definite cultural impact, although in what might be termed traditional terms rather than any sense being modernist. Mention has been made already of the effect of the war upon popular song and art and, indeed, of the renaming of football ground ends. There was also a considerable amount of war poetry generated by the war reflecting the development of literacy in Britain since the 1870 Education Act.

Moreover, the war did generate substantial administrative reform so far as the army was concerned, though this should also be seen in the context of wider security fears, and it had a profound psychological impact in the growing concern with the apparent deterioration of the imperial race. One manifestation was the article by the journalist Arnold White, in the *Weekly Sun*, pointing out that three out of every five men who came forward to enlist in Manchester between October 1899 and July 1900 had been rejected as unfit for military service. White followed this with a pamphlet, *Efficiency and Reform*, giving actual figures for Manchester of 8000 out of 11,000 men rejected. The theme was also taken up by Major-General Sir Frederick Maurice in the *Contemporary Review* in January 1902 under the pseudonym, 'Miles'. Maurice's concern had been prompted originally by his chairing of a lecture at the Royal United Service Institution in October 1899 by Lieutenant-Colonel C. M. Douglas, brigade surgeon in the Northern District. Maurice and the rest of the audience had been outraged at that time by Douglas's assertion that the 'army of the past had many blackguards in it no doubt but it had fewer degenerates'.[12] The experience of the war changed his mind, a second article appearing under his own name in January 1903.

The concern prompted the establishment of the Royal Commission on Physical Training in Scotland in 1902 and, especially, the Interdepartmental Committee on Physical Deterioration in September 1903. The evidence presented to the former included the claim by Dr Thomas Savill of the British College of Physical Education that the war had been 'lost' because Boer snipers had better eyesight than British regulars. The report of the Interdepartmental Committee in July 1904 was hardly comforting, despite its declaration that the physique of army recruits was not necessarily an accurate representation of the nation as a whole. Its recommendations included a range of ideas for school medical inspection, school meals, better distribution of milk, child care instruction for mothers and so on.

Faced with the overall cost of the war, the Unionist government did not respond and also suspended any consideration of old-age pensions, but the Liberal government did take up some of the recommendations after 1906. Indeed, it is generally accepted that the provision of school meals in 1906 and school medical inspection in 1907 was a direct result of the war. The war also gave added stimulus to social investigation of the condition of the working class, as evinced by Charles Booth's study of London's poor, published in 1902, and Seebohm Rowntree's study of York in 1901. Similarly, it gave new impetus to existing attempts to improve the welfare of mothers and children, the 1902 Midwives Act being a particular example. Generally, therefore, it is argued that the war did see the tentative beginning of the welfare state.

A new interest in eugenics and national efficiency was at the back of such new manifestations of concern as the National Service League, the National Social Purity Crusade, the Aliens Act of 1905 and, of course, the Boy Scouts in 1907. British soldiers were prominent in the debate, the experience of the war having led to a reassertion among them of rural values and the need to obtain better and healthier recruits from urban areas. The Social Darwinist military writer Colonel F. N. Maude believed that a healthier nation would be better prepared in terms of morale to bear heavier casualties in future wars, remarking that, in 1899, the country 'did not know that bloodshed was a usual consequence of the armed collision of combatants. Hence, the outbreak of hysteria with which they received the news of our casualties'.[13]

The extent of participation by volunteers and the involvement of the British public in the war, albeit at a distance, meant that it also had an impact on what might be termed the popular memory, signposting the effect of the First World War. Prior to the South African War, it was unusual in Britain to commemorate individual private soldiers. It was the sense of national involvement in the South African War which changed this. In fact, over nine hundred Boer War memorials were erected in Britain, Sir James Gildea producing a record of many of them in 1911. As in the aftermath of the Great War, leading sculptors were involved, such as Sir William Hamo Thorneycroft, who designed the memorials at Durban and Manchester; Sir George Frampton, who contributed those at Radley School and Bury; and Sir William Goscombe John who designed that to the King's Regiment in Liverpool. Many were striking, such as the obelisk on Plymouth Hoe and that on the highest point of the Chilterns at Coombe Hill in Buckinghamshire.

The memory of the war was preserved in other ways. In Leicester, for example, Ladysmith Day (28 February) was used to make church collections for a memorial in 1903, while Liverpool had an annual ceremony on that day from 1907 onwards when Goscombe John's memorial was specially decorated. In London, the Union Jack Club opened its doors as a memorial in the same year of 1907. In another precursor of the future, the Graves Fund was begun with royal patronage in December 1900 to allow the bereaved to visit distant graves, while Milner was trying to discourage tourists from visiting the war zone as early as April 1900.

It is generally accepted that the impact of total war will be greater in states that are defeated, occupied or newly created as a result of war. Moreover, through accidents of location, some states will suffer more than others. Societies are not uniform in their development and the likely effect of war will also vary depending upon the nature of a particular society and the intensity of its war experience. It renders generalisation exceptionally hazardous.

Clearly, the impact of the war was greater for Afrikaners and Africans than for the British. Indeed, like many so-called limited conflicts since 1945, the South African War might be regarded as more 'total' for one side than the other. Recently, indeed, it has argued that the war had little long-term impact on Britain: it merely served to heighten the attention increasingly being devoted to a range of wider social, economic and political issues, the search for the solution of which pushed South African and imperial affairs rapidly off the political agenda. Nonetheless, even for Britain, this conflict was of a far greater magnitude than anything else experienced since 1815. Most recently, the war has been characterised as well up the evolutionary scale towards total war.[14] Certainly, it was a precursor of the greater conflict to come between 1914 and 1918 in many ways, and not just in terms of the level of military violence and the erosion of distinctions between combatants and non-combatants in South Africa itself. Indeed, the South African War was much more than a colonial war writ large and, arguably, in terms of the evolution of Marwickian totality, the most significant conflict since the American Civil War.

22

No End of a Lesson

It appears to have been Robert Louis Stevenson who coined the phrase that it is better to travel hopefully than to arrive. One is reminded constantly of this when surveying British expectations of the prospects of war. 'The finest army that has ever left these shores.' 'The Army was never in better condition either as regards the zeal and skill of its officers from the highest to the lowest, the training and discipline of the men, or the organisation of all the branches of the service.' 'In every respect ... incomparably the best trained, best organised and best equipped British Army that ever went forth to war.' The first and last of these three quotations may sound familiar. Only one – the third – was arguably true, this being Sir James Edmonds's conclusion with regard to the BEF in 1914. The first was the initial verdict of *The Times* on the expeditionary force being sent to the Crimea in 1854. The second, of more immediate relevance to our concern here, was the judgement of the military commentator Henry Spenser Wilkinson at the beginning of the South African War.[1]

Within a few short weeks, events in South Africa suggested that Spenser Wilkinson had been all too optimistic, although, in part, it had been his intention from the start to contrast the apparent efficiency of the army with what he perceived to be the inadequacy of the higher organisation of defence. By the end of the war, the generally accepted conclusion with regard to the British army's performance accorded with that of Leo Amery's influential *The Times History of the War in South Africa*, which took a highly critical view of the British military performance.

Many contemporaries recognised the flawed nature of Amery's creation. With some irritation, for example, Major-General Sir Frederick Maurice pointed out in the second volume of the War Office's official history that it was too easy to forget that the British army had initially been numerically inferior to a well-armed and organised enemy and to 'throw the whole blame on our "ignorant generals" and our "stupid soldiers"'.[2] Amery's conclusions, however, continued to shape the received version of the war for almost seventy years, authors of the popular accounts that appeared when interest in the war revived in the 1950s and 1960s appearing oblivious to his motives.

Thus, from an assumption of unmitigated military failure, and of obvious lessons deriving from the South African experience, the impact of the war upon the British army has been largely seen as administering, to quote Kipling, 'no end of a lesson', ushering in a period of substantial and much needed reform. Clearly there were major changes, not least in higher military organisation. In many ways, however, the impact of the war was not as great as sometimes supposed, since the apparent lessons of war were far from unambiguous. But, then, they seldom are.

The war clearly had significance in that it was the first occasion on which the British army was faced with modern conditions of warfare on a large scale. As Maurice further commented, the effectiveness of the weapons available to both sides in South Africa was 'about in the same proportion to those which thirty years earlier the contest between France and Germany had been fought out then stood to the Brown Bess of Waterloo'.[3] The results were early apparent, as Major-General Neville Lyttelton noted. Commanding the 4th (Light) Brigade at Colenso, Lyttelton was startled by the contrast with his experience of commanding a British brigade at Omdurman a year previously: 'In the first 50,000 fanatics streamed across the open regardless of cover to certain death, while at Colenso I never saw a Boer all day till the battle was over, and it was our men who were the victims.'[4] Apart from the effects of firepower, South Africa was also noted for the use of railways, the telegraph, steam tractors, armoured trains, aerial reconnaissance by balloon, electric illumination, blockhouses, wire entanglements, entrenchment and other technological advances.

How far the war was, or was not, a 'total' conflict is a rather larger question, but the scale of the war clearly dwarfed earlier colonial conflicts in which Britain had been involved. Again, the South African War was also clearly a transitional conflict on the cusp between the traditional and the modern (although, so for that matter, was the First World War). Notwithstanding the paradoxes, many contemporary commentators

were convinced that the lessons of the war were obvious. In offering
his collected articles from the *Morning Post* to the public in March 1900
under the title of *Lessons of the War,* for example, Spenser Wilkinson
made the confident assertion that the war's lessons were already far
from obscure for 'those whose occupations have led them to indulge in
any close study of war'.[5]

By contrast, St John Brodrick, who became Secretary of State for War
in October 1900, scaled down the scope of the official history because
he did not think the war offered any useful lessons after the end of its
conventional phase. It is apparent that financial restrictions were the
real cause of Brodrick's stance, but in fact many other commentators
believed the South African War so abnormal as to render its lessons, in
the words of Major-General Robert Baden Powell's brother, Major
B. F. S. Baden Powell, 'hardly worth study'. Baden Powell shared his
brother's views. G. F. R. Henderson, originally chosen as the official
historian, had also believed conditions on the veldt 'peculiar'.[6]

Appearing before the Royal Commission on the War in South Africa,
Major-General J. P. Brabazon similarly declared that 'It was a most
extraordinary war, fought under absolutely different conditions (it was
my sixth campaign) from those of any other war I had ever seen'. The
value of Brabazon's observation, however, was perhaps offset by his
advocacy of shock tactics by cavalry armed with tomahawks. As Lord
Esher remarked, 'He drew graphic pictures of a cavalry charge under
these conditions, so paralysing to the imagination of the Commissioners
that they wholly failed to extricate the General or themselves from the
discussion of this engrossing subject'.[7] Even some external observers
were struck by the unique conditions, the American naval theorist,
Alfred Thayer Mahan, declaring the war an anomaly in his account of
the war published in July 1900, although Jean de Bloch did believe the
war essentially modern.

To some extent, these peculiarities derived from the climate and
terrain. Only Natal had a climate resembling any part of Europe. The
area around Mafeking was, for all intents and purposes, semi-desert,
while temperatures on the high veldt, between 5000 and 7000 feet above
sea level, were subject to the most extreme variations. Of particular
significance with regard to the assessment of firepower, whether rifles
or artillery, was the atmospheric clarity of the veldt, and the lack of

either large-scale topographical features or natural obstacles. This enhanced the effectiveness of fire at long range, with unaimed fire to the maximum range of magazine rifles quite capable of killing distant opponents.

If many of these conditions were unlikely to be reproduced in Europe, there was also the nature of the Boers themselves. In the first edition of his celebrated *Small Wars: Their Principles and Practice*, published in 1896, Colonel Charles Callwell had already placed the Boers in a category of their own, separate from all other colonial opponents faced by the British. The third edition published in 1906, and embracing the lessons of the second Anglo-Boer conflict, did not alter this assessment. Indeed, Callwell remarked of the methods eventually evolved to defeat the Boers that 'it would rarely happen that such heroic remedies would be necessary in operations against the class of enemy ordinarily met with in small wars'.[8]

Nonetheless, in passing, it should be emphasised that the highly successful pacification methods evolved in South Africa, including the use of wire, blockhouses, mobile columns and reconcentration, were to inform British counter-insurgency practice throughout the twentieth century. In any case, leading British military theorists like Henderson and Maurice were too pragmatic to assume that any conflict did more than add to the accumulation of practical experience. Moreover, those lessons from South Africa deemed to be applicable to a modern European war were soon to be contradicted in many cases by those of the Russo-Japanese War.

Turning first to infantry tactics, J. F. C. Fuller's claim that British generals displayed a 'Brown Bess' or 'Peninsular' mentality of 'shoulder to shoulder formations, of volleys in rigid lines and of wall-like bayonet assaults' is quite ludicrous.[9] Admittedly, peacetime training in the 1890s showed that some battalions still clung to the close formations long officially abandoned, and Fitzroy Hart's brigade was committed in close order at Colenso (15 December 1899). It has been argued, however, that after the reverses as Colenso, Spion Kop (24 January 1900) and Vaal Krantz (5 February 1900), the final advance of the Natal Field Force to relieve Ladysmith saw troops move in short rushes, using available cover and with the support of creeping barrages. In fact, those used to recent

Indian warfare had already become painfully aware of the potentially destructive effects of modern breechloaders during the great rising on the North-West Frontier in 1897. Ian Hamilton deployed successfully in extended order at Elandslaagte (21 October 1899) and Lord Methuen also deployed successfully in extended order at Belmont (23 November 1899), though unfortunately his troops were caught while deploying at Magersfontein (11 December 1899).

It has also been argued that the whole thrust of British tactical thought and training through the 1890s was towards more flexibility. In these terms, the 'Notes for Guidance in South African Warfare', issued by Roberts on 26 January 1900, and emphasising the need to avoid frontal attacks and to use extended order, were no more than a textbook summary of the advanced tactical ideas of the previous three decades.[10] Consequently, it could be argued that the reverses in the early part of the war derived from a failure to act in accordance with actual doctrine, although the war occurred at a moment when the practical application of new tactical ideas were at an early stage.

The principal infantry lessons of the war, therefore, certainly appeared to be that firepower was the most decisive factor in warfare, and that manoeuvre was required to avoid its destructive effect, although the success of manoeuvre was also taken to rely upon the offensive power of modern weapons. Henderson, indeed, in stressing the importance of envelopment, argued that 'it is not always realised that anything which gives new strengths to the defence at the same time adds something to the advantage of the army which attacks'.[11] If the war suggested the significance of infantry firepower, through the perceived reluctance on occasions of officers and men to face fire, there was also a new emphasis upon morale and the offensive spirit. Soldiers such as Maurice were in the forefront of the growing concern with the apparent deterioration of the imperial race as suggested by the physical deficiencies of many wartime recruits.

The Russo-Japanese War reinforced this particular emphasis, although its lessons were equally ambiguous. To quote Major-General E. A. Altham, the experience in Manchuria 'has wiped out the mistaken inference from South African experience that bayonet fighting belongs to the past'.[12] Similar conclusions were reached by Major-General Lancelot Kiggell, Douglas Haig's successor as Director of Staff Duties at the War Office in 1909, who also believed that Manchuria had proven erroneous the assumptions about firepower derived from South Africa.

A greater emphasis was given to musketry training as a result of the South African War, although financial considerations led to the scaling back of the new practice ammunition allowance of 1902–3 in 1907, and also to the compromise adoption of the Short Lee Enfield in 1905. However, the significance accorded firepower and the methodical caution in attack apparent in the new manuals, *Combined Training* in 1902 and *Infantry Training* in 1905, was reversed in *Field Service Regulations* in 1909, which downgraded firepower and subordinated the defensive to the moral effect of the vigorous offensive.

The lessons of the war with regard to cavalry were even less clear-cut. It is usually assumed that traditional cavalry wedded to shock tactics proved unsuccessful and that mounted infantry was the key to the future of the mounted arm. As is well known, Roberts and his supporters, such as Amery and Erskine Childers, the author of the fifth volume of *The Times* history, were highly critical of the cavalry's record in South Africa. Childers, indeed, famously questioned the utility 'if any, of the *arme blanche*, in the conflicts of the future'.[13] The new manual, *Cavalry Training*, in 1904 therefore emphasised the importance of the rifle and of dismounted action rather than of the sword and of mounted action.

It has been argued, however, that the limitations of the cavalry in South Africa owed most to the woeful neglect of the 'horsemastership' essential in the particular climatic conditions of the veldt. Thus, the perceived failure of the cavalry at Poplar Grove (6 March 1900) was due to the poor condition of the horses. Moreover, actual doctrine as suggested by the 1896 *Cavalry Drill Book* endorsed the combination of mounted and dismounted action, though without devoting much space to the latter. Indeed, British cavalry traditionalists, such as Sir John French and Douglas Haig, were able to argue that the principles of offensive mounted action remained unchanged as a result of the war.

Traditional cavalry action had worked well at Elandslaagte. Similarly, French demonstrated what Stephen Badsey has described as 'the immense tactical flexibility of his reformed cavalry' at Klip Drift (15 February 1900), and the combination of mounted and dismounted action proved successful at both Zand River (10 May 1900) and Diamond Hill (11 June 1900).[14] Subsequently, there were many examples of cavalry charging successfully during the guerrilla phase of the conflict, albeit with rifles rather than swords. Even Childers recognised this and, while believing the sword unnecessary, was not actually an opponent of the cavalry charge per se.

Consequently, Haig, as successively Director of Military Training and Director of Staff Duties between 1906 and 1909, and French, as Inspector-General of the Forces from 1907 to 1911, reversed the emphasis upon mounted infantry. Haig's *Cavalry Studies*, published in 1907 in collaboration with Lonsdale Hale, and French's preface to the translation of Bernhardi's *Cavalry in Peace and War* in 1910, both upheld traditional principles of offensive action. The balance, however, shifted back towards mounted infantry in the 1912 edition of *Cavalry Training*. In fact, the cavalry was trained adequately for both mounted and dismounted action by 1914, although the combination of tactical roles ascribed the cavalry was overly ambitious, and one the more traditionally minded officers found difficult to grasp.

Unlike the infantry debate, Manchurian experience was of little further guidance since cavalry played virtually no part in the Russo-Japanese War. The latter conflict, however, was of more significance for artillery lessons, which were obscured in the case of South Africa by the war being primarily used to justify the rearmament and reorganisation of the Royal Artillery without any regard to actual experience. British soldiers entered the war already believing in the need for European-style quick-firing guns. Consequently, the Director-General of the Ordnance, Sir Henry Brackenbury, persuaded the government to consider rearming the Royal Artillery in January 1900. An order was immediately placed for German Ehrhardt guns and agreement reached on a three-year programme of rearmament in January 1901. It should be emphasised, however, that the Boers possessed no such quick-firing guns and that the only ones actually deployed in South Africa were naval guns. These were too heavy for use in the field, and fired only an estimated 2 per cent of those shells discharged by the British during the war. The war was thus merely a means of justifying rearmament, the only actual perceived lessons being refinements in armament characterised by 'greater mobility for Horse Artillery, increased firepower for Field Artillery, and a longer-range capability for both'.[15]

These requirements were satisfied by the adoption of the thirteen

pounder for horse artillery, and the eighteen pounder and 4.5 inch
howitzer for field artillery. In fact, not all artillery officers shared these
perceptions, and many erroneously thought that the new quick-firers
would make little difference to artillery tactics. Colonel Long utilised at
Colenso tactics which had worked at Omdurman. Indeed, despite
the poor results of artillery fire at Magersfontein and Colenso, largely
as a consequence of a misplaced faith in the effectiveness of lyddite as
a propellant, an emphasis was retained on the necessity for preliminary
bombardment. Shrapnel, which had also proved largely ineffective, was
retained precisely because lyddite had failed as a high explosive.

Even those who grasped the importance of indirect fire, and the need
to accentuate the volume of fire as a necessary precondition to movement, were haunted to some extent by the accusation that, in 'hiding
behind hills', they sought to avoid delivering close support to the infantry
in the firing line. Subsequently, the experience of the Russo-Japanese
War, and observation of French artillery tactics, demonstrated that
simply rearming, without a due consideration of the tactical implications
of doing so, had been somewhat premature.

In many respects, the least ambiguous lessons of South Africa were
those relating to the army's support services. Most, with the noted
exception of the Royal Army Medical Corps, had performed adequately.
Indeed, despite much contemporary criticism, the Army Service Corps
had done especially well when the disastrous meddling of Roberts and
Kitchener in regimental transport is taken into account. All services,
however, had been grossly understaffed and underresourced. Consequently, the Royal Engineers and the RAMC were both expanded after
the war, which had provided useful lessons in such areas as military
railway management, military nursing, ambulance design and hospital
trains. A variety of smaller lessons were also taken on board with respect
to equipment such as puttees, the lighter aluminium canteen, new water
carts, looped cartridge belts and universal khaki service dress.

The shortages of matériel, especially ammunition, in 1899 were also
addressed, though since the war ended before an even greater economic
mobilisation became necessary, the lessons were not absorbed.
Reserves of ammunition continued to be predicated on the South
African War experience, the lesson drawn from the Russo-Japanese
War being the need to ensure fire economy rather than increasing the

ammunition available. In part, this reflected continued financial re-
straints. Predictably, the same kind of shell shortages occurred in
1914–15.

The war's greatest and most important military impact, however, was
in what has been characterised as the 'managerial revolution',[16] emanat-
ing from the official enquiries by Royal Commissions and Parliamentary
Committees instituted as a result of the war. Two met while the war
was still in progress, the Select Committee on War Office Organisation,
chaired by Clinton Dawkins, reporting in May 1901; and that on the
Education and Training of Officers of the Army, chaired by A. Akers-
Douglas, in 1902. Principally, however, organisational reform was driven
by the Royal Commission on the War in South Africa, chaired by Lord
Elgin, which reported in July 1903; the War Office (Reconstitution)
Committee, chaired by Lord Esher, which reported in January and
March 1904; and the Royal Commission on the Militia and Volunteers,
chaired by the Duke of Norfolk, which reported in May 1904.

A measure of greater higher defence organisation had been instituted
before the war through the establishment of such bodies as the Colonial
Defence Committee (1885), Joint Naval and Military Committee (1891)
and Standing Defence Committee of the Cabinet (1895), although, like
changes within the War Office in 1895, these had not been notably
successful. Indeed, the Elgin Commission revealed the frequent confusion as to the respective functions of such bodies. It did, however, point
to the success of mobilisation in 1899, an unprecedented event, which
was itself the product of the Stanhope Memorandum of 1888.

Elgin also pointed to the accuracy of the predictions of the small and
poorly-funded Intelligence Department within the War Office, a new
post of Director General of Mobilisation and Military Intelligence having
already been created in November 1901. Despite its attention to the
decision-making process, however, the Elgin Commission made few
positive recommendations and it was Esher, who had dissented from
the majority report, whose own committee produced the most significant organisational reforms of all.

The general outline of the reforms are familiar: abolition of the post
of Commander-in-Chief; the creation of that of Chief of the General
Staff and, in due course, the creation of a General Staff; an Army
Council; a permanent secretariat for the Committee of Imperial Defence

established by Balfour in December 1902; the reorganisation of the Staff College; and the greater professionalisation of officer education. Some of these were old ideas, the Hartington Commission having advocated the replacement of Commander-in-Chief with a Chief of Staff in 1890. There were also the successive attempts at organisational reform between 1901 and 1905 by Brodrick and Arnold-Forster as Secretaries of State for War. Brodrick and Arnold-Forster, however, did not succeed, and it was left to Haldane to effect wider reforms after 1906, which were guided more by financial considerations than either strategic calculations or lingering reflections on the military lessons of the South African War.

Nonetheless, just as much as his two immediate predecessors, Haldane still needed to take into account the reorientation of British strategic interests, which were driven partly by the cost of the war. The process had begun in many respects with the abandonment of the traditional concern for the independence of the Ottoman Empire and the freedom of the Straits in 1896. It was accelerated, however, by the fears arising from British diplomatic isolation during the war. Concessions had to be made to the United States over the Venezuelan episode in 1901; there were the tentative negotiations with Germany in the same year; and the conclusion of the alliance with Japan in 1902.

The spectre of invasion had arisen once more during the war, at least in the public mind, and the army schemes advocated by Brodrick, Arnold-Forster and Haldane all addressed the effort required to meet British commitments at both home and abroad. As a whole, it is estimated that 14.2 per cent of the male population of the United Kingdom between the ages of eighteen and forty were in uniform at some stage between 1899 and 1902. By March 1900, however, only one regular infantry battalions remained in Britain, with the volunteer force the only additional defence against possible invasion. Hence the concern to reform the auxiliary forces as well as the regular army, the process ultimately resulting in 1908 in Haldane's abolition of the militia and the merger of volunteers and yeomanry in the Territorial Force.

The South African War caught the British army at a moment of transition. There is some debate as to the degree of real change within the army as a result of its experience. This mirrors in some respects the wider historical debate about continuities and discontinuities with respect to the effect of war upon social change. Since the lessons were so ambiguous, what mattered most about the impact of the South African War upon the army was the general sense of the need for reform. The army was undoubtedly better for the experience and, in August 1914, the fact that the BEF was such a finely honed military instrument owed much to the South African War. Unfortunately, an assumed wastage rate of 40 per cent for the first six months of war, and between 65 and 75 per cent for twelve months, calculated as an average between those of the South African and Russo-Japanese Wars, tragically proved a considerable underestimate: the actual casualty rate was 63 per cent in the first three months. In other words, while some lessons had been absorbed, the South African experience had not fundamentally altered the limited way in which the British envisaged waging war in the future. A profounder lesson awaited them. As Cyril Falls later wrote of the BEF: '*Armées d'élite* would be invincible if wars were fought without casualties. Things being what they are, *armées d'élite* are unlikely to remain so for long.' [17]

Notes

Notes to Chapter 1: An English Confederacy

1. James Rawley, ed., *The American Civil War: An English View by Field-Marshal Viscount Wolseley* (Charlottesville: University Press of Virginia, 1964), p. 107.
2. B. Liddell Hart, *The Remaking of Modern Armies* (London: Murray, 1927), pp. 170–71.
3. Hove, W/P 3/17, Wolseley to his wife, 16 December 1873.
4. G. W. Steevens, *With Kitchener to Khartoum* (Edinburgh: Blackwood & Sons, 1898), p. 22.
5. RA, N41/78, Hardinge to the Queen, 12 February 1885.
6. Hove, W/P 8/19, Wolseley to his wife, 8–13 August 1879.
7. IOL, MSS Eur F 127/1, Strachey to Strachey, 28 January 1880.
8. RA, Add. E1/8596, Stanley to Cambridge, 20 March 1879.
9. E. N. Bennett, *The Downfall of the Dervishes: Being a Sketch of the Final Sudan Campaign of 1898* (London: Methuen, 1898), p. 70.
10. SUSM, M1994/112/93, pp. 8–9.
11. Adrian Preston, ed., *Sir Garnet Wolseley's South African Journal, 1879–80* (Cape Town: A. A. Balkema, 1973), p. 38; Wolseley journal entry, 21 June 1879.
12. NLS, MS 12380, Pretyman to Minto, 1 July 1900.
13. Earl of Midleton, *Records and Recollections, 1856–1939* (London: John Murray, 1939), p. 120.
14. Adrian Preston, ed., *In Relief of Gordon: Lord Wolseley's Campaign Journal of the Khartoum Relief Expedition, 1884–85* (London: Hutchinson, 1967), pp. 45–46; Wolseley journal entry, 22 Oct. 1884.
15. Field-Marshal Viscount Wolseley, *The Story of a Soldier's Life* (London: Archibald Constable & Co., 1902), ii, p. 135.

Notes to Chapter 2: Cleansing the East with Steel

1. *The Times*, 25 May 2002.
2. Olive Anderson, 'The Growth of Christian Militarism in Mid-Victorian Britain', *English Historical Review*, 86 (1971), pp. 46–72.
3. D. A. Kinsley, *They Fight Like Devils* (New York: Sarpedon, 2001), p. 1.
4. *The Times*, 25 September 1857, p. 7.
5. Graham Dawson, *Soldier Heroes: British Adventure, Empire and the Imagining of Masculinities* (London: Routledge, 1994), p. 81.
6. J. C. Marshman, *Memoirs of Major-General Sir Henry Havelock* (London: Longmans, Green & Co., 1909), pp. 162–67, 191–212.
7. J. C. Pollock, *Way to Glory: The Life of Havelock of Lucknow* (London: John Murray, 1957), p. 153.
8. Anderson, 'Growth of Christian Militarism', p. 51.
9. Stephen Wood, 'Temperance and its Rewards in the British Army', in Marion Harding, ed., *The Victorian Soldier: Studies in the History of the British Army, 1816–1914* (London: National Army Museum, 1993), pp. 86–96.
10. Christopher Hibbert, *The Great Mutiny: India, 1857* (New York: Viking Press, 1978), p. 198.
11. Ibid., p. 203.
12. 'Our Indian Empire', *Blackwood's Edinburgh Magazine*, 82, 506 (1857), p. 650.
13. Sir John Kaye, *History of the Sepoy War in India, 1857–58* (London, 1880), ii, p. 397.
14. Hibbert, *Great Mutiny*, p. 255.
15. Kinsley, *They Fight Like Devils*, p. 32.
16. Hibbert, *Great Mutiny*, p. 420.
17. Marshman, *Memoirs*, p. 446.

Notes to Chapter 3: The Hand on the Throttle

1. RA, O38/178, Wood to the Queen, 8 February 1881.
2. William Butler, *The Life of Sir George Pomeroy-Colley* (London: John Murray, 1899), p. 88.
3. RA, O38/276, Wood to the Queen, 27 February 1881.
4. John Charteris, *Field Marshal Earl Haig* (London: Cassell, 1929), p. 32.
5. Hatfield House, A/112/19, Cromer to Barrington, 3 March 1899.
6. Hove, W/P 16/85 Wolseley to wife, 11 October 1887.
7. Warwick CRO, CR895/92 Dormer to wife, 28 October 1878.

8. Hove, W/P 24/76, Wolseley to wife, 1 August 1895.

9. Hove, W/W. 4/140, Wolseley to George Wolseley, 1 November 1900.

10. BL, L(5)44, Bigge to Lansdowne, 16 and 18 August 1900.

11. RA, Vic Add. MS U. 32, Queen to Princess Royal, 26 August 1895.

Notes to Chapter 4: The Devil's Pass

1. Ron Lock, *Blood on the Painted Mountain* (London: Greenhill Books, 1995), p. 208.

2. M. J. Crook, *The Evolution of the Victoria Cross: A Study in Administrative History* (Tunbridge Wells: Midas Books, 1975), pp. 279–82.

3. H. M. Bengough, *Memories of a Soldier's Life* (London: Arnold, 1913), p. 133.

4. Devon CRO, 2065M/SS4/10, Buller to Browne, 30 January 1880.

5. Ibid., Hutchinson to Buller, 12 July 1880.

6. PRO, WO 32/7317, Storks to Peel, 14 November 1858.

7. Adrian Preston, ed., *Sir Garnet Wolseley's South African Journal* (Cape Town: A. A. Balkema, 1973), pp. 70, 256–57, journal entries for 3 August 1879 and 19 March 1880.

8. RA, Add. E1/8675, Chelmsford to Cambridge, 21 May 1879.

9. KCL, KCM 89/9/27/3, Gardner to Wood, 22/23 January 1879.

10. Sonia Clark, ed., *Zululand at War, 1879: The Conduct of the Anglo-Zulu War* (Houghton: Brenthurst Press, 1984), pp. 131–32, quoting Clery to Alison, 16 May 1879.

11. Buller Family MSS, Buller to Lucy, 18 February 1879.

12. Hove, Autobiographical Collection, Brackenbury to Wolseley, 13 August 1885; Buller to Wolseley, 5 August 1879; Graham to Wolseley, 18 May 1884.

13. Ibid., 163iv, Wolseley to his mother, 30 March 1874.

14. Ibid., W/P 11/23, Wolseley to wife, 28 September–1 October 1882.

15. RA, Add. E1/8744, Baker to Cambridge, 20 June 1879.

16. William Trousdale, ed., *War in Afghanistan, 1879–80: The Personal Diary of Major-General Sir Charles Metcalfe MacGregor* (Detroit: Wayne State University Press, 1985), p. 13.

17. Sir Ian Hamilton, *Listening for the Drums* (London: Faber & Faber, 1944), p. 93.

Notes to Chapter 5: The Race for the Peerage

1. Field-Marshal Lord Roberts, *Forty-One Years in India* (Longmans, Green & Co., London, 1904), p. 468.

2. NAM, 8108–9–30–2, memo by Haines, 1 August 1880.

3. E. F. Chapman, 'The March from Kabul to Kandahar in August and the Battle of the 1st of September 1880', *Journal of the Royal United Service Institution*, 25, 110 (1881), pp. 282–315.

4. Roberts, *Forty-One Years*, pp. 481, 485; Brian Robson, *The Road to Kabul: The Second Afghan War, 1878–81* (Arms and Armour Press, London, 1986), p. 249.

5. William Trousdale, ed., *War in Afghanistan, 1879–80: The Personal Diary of Major-General Sir Charles Metcalfe MacGregor* (Wayne State University Press, Detroit, 1985), p. 236.

6. Captain C. Hoskyns, RE, 'A Short Narrative of the Afghan Campaigns of 1879–80–81 from an Engineer's Point of View', *Journal of the Royal United Service Institution*, 26, 116 (1882), pp. 431–55.

7. Trousdale, *War in Afghanistan*, p. 226.

8. NAM, 8108–9–30–46, Ripon to Haines, 17 August 1880.

9. RA, Add. E1/9301, Warre to Cambridge, 19 August 1880.

10. RA, Add. E1/8862, Johnson to Cambridge, 25 August 1879.

11. NAM, 8108–9–24, Lytton to Haines, 21 February 1880; IOL, F132/26, Stewart to Lyall, 29 January 1880.

12. RA, Add. E1/9326, Ripon to Cambridge, 7 September 1880.

13. IOL, F132/24, Roberts to Lyall, 9 September 1880; RA, Add. E1/9360, Warre to Cambridge, 15 October 1880.

14. RA, Add. E1/9380, Cambridge to Haines, 29 October 1880.

15. Robson, *Road to Kabul*, p. 213.

16. Gough MSS, Hanna Correspondence, Gough to Hanna, 9 January 1893.

Notes to Chapter 6: Paths of Duty

1. General Sir Ian Hamilton, *Listening for the Drums* (London: Faber & Faber, 1944), pp. 7–8.

2. William Butler, *The Great Lone Land: A Narrative of Travel and Adventure in the North West of America* (London: Sampson Low, 1872), pp. 199–200.

3. Sir Charles Watson, *The Life of Major-General Sir Charles William Wilson* (London: John Murray, 1909), pp. 391, 401–4.

4. BL, L(5)16, Brodrick to Lansdowne, 11 September 1895.

5. Ibid, L(5)47, Roberts to Lansdowne, 29 January 1900.

Notes to Chapter 7: Doing a Billy Hicks

1. Brian Robson, *Fuzzy Wuzzy: The Campaigns in the Eastern Sudan, 1884–5* (Tunbridge Wells: Spellmount, 1993), p. 21.

2. SAD, 600/1/11–15 Hicks to wife, 24–30 January 1883; ibid., 643/12/5 Hicks to daughter, 12 September 1883.

3. SAD, 643/12/3–5, Hicks to daughter, 13 July 1883.

4. Bennet Burleigh, *Desert Warfare: Being the Chronicle of the Eastern Soudan Campaign* (London: 1884), p. xx.

5. Bodleian, MSS. Eng. lett. c. 452, Alison to Cambridge, January 1883.

6. SAD, 600/2/30–31, Hicks to Minister of War, 25 and 26 August 1883.

7. H. E. Colvile, *History of the Sudan Campaign* (London: War Office Intelligence Division, 1889), i, p. 13.

8. Field-Marshal Sir Evelyn Wood, *From Midshipman to Field-Marshal* (New York: E P Dutton & Co., 1906), ii, p. 158.

9. Winston S. Churchill, *The River War* (London: Longmans, Green & Co., 1900), i, p. 52; J. Colborne, *With Hicks Pasha in the Sudan* (London, 1884), p. 93; SAD, 600/1/89–90, Hicks to wife, 30 September 1883.

10. F. R. Wingate, *Ten Years' Captivity in the Mahdi's Camp* (London, 1898), pp. 27–32.

11. Colvile, *History of Sudan Campaign*, p. 16; F. R. Wingate, *Mahdism and the Egyptian Sudan* (2nd edn, London: Frank Cass, 1968), p. 90.

12. Lord Elton, ed., *General Gordon's Khartoum Journal* (New York: Vanguard Press, 1961), p. 195.

13. Earl of Cromer, *Modern Egypt* (London: Macmillan & Co., 1908), i, p. 369.

Notes to Chapter 8: The Excitement of Railway Carriages

1. PRO, WO132/1, Buller to 'Aunt Georgina', 30 March 1879.

2. RA, R8/82, notes by the Queen, 9 September 1879; ibid., R10/1, Wood to the Queen, 25 April 1880.

3. RA, O31/20, note by Queen, 3 November 1898.

4. Hove, W/P 5/11, Wolseley to wife, 2 May 1875; Adrian Preston, ed., *Sir Garnet Wolseley's South African Diaries (Natal) 1875* (Cape Town: A. A. Balkema, 1971), p. 75.

5. Anne Baker, *A Question of Honour: The Life of Lieutenant-General Valentine Baker Pasha* (London: Leo Cooper, 1996), p. 88.

Notes to Chapter 9: War, Truth and History

1. IOL, MSS Eur F 108/66, à Court to White, 6 January 1901.

2. LHCMA, 1/25/93, 95 Liddell Hart to Edmonds, 6 and 13 November 1934.

3. J. H. M. Abbott, *Tommy Cornstalk* (London: Longman, Green & Co., 1902), p. ix.

4. A British Officer, 'The Literature of the South African War, 1899–1902', *American Historical Review* 12 (1907), pp. 299–321.

5. J. Barnes and D. Nicholson, eds, *The Leo Amery Diaries*, i, *1896–1929* (London: Hutchinson, 1980), p. 33.

6. Arthur Conan Doyle, *Memories and Adventures* (London: Hodder, 1924), pp. 181–210; Julian Symons, *Portrait of an Artist: Conan Doyle* (London: John Murray, 1949), pp. 65–67.

7. Times Archive, Bell letter books, 23, Bell to Amery, 23 March 1900.

8. IOL, MSS Eur F 108/66, Amery to White, 22 February 1901; *The Times History of the War in South Africa* (London: Sampson Low, Marston & Co., 1900–1909), ii, p. vii.

9. *The History of The Times, 1912–1948* (London: The Times, 1952), ii, p. 1051.

10. IOL, MSS Eur F108/66, Amery to White, 22 February 1901.

11. *Royal Commission on the War in South Africa, Minutes of Evidence, ii* (London, 1903), Cmd 1791, 659.

12. IOL, MSS Eur F 108/66, White to Bell, n.d.

13. *Times History of the War*, ii, pp. viii, 33, 40; ibid., iii, p. vi.

14. Brian Robson, 'The Strange Case of the Missing Official History', *Soldiers of the Queen*, 76 (1984), pp. 3–6.

15. *History of the War in South Africa* (London: Hurst and Blackett, 1906–10), ii, 'Note to Reader'.

16. LHCMA, Maurice 2/3/90, Buller to Maurice, 5 May 1904.

17. LHCMA, Maurice 3/2/101, Pole-Carew to Maurice, 4 October 1906.

18. *History of the War in South Africa*, iv, pp. v–vi.

19. IOL, MSS Eur 108/66, à Court to White, 9 March 1901.

Notes to Chapter 10: Command in South Africa

1. RA, Add. E1/ 7569, Cunynghame to Cambridge, 20 March 1875.

2. BL, L(5)48, Lansdowne to Roberts, 1 June 1900.

3. Graham Dominy, 'The Imperial Garrison in Natal with Special Reference to Fort Napier, 1843–1914: Its Social, Cultural and Economic Impact', unpublished Ph.D. thesis, University of London (1995), p. 165.

4. Sir Arthur Cunynghame, *My Command in South Africa, 1874–8* (London: Macmillan, 1879), pp. 361–71.

5. BL, Add. MS 60800, Hardy to Cunynghame, 29 January 1878.

6. John Laband, *Lord Chelmsford's Zululand Campaign, 1878–9* (Stroud: Sutton Publishing, 1994), pp. xxxi–xxxvi.

7. Brian Bond, 'The South African War, 1880–1', in Brian Bond, ed., *Victorian Military Campaigns* (London: Hutchinson, 1967), pp. 199–240.

Notes to Chapter 11: Islands in the Sun

1. C. C. Eldridge, *England's Mission* (London: Macmillan, 1973), p. 224.
2. RA, Add. E1/8316, Chamberlain to Cambridge, 16 May 1878.
3. J. L. Vaughan, 'The Indian Expeditionary Force' *Contemporary Review*, 32 (July 1878), pp. 665–74.

Notes to Chapter 12: Cavagnari's Coup de Main

1. G. W. Forrest, *Life of Field-Marshal Sir Neville Chamberlain* (Edinburgh: William Blackwood & Sons, 1909), p. 494.
2. R. S. Rait, *The Life of Field-Marshal Sir Frederick Paul Haines* (London: Constable & Co., 1911, p. 244.
3. IOL, Eur MSS D951/11, Colley to Burne, 3 November 1878 and 20 January 1880.
4. Rait, *Haines*, pp. 213–14.
5. NAM, 3108–9–12, Haines to Lytton, 3 October 1878.
6. IOL, D951/11, Colley to Burne, 3 November 1878.

Notes to Chapter 13: Chelmsford's Major-Generals

1. Hove, W/P 8/9, Wolseley to wife, 4–7 July, and 10–11 July 1879.
2. Wolseley, 30 May and 27 July 1879, quoted in Adrian Preston, ed., *Sir Garnet Wolseley's South African Journal, 1879–1880* (Cape Town: A. A. Balkema, 1973), pp. 34–36, 64–65.
3. RA, Add. A36, box 20, Ponsonby to wife, 3 March 1881; ibid., Add. E1/8633 and 8776, Clifford to Cambridge, 17 April and 6 July. 1879; KCL, KCM 89/9/27/9, Herbert to Wood, 3 April 1879.
4. Hove, S. A. 1., Wolseley to Hicks Beach, 10 October 1879; ibid., S. A. 2., Wolseley to Cambridge, 30 June, 18 July and 28 September 1879.
5. RA, E1/8606, Cambridge to Crealock, 27 March 1879.
6. RA, Add. E1/8648, Clifford to Cambridge, 2–4 May 1879; E1/8852, Cambridge to Clifford, 12 August 1879.
7. Crealock to Alison, 21 July 1879, quoted in Sonia Clarke, *Zululand at War* (Houghton: Brenthurst Press, 1984), pp. 249–51; Wolseley, 27 and 30 May 1879, quoted in Preston, *Wolseley's Journal*, pp. 33, 36–37.

Notes to Chapter 14: Stanhope's Storehouse

1. W. St John Brodrick, 'Edward Stanhope' *National Review* (February 1894), pp. 842–49.
2. KAO, U1590, 0250/1, Queen to Stanhope, 25 July 1890.
3. T. J. Spinner, *G. J. Goschen: The Transformation of a Victorian Liberal* (Cambridge: Cambridge University Press, 1973), p. 165.
4. W. S. Hamer, *The British Army: Civil-Military Relations, 1885–1905* (Oxford: Oxford University Press, 1970), p. 49.
5. RA, E1/12182, Cambridge to Stanhope, 27 April 1888.
6. Hove, W/P 17/18, Wolseley to wife, 9 April 1888
7. KAO, U1590, 0254/2, Stanhope to Cambridge, 9 November 1887.
8. RA, E1/12030, Stanhope to Cambridge, 15 December 1887.
9. NAM, 7101–23–82–23, Stanhope to Roberts, 27 November 1890.
10. Hove, Wolseley Autograph Collection, Stanhope to Wolseley, 18 July 1892.

Notes to Chapter 15: One and a Half Battalions

1. Warwick CRO, CR895/94, various press obituaries.
2. PRO, WO33/48, A152, Baring to Foreign Office, 6 December 1888.
3. RA, Add. E1/12324, Stanhope to Cambridge, 4 December 1888.
4. KAO, U1590, 0254/2, Stanhope to Cambridge, 5 December 1888.
5. PRO, WO33/48, A152, Grenfell to War Office, 20 December 1888.
6. PRO, CAB37/23.2; KAO, U1590, 0308, Salisbury to Stanhope, 7 January 1889.
7. RA, Lady Geraldine Somerset's diary, 16 January 1889.
8. RA, E1/12380 (and Hatfield, F94), Salisbury to Cambridge, 23 January 1889.

Notes to Chapter 16: The Improbable Probability

1. KAO, U1590, 0313, Stanhope to Wantage, 3 June 1891. The Stanhope Memorandum itself is reproduced in Edward Spiers, *The Late Victorian Army, 1868–1902* (Manchester: Manchester University Press, 1992), p. 337.
2. HC 236, pp. v (para 13), 5 (1908), vii, 369, 379.
3. RA, Add. E1/12658, Cambridge to Stanhope, 24 September 1890.
4. NAM, 7101–23–12–95, Brownlow to Roberts, 13 December 1890.
5. PRO, 30/40/2, Wilson to Ardagh, 15 August 1889.
6. Howard Bailes, 'Technology and Imperialism: A Case Study of the Victorian Army in Africa', *Victorian Studies*, 24 (1980–81), pp. 82–104.

Notes to Chapter 17: The First Modern War?

1. General Sir Evelyn Wood, *The Crimea in 1854 and 1894* (London: Chapman & Hall, 1896), p. viii.
2. Correlli Barnett, *Britain and Her Army, 1509–1970* (New York: William Morrow & Co., 1970), p. 290.
3. Christopher Hibbert, *The Destruction of Lord Raglan: A Tragedy of the Crimean War* (Boston: Little, Brown & Co., 1961), p. 213.
4. A. W. Kinglake, *The Invasion of the Crimea* (Edinburgh: William Blackwood & Sons, 1868), iv, p. 63.
5. Paul Usherwood and Jenny Spencer-Smith, *Lady Butler: Battle Artist, 1846–1933* (Gloucester: Alan Sutton for National Army Museum, 1987), p. 36.
6. Hibbert, *Destruction of Lord Raglan*, p. 259.
7. *The Times* 23 December 1854.
8. *Punch*, 26 May 1855, quoted in Olive Anderson, *A Liberal State at War: English Politics and Economics during the Crimean War* (London: Macmillan, 1967), p. 112.

Notes to Chapter 18: War, Technology and Change

1. Jay Luvaas, *The Education of an Army: British Military Thought, 1815–1940* (Chicago: University of Chicago Press, 1964), p. 212; Tim Travers, *The Killing Ground* (London: Allen & Unwin, 1987), p. 39.
2. Howard Bailes, 'Patterns of Thought in the Late Victorian Army', *Journal of Strategic Studies*, 4, 1 (1981), pp. 29–45.
3. Hew Strachan, *From Waterloo to Balaclava: Tactics, Technology and the British Army, 1815–54* (Cambridge: Cambridge University Press, 1985), pp. 40–41.
4. Winston S. Churchill, *The River War* (London: 1915 edn), p. 372.
5. Strachan, *Waterloo to Balaclava*, pp. 40–44, 142; ibid., *Wellington's Legacy: The Reform of the British Army, 1830–54* (Manchester: Manchester University Press, 1984), pp. 18–27, 121–24, 131–34.
6. Anthony Cantwell and David Moore, 'The Victorian Army and Submarine Mining' *Fortress*, 18 (1993), pp. 32–47.
7. Jon Tetsuro Sumida, *In Defence of Naval Supremacy: Finance, Technology and British Naval Policy, 1889–1914* (London: Routledge, 2nd edn, 1993), pp. xvi–xvii, 8–10, 18–19; Paul Smith, 'Ruling the Waves: Government, the Service and the Cost of Naval Supremacy, 1885–99', in Paul Smith, ed., *Government and the Armed Forces in Britain, 1856–1990* (London: Hambledon Press, 1996), pp. 21–52.

8. Jay Luvaas, *The Military Legacy of the Civil War: The European Inheritance* (Chicago: University of Chicago Press, 1959), p. 185.

9. Keith Neilson, 'That Dangerous and Difficult Enterprise: British Military Thinking and the Russo-Japanese War' *War and Society*, 9, 2 (1991), p. 30.

10. Brian Robson, 'Mounting an Expedition: Sir Gerald Graham's 1885 Expedition to Suakin', *Small Wars and Insurgencies*, 2, 2 (1991), pp. 232–39; ibid., *Fuzzy Wuzzy*, pp. 176–77, 184–85.

11. Ian F. W. Beckett, *Riflemen Form: A Study of the Rifle Volunteer Movement, 1859–1908* (Aldershot: Ogilby Trusts, 1982), pp. 200–1.

Notes to Chapter 19: 'Troopin'

1. Winston S. Churchill, *The River War* (London: 3rd edn, Eyre & Spottiswoode, 1949), p. 162.

2. PRO, MT 23/15, T3504 and 3351–52.

3. *Rudyard Kipling's Verse: Inclusive Edition, 1885–1918* (London: Hodder & Stoughton, n.d.), pp. 478–79.

4. General Sir Hubert Gough, *Soldiering On* (New York: Robert Speller & Son, 1957), pp. 38–39.

5. PRO, MT23/102, T42943.

6. PRO, MT23/102, T3941 and 3981.

7. P. J. O. Tayler, *A Companion to the Indian Mutiny of 1857* (Delhi: Oxford University Press, 1996), p. 256.

8. Sir Alexander Tulloch, *Recollections of Forty Years' Service* (Edinburgh: Blackwood & Sons, 1903), p. 237.

9. War Office Intelligence Branch, *Narrative of the Field Operations Connected with the Zulu War of 1879* (London: War Office, 1881), p. 154.

10. J. F. Maurice, *The Campaign of 1882 in Egypt* (London: HMSO, 1887), pp. 108–10.

11. Howard Bailes, 'Technology and Imperialism: A Case Study of the Victorian Army in Africa', *Victorian Studies*, 24 (1980), pp. 83–104.

12. Sir Frederick Maurice and Sir George Arthur, *The Life of Lord Wolseley* (William Heinemann, London, 1924), p. 319.

13. Desmond Chapman-Huston and Owen Rutter, *General Sir John Cowans* (London: Hutchinson, 1924), i, pp. 103–5; PRO, MT23/106, T5974, 6466 and 6598; MT23/123, T2958.

14. Leo Amery, *The Times History of the War in South Africa, 1899–1902* (London: Sampson, Low, Marston & Co., 1909), vi, p. 293.

15. Ibid., vi, p. 296.

Notes to Chapter 20: A Frenchman's Horse

1. HEHL, Stowe, STG 208, Morgan to Fremantle, 11 June 1888.
2. H. S. Gaskell, *With Lord Methuen in South Africa* (London: Henry Deane, 1906), p. 7.
3. Unpublished manuscript in private collection, John Brown, 'A Rough Sketch of the South African War as Experienced by the Undersigned in the 10th Regiment Imperial Yeomanry from January 1900 to June 1901', p. 142.
4. Field-Marshal Lord Birdwood, *Khaki and Gown: An Autobiography* (London: Ward, Lock & Co. 1941), pp. 119–20.
5. Hon. Sidney Peel, *Trooper 8008 IY* (London: Edward Arnold, 1901), p. 32.
6. Gaskell, *With Methuen in South Africa*, p. 101.
7. HBA, Lawson to wife, 13 February 1900.
8. C. N. Robinson, *Celebrities of the Army* (London: George Newnes, 1900), p. 107.

Notes to Chapter 21: A Question of Totality

1. Béla Király, 'Elements of Limited and Total War', in Robert A. Kann, Béla Király and Paula Fichtner, eds, *The Habsburg Empire in World War I* (New York, 1977), pp. 135–56.
2. Stig Förster and Jörg Nagler, 'Introduction', in Stig Förster and Jörg Nagler, eds, *On the Road to Total War: The American Civil War and the German Wars of Unification, 1861–71* (Cambridge: Cambridge University Press, 1997), pp. 1–28; Mark E. Neely, 'Was the Civil War a Total War?' in ibid., pp. 29–52; Roger Chickering, 'The American Civil War and the German Wars of Unification: Some Parting Shots' in ibid., pp. 683–91.
3. Glenn A. May, 'Was the Philippine-American War a "Total War"?', in Manfred F. Boemeke, Roger Chickering and Stig Förster, eds, *Anticipating Total War: The German and American Experiences, 1871–1914* (Cambridge: Cambridge University Press, 1999), pp. 437–57.
4. Marc Yakutiel, 'Treasury Control and the South African War, 1899–1905', unpublished D. Phil. thesis, University of Oxford (1989), pp. 23, 26; James Cronin, *The Politics of State Expansion: War, State and Society in Twentieth Century Britain* (London, 1991), p. 28; Craig Robinson, 'General Buller's Telegrams Regarding the Abandonment of Spion Kop and Trichard's Drift, and their Impact upon the Garrison Towns of Lancashire: An Analysis', unpublished M.A. dissertation, University of Leeds (1997), p. 26.
5. *Report of the Royal Commission on the War in South Africa*, Cmd 1789 (London: HMSO, 1903), paras 158–61, pp. 84–87; Clive Trebilcock, 'War

and the Failure of Industrial Mobilisation: 1899 and 1914' in Jay Winter, ed., *War and Economic Development: Essays in Memory of David Joslin* (Cambridge: Cambridge University Press, 1975), pp. 139–64.

6. F. W. Hirst, *The Consequences of the War to Great Britain* (Oxford: Oxford University Press, 1934), p. 298.

7. Major-General Sir J. F. Maurice and Captain M. H. Grant, *History of the War in South Africa*, 4 vols (London: HMSO, 1906–10), ii, p. 204; Colonel G. F. R. Henderson, *The Science of War* (London: Longmans, Green & Co., 1910), p. 372

8. Molly Sutphen, 'Striving to be Separate?': Civilian and Military Doctors in Cape Town during the Anglo-Boer War', in R. Cooter, M. Harrison and S. Sturdy, eds, *War, Medicine and Modernity* (Stroud: Sutton Publishing, 1998), pp. 48–64.

9. Stephen Badsey, 'A Print and Media War', in Craig Wilcox, ed., *Recording the South African War: Journalism and Official History, 1899–1914* (London: Robert Menzies Institute, 1999), pp. 5–16.

10. The debate can be followed in Henry Pelling, *Popular Politics and Society in Late-Victorian Britain* (London, 1968), pp. 82–100; Ross McKibbin, *The Ideologies of Class: Social Relations in Britain, 1880–1950* (Oxford: Oxford University Press 1991), pp. 23–24; Richard Price, *An Imperial War and the British Working Class: Working Class Reactions to the Boer War, 1899–1902* (London: Routledge and Kegan Paul, 1972), pp. 97–232; idem, 'Society, Status and Jingoism: The Social Roots of Lower Middle-Class Patriotism, 1870–1900', in Geoffrey Crossick, ed., *The Lower Middle Class in Britain, 1870–1914* (London: Croom Helm, 1977), pp. 89–122.

11. Ian F. W. Beckett, *The Amateur Military Tradition, 1558–1945* (Manchester: Manchester University Press, 1991), pp. 198–209; idem, *Riflemen Form: A Study of the Rifle Volunteer Movement, 1859–1908* (Aldershot: Ogilby Trusts, 1982), pp. 103–7, 211–26.

12. C. M. Douglas, 'The Recruit from a Depot Medical Officer's Point of View', *Royal United Service Institution Journal*, 44 (1900), pp. 1–18; Miles, 'Where to get Men?', *Contemporary Review* 81 (1902), pp. 78–86; Sir Frederick Maurice, 'National Health: A Soldier's Study', ibid., 83 (1903), pp. 41–56.

13. F. N. Maude, *Notes on the Evolution of Infantry Tactics* (London, 1905), p. 134.

14. Andrew Porter, 'The South African War (1899–1902) and Imperial Britain: A Question of Significance?', conference paper presented to 'Rethinking the South African War', UNISA, August 1998; Bill Nasson, *The South African War, 1899–1902* (London: Edward Arnold, 1999), p. 8.

Notes to Chapter 22: No End of a Lesson

1. Christopher Hibbert, *The Decline of Lord Raglan: A Tragedy of the Crimean War* (Harmondsworth: Penguin, 1963), p. 38; Henry Spenser Wilkinson, *Lessons of the War: Being Comments from Week to Week to the Relief of Ladysmith* (London: Constable, 1900), p. 3; Sir James Edmonds, *Official History of the Great War: Military Operations, France and Belgium, 1914* (London: HMSO, 1922), i, pp. 10–11.

2. Major-General Sir Frederick Maurice and Captain M. H. Grant, *History of the War in South Africa* 4 vols (London: Hurst & Blackett, 1906–10), ii, p. 206.

3. Ibid., p. 204.

4. General Sir Neville Lyttelton, *Eighty Years: Soldiering, Politics, Games* (London, 1927), p. 212.

5. Wilkinson, *Lessons of War*, pp. vii–ix.

6. Tim Travers, *The Killing Ground* (London: Allen & Unwin, 1987), pp. 44, 57 n. 20; G. F. R. Henderson, *The Science of War* (London: Longman, Green & Co., 1910), pp. 371–72.

7. John Gooch, *The Plans of War: The General Staff and British Military Strategy, c. 1900–1916* (London: Routledge & Kegan Paul, 1974), p. 34.

8. Charles Callwell, *Small Wars: Their Principles and Practice* (3rd edn, London: HMSO, 1906), pp. 31, 143.

9. J. F. C. Fuller, *The Last of the Gentleman's Wars* (London: Faber & Faber, 1937), pp. 19–20.

10. Howard Bailes, 'Technology and Tactics in the British Army, 1866–1900', in Ronald Haycock and Keith Neilson, eds, *Men, Machines and War* (Waterloo: Wilfred Laurier University Press, 1988), pp. 23–47.

11. Henderson, *Science of War*, p. 4.

12. Travers, *Killing Ground*, p. 45.

13. Erskine Childers, *The Times History of the War in South Africa* (London: Sampson Low, Marston & Co., 1900–1909), v, pp. xii–xiii.

14. Stephen Badsey, 'Mounted Combat in the Second Boer War', *Sandhurst Journal of Military Studies*, 2 (1991), pp. 11–28.

15. Edward Spiers, 'Rearming the Edwardian Artillery', *Journal of the Society for Army Historical Research*, 57 (1979), pp. 167–76.

16. John Gooch, 'Britain and the Boer War', in George J. Andrepoulos and Harold E. Selesky, eds, *The Aftermath of Defeat: Societies, Armed Forces, and the Challenge of Recovery* (New Haven: Yale University Press, 1994), pp. 40–58.

17. Cyril Falls, *The First World War* (London: Longman, 1967), p. 16.

Bibliographical Note

A number of the essays in this volume are based upon previously published academic articles and chapters, or upon public lectures. In every case, however, they have been rewritten (sometimes substantially) for a general readership with a minimum of footnotes. For those readers interested in the full sources drawn upon, the following gives an indication of the original versions of those essays previously published in other forms.

'Introduction'. Partly based upon 'Personality and the Victorian Army: Some Reflections', *Soldiers of the Queen*, 100 (2000), pp. 3–5.

'An English Confederacy'. Partly based upon 'Command in the Late Victorian Army', in Gary Sheffield, ed., *Leadership and Command: The Anglo-American Military Experience since 1861* (London: Brasseys, 1997), pp. 37–56; and 'Wolseley and the Ring', *Soldiers of the Queen*, 69 (1992), pp. 14–25.

'The Hand on the Throttle'. Based upon 'Women and Patronage in the Late Victorian Army', *History*, 85 (2000), pp. 463–80.

'War, Truth and History'. Based upon 'The Historiography of Small Wars: Early Historians and the South African War', *Small Wars and Insurgencies*, 2 (1991), pp. 276–98; and 'British Official History' in Craig Wilcox, ed., *Recording the South African War: Journalism and Official History, 1899–1914* (London: Sir Robert Menzies Centre for Australian Studies, 1999), pp. 33–42.

'Command in South Africa'. Based upon 'Military High Command in South Africa', in Peter Boyden, Alan Guy and Marion Harding, eds, *Ashes and Blood: The British Army in South Africa, 1795–1914* (London: National Army Museum, 1999), pp. 60–71.

'Islands in the Sun'. Based upon 'The Indian Expeditionary Force on Malta and Cyprus, 1878', *Soldiers of the Queen*, 76 (1994), pp. 6–11.

'Cavagnari's Coup de Main'. Based upon 'Cavagnari's Coup de Main', *Soldiers of the Queen*, 82 (1995), pp. 24–28.

'Chelmsford's Major-Generals'. Based upon 'Such Generals as They Have Sent Out: Chelmsford's Major-Generals', *Soldiers of the Queen*, 84 (1996), pp. 16–19.

'Stanhope's Storehouse'. Based upon 'Edward Stanhope at the War Office, 1887–1892', *Journal of Strategic Studies*, 5 (1982), pp. 278–307.

'One and a Half Battalions'. Based upon 'Edward Stanhope at the War Office, 1887–1892', *Journal of Strategic Studies*, 5 (1982), pp. 278–307.

'The Improbable Probability'. Based upon 'The Stanhope Memorandum of 1888: A Reinterpretation', *Bulletin of the Institute of Historical Research*, 57 (1984), pp. 240–47.

'War, Technology and Change'. Based upon 'Victorians at War: War, Technology and Change', Paper delivered to the 'Locating the Victorians' Conference, Science Museum, London, July 200; and 'The Pen and the Sword: Reflections on Military Thought in the British Army, 1854–1914', *Soldiers of the Queen*, 68 (1992), pp. 3–7.

'Troopin'. Based upon 'Going to War: Southampton as a Port of Embarkation and Disembarkation in Peace and War', paper delivered to 'Southampton: Gateway of Empire' Conference, University of Southampton, March 2002.

'A Frenchman's Horse'. Based upon 'Lord Chesham, the Imperial Yeomanry and the South African War', lecture given in various locations in Buckinghamshire, 2000–2001.

'A Question of Totality'. Based upon 'Britain's Imperial War: A Question of Totality?', *Joernaal vir Eletydse Geskiedenis*, 25 (2000), pp. 1–22.

'No End of a Lesson'. Based upon 'The South African War and the Late Victorian Army' in Peter Dennis and Jeffrey Grey, eds, *The Boer War: Army, Nation and Empire* (Canberra: Army Historical Unit, 2000), pp. 31–44.

Index

2-15-04